Praise

The mystery of how to have continuous color in a perennial garden has been carefully and methodically solved in Cyndie's book, *Northern Garden Symphony.* Plant sellers and plant buyers alike will find it an invaluable asset when planning, growing, and maintaining a new or established perennial garden. Reading it, with its charts and beautiful photos, will coax you into a plan of action for your own garden. You will be doing yourself a favor when you add *Northern Garden Symphony* to your gardening library!

 —NANCY MACFARLANE Danamac Acres Greenhouse, owner 1980-2012, Palmer, Alaska

On a blustery, gray day in April, a friend took me to The Plant Kingdom Nursery in Fairbanks. Nothing in my years of haunting nurseries prepared me for the incredible riot of color that greeted me as I entered Cyndie Warbelow's greenhouses. Her unabashed and incredibly creative color sense was on full display, especially in the vast array of hanging baskets. It was too early in the season to have the opportunity to enjoy her perennial display gardens, but now, through *Northern Garden Symphony*, her much-needed and photo-filled book on perennial gardening in Interior Alaska, we can all experience them. Cyndie freely shares her talent and techniques for creating vibrant and well-designed perennial gardens in a part of the world that many Outsiders think of as hostile to plants.

After carefully guiding her readers through the concepts of designing perennial gardens, including emphasis on bloom succession, balance, continuity, and the importance of eye movement, Cyndie has added a unique and incredibly useful series of charts depicting the attributes of more than 200 hardy perennials. She then takes the next vital step and demonstrates exactly how to use the charts by providing examples of five varied gardens. Moreover, Cyndie includes excellent descriptions of each of the plants. The result is an easy-to-follow, step-by-step process that every gardener can employ whether a first-timer or an old hand looking for fresh ideas.

As a true native of Interior Alaska who grew up surrounded by plants in a family of gardeners, Cyndie is the ideal guide for anyone who desires a dazzling and enticing garden as a respite from long cold winters. In *Northern Garden Symphony*, her enthusiasm for perennials and gardening in the Interior will encourage and empower all gardeners to try their hand at creating a perennial garden of their own.

 —BRENDA C. ADAMS author of award-winning *Cool Plants for Cold Climates* as well as *There's a Moose in My Garden*; speaker, educator and international award-winning garden designer

The author writes so clearly and positively that even the most timid folks should have the confidence to try their hands at perennial gardening. She makes it sound like fun, like putting together a pretty puzzle. Warbelow writes with such joy and optimism that the reader is drawn in and on. I didn't want to put the book down. This is a welcome addition to the literature on northern gardening. Well done. Reading Cyndie's book is like talking to her in person. She's brilliant, and writes with humor. My favorite kind of writer.

 —LES BRAKE Coyote Garden, Willow, Alaska

T0344980

This book is a wonderfully written and researched garden tell-all---engaging not just for Alaska green thumbs but for any garden enthusiasts in the northern hemisphere. Loved it...simply brilliant!

—KIM THISTLE owner, The Greenhouse, Newfoundland and Labrador, Canada

Northern Garden Symphony is a book written with great experience and knowledge and with beautiful pictures to give an idea of what opportunities there are to grow perennials in gardens and borders in colder climates. This is a climate that most people are thinking is one where you cannot grow any perennials. For me Nico Rijnbeek, a perennial grower from the Netherlands with experience for more than fifty-five years, it has also opened my eyes. I want to tell everybody: please read this book to get more knowledge about perennial gardens and borders and the number of combinations you can make.

—NICO RIJNBEEK Rijnbeek and Son–Perennials, Boskoop, Holland

Northern Garden Symphony would be a valuable resource for anyone planning a perennial garden in Interior Alaska, as well as a wonderful resource for existing gardeners looking for inspiration!

—DENNIS ROGERS perennial gardener continuing the legacy of his life partner, the talented plantsman, Ken McFarland, Fairbanks, Alaska

I have never been a skeptic about Alaskan gardening. In fact, when I visit that great state, I come away thinking that gardens there are every bit as beautiful as gardens in Cornwall, UK and Atlanta, GA.

However, reading through Cyndie's common sense approach to far-north gardening and seeing her spectacular photography leaves me speechless. She not only explains the plants that work, but also takes us through the planning steps for designing a successful garden. If that was not enough, she has prepared in-depth plant lists that allow us to quickly find information about the plants that succeed in the far north.

In summary, Cyndie has shown us how to garden in Fairbanks, but this stunning book is valuable for any northern gardeners in Canada and the United States. I can't wait to visit.

—DR. ALLAN ARMITAGE Professor Emeritus of Horticulture, University of Georgia

Inspiring and informative! Wonderful descriptive photos, charts providing progressive bloom times, heights, colors, plant information. This book provides for all gardening levels. Cyndie's extensive plant and design knowledge shines through in *Northern Garden Symphony*!

—PATRICIA WOLCZKO a long-time Interior Alaska gardener

An Alaska summer would not be complete for gardeners and landscapers without a trip to the Plant Kingdom greenhouses and a walk-about through their perennial trial gardens. Cyndie Warbelow's talent lies in her grounding in basic plant biology layered with a gift of art and music that have allowed her to create stunning landscapes using hardy plants as her palette and northern soils as her canvas. Cyndie shows that spectacular gardens can be the rule, not the exception in northern environments. Her book is filled with lists of hardy perennials, methods of design, and examples of garden layouts that will help gardeners create their own summer-long perennial showcase gardens. It is a well-balanced idea book for novice as well as seasoned northern gardeners.

—DR. PATRICIA S. HOLLOWAY Professor Emerita, Horticulture, Horticultural Consultant, A.F. Farmer, LLC, University of Alaska Fairbanks

Northern Garden Symphony

♪

A bed of annual phlox tucked in against a backdrop of junipers and ornamental shrubs.

Shrubs and a tree add structure and texture even as the first snow of winter dusts this garden.

Northern Garden Symphony

Combining Hardy Perennials for Blooms All Season

CYNDIE WARBELOW

SNOWY
OWL
BOOKS

University of Alaska Press

Published by

University of Alaska Press

P.O. Box 756240

Fairbanks, AK 99775-6240

Cover and interior design by UA Press.

All images courtesy Cyndie Warbelow unless otherwise noted.

Cover image: *Lilium* 'Salmon Twinkle' and *Achillea* 'Laura' show their colors against the foliage backdrop of *Aegopodium* 'Variegata.'

Library of Congress Cataloging-in-Publication Data

Names: Warbelow, Cyndie, author.

Title: Northern Garden Symphony: Combining Hardy Perennials for Blooms All Season
        / Cyndie Warbelow.

Description: Fairbanks, AK : University of Alaska Press, [2021] | Includes
        bibliographical references and index.

Identifiers: LCCN 2020030578 (print) | LCCN 2020030579 (ebook) | ISBN
        9781602234413 (paperback) | ISBN 9781602234420 (ebook)

Subjects: LCSH: Perennials—Alaska. | Gardens—Design. | Gardening—Alaska.
        | Color in gardening—Alaska.

Classification: LCC SB434 .W37 2021 (print) | LCC SB434 (ebook) | DDC
        635.9/3209798—dc23

LC record available at https://lccn.loc.gov/2020030578

LC ebook record available at https://lccn.loc.gov/2020030579

PRINTED IN CANADA

This book is dedicated to my mother,
Willy Lou.

I love perennials!
There's this wonderful thing about them—
that they can survive our long winters.
It gives me a kinship with them.

Marion Avrilyn Jones
Fairbanks perennial gardener
July 2016

Lilium 'Salmon Twinkle' and *Achillea* 'Laura' show their colors against the foliage backdrop of *Aegopodium* 'Variegata.'

Contents

Foreword

Roots: Growing Up North

In October 1945 Marvin and Willy Lou Warbelow left their farming roots in Wisconsin to ride a steamship, train, small airplane and then dogsled to Shungnak, Alaska, a small Iñupiat village about forty miles north of the Arctic Circle. Marvin's venture north as an Alaska Native Service teacher in the village of Elim a few years earlier had been cut short, when the increasing likelihood of his being drafted, had convinced him to enlist in the Merchant Marine. As soon as the war ended, he looked up his college classmate Willy Lou. Seven weeks later they were married, and with teaching contracts in hand, they were on the way to Alaska.

When they arrived in Shungnak, the ground was frozen and covered with snow. As soon as the soil thawed a few inches in early June of that first summer, they were spading up a garden spot and planting seeds. Willy Lou wrote home to her sister describing Marvin's amazing success with two hundred celery plants, rows of lettuce, and hills of potatoes grown from the few remainders of their once-a-year supply of groceries. She admitted to a few failures as well. Carrots grew at right angles when they met the icy soil just below the surface. Marvin buried fish heads along some of the garden rows with the expectation that they would compost in place and add nutrients to the soil. When they harvested the garden at the end of the season in August, they found the fish heads still intact, preserved by the cold soil. In letters mailed back to Wisconsin that fall, Willy Lou related the ongoing saga of the two hundred celery stalks. Celery was on the menu for days. It was traded for wild meat and fish. But even so, there was excess to give to everyone in the village.

Marvin and Willy Lou instilled this fascination with gardening in their four children, my brothers and me, as we grew up first in several Iñupiat and Athabascan villages. In each village, early June would find my parents spading up cold soil and planting

Marvin and Willy Lou Warbelow (opposite, top). The author, her brothers and their childhood pony, Pepper, at Cathedral Bluffs (opposite, bottom).

vegetable seeds. In 1958 the entrepreneurial and adventurous spirits of my parents led to a new direction for our family. We lived the next fourteen years at Cathedral Bluffs Lodge, a roadhouse on the Alaska Highway, where my father operated a bush flying service transporting miners, hunters, scientists, and sightseers as well as delivering mail to remote villages and responding to medical emergencies. Each summer my mother and her staff, my brothers and I, hosted a world of fascinating visitors---tourists visiting Alaska as well as geologists, road construction crews and survey parties using the roadhouse as a base. During the winter, she home-schooled the four of us because the nearest school was twenty-five miles away. My parents were more than busy so now the gardening fell to my brothers and me. Cathedral Bluffs was positioned right at the base of the Alaska Range whose peaks were snow-covered for at least half of the growing season. Undeterred by the climatic limitations of our location, my brothers and I grew a small garden every summer. Our primary, and in fact only, crops were nasturtiums and shell peas. The part of the garden that survived the less than optimal temperatures was often fodder for our free-ranging Shetland pony. Pepper's favorite pass times were forbidden activities: rubbing against the tail feathers of one of the airplanes, poking his head in the open windows of visitors' cars to either get into their travel snacks or to bite the passengers, and stealing nasturtiums and peas from our garden.

From Cathedral Bluffs I went off to the University of Alaska where I studied biology. In graduate school I pursued the zoology path rather than botany. One spring day ten years later I walked into Ann's Greenhouses in Fairbanks and looked down the length of a hoop house full of bedding plants. I knew I was home. The following spring I worked for Ann during the bedding plant season. That started a lifelong friendship with Ann and her daughter, Linda, and a serious addiction to plants and the field of horticulture. Within a few years I was living with my husband on thirty acres east of Fairbanks. We cleared land and grew vegetables for the local farmers market and for restaurants, but I was soon sneaking a few flowers into the vegetable seedling greenhouse. The truck farming operation grew into two children, ten greenhouses and a general store, café, post office, and gas station. Twenty years later I moved to a beautiful south hillside three miles from Fairbanks and carved out The Plant Kingdom Greenhouse and Nursery. It is here that I have been able to pursue my love of perennials, to build display gardens, to share and learn through classes I teach and gardeners I meet, and to spend hours and hours in my own garden marveling at how lucky I am to live in a world with plants.

Acknowledgments

As I sit before this blank page of paper with the intent of thanking all those who have participated in bringing this book to fruition, I realize that this is a list too extensive to write here. So many people along my path of life have taught me, encouraged me, shared their love of plants, offered their friendship. You are all the reason this book came to be. *Northern Garden Symphony* would not have happened without our collective efforts. It is our book. Thank you, everyone, for your part.

Within this lifelong community of support there are certain individuals who have been the posts and beams of my life, the bones of my garden. And so I want to express a special thank you:

To my parents, Marvin and Willy Lou Warbelow, and to my "third parent," Helen Foster. Thank you for showing me, by your example, the value of education and hard work and for supporting me in my decisions and choices, however strange they sometimes seemed.

The author's children,
Brett (left) and Kaarin (right).

To my three bush pilot brothers: Ron, Charlie, and Art. Thank you for always being my sounding board, my source of timely advice, my best friends, even though I never shared your ability to fly and instead have always had my feet firmly planted in the earth.

To my children, Kaarin and Brett. Thank you for being willing to grow up in my garden, and for helping me understand that there is more to a garden than plants.

To my mentors in the early years of my gardening career, Ann Dolney and Lee Risse. At the time I thought you knew everything there was to know about growing plants—and now I know you did. Thank you for being so generous with your knowledge. If only you knew how often I heed your words of advice from so many years ago.

To my customers and co-workers in the greenhouses at Tacks' General Store and The Plant Kingdom. Thank you for sharing your gardens, your experience, your questions, and your love for perennials. I am especially grateful to Patty Wolczko for our years of working together, for all that I learned from you about horticulture, and for your appreciation of all living things, including perennial plants.

To Pat Holloway, Nancy Macfarlane, and Susie Zimmerman. Thank you for reviewing this manuscript and for your thoughtful, insightful recommendations, all of which have now been incorporated to the benefit of *Northern Garden Symphony*. I consider each of you an expert on Alaska perennials, and so I am honored that you were willing to give of your time and knowledge for the peer review.

To Brenda Adams. Thank you for sharing your proofreading eyes, your experience as an author, and your love of perennial gardening.

To Jennifer Jolis. Thank you for the luncheon conversation, which led me to the door of UA Press and the opportunity to present the embryonic manuscript.

To Nate Bauer at the University of Alaska Press. Thank you for your enthusiastic support for the initial concept of this book, for the direction on the first revision, and for your subsequent guidance of *Northern Garden Symphony* through the publication process. To Krista West. Thank you for sharing your creative talent in the design of this book and for your willingness to consider my input along the way. To all the behind-the-scenes staff at UA Press. Thank you for your part in the many steps of the path to the finished book.

Introduction

I have a multitude of goals, ideas, and plans in writing *Northern Garden Symphony.* If I were to pare it down to just a few words, here is how I would describe my motivation for this book.

First there is the Garden Symphony to consider. The successful perennial garden has much in common with its annual counterpart. Both rely on gradations in plant height, variations in textures and foliage, and a spontaneous expression of the gardener's carefully chosen color palette. But here is where annual and perennial gardens diverge. Happy annuals bloom continuously through the growing season. In the case of perennials, each variety has a specific time during the growing season when it blooms. In order to provide sequential blooming all season long, the perennial gardener must consider the bloom time of each plant in the garden.

String instruments adding their own music to the garden symphony.

A garden in mid June (top) and the same garden in mid July (opposite, top). Note the blooming perennials to the left of the sidewalk, which change from pink and blue columbine and yellow-flowered *Trollius* in June to peonies and orange flowered *Trollius* in July. The lilac and the Siberian pea are blooming in June but the *Spirea* has taken over in July.

This added challenge is what makes perennial gardening so exciting and rewarding. It takes careful orchestration of the details to create this lively, colorful garden symphony where each plant is playing its part at the correct time for the perfect symphony, one that brings pleasure to the eye and to the soul and that repeats its performance year after year. The garden symphony is not unlike a music symphony. The players may be different in different climates and in different concerts, but gardening and music are universal languages. Discussions about the garden and the music may be in many languages but the Latin names and the notes are common to all of them, and so gardeners the world over speak the same language just as musicians do. The use and the interpretation of the plants and of the notes are in the hands of the gardener and the conductor. That is why making gardens and making music are so much fun.

And then there is the Northern aspect to consider: the magic and joy of perennial gardening in northern climates, including really northern, like 64 degrees north as in Fairbanks, Alaska. Although gardeners this far north are a serious and enthusiastic breed, we may be defined by our dedication to 24-hours-a-day gardening more than we are by the total number of species that we can grow compared to gardeners in more temperate climates. However, those species, varieties, and cultivars that do like the north, thrive and grow with a vigor unique to the latitude and its special growing conditions.

My hope is that in the pages that follow, I am able to convince you of the magic of perennial gardening. I will show you how to choose players specific to the northern

garden symphony and to learn how to tweak their parts according to the venue. I want to give you the tools and the confidence to nurture your own innate abilities as a perennial gardener. With this empowerment, you can have fun and success as you plant and grow your own perennial garden that sings with color all season long. And as a final note, although some of what I am going to share with you is proprietary to northern climates, most of the information that follows applies to growing a colorful perennial garden symphony any place there is a garden.

Let me explain the arrangement of the book. Part I defines the terms that will assure we all have our feet on the ground in the same garden, speaking the same language. Part II examines methods for planning and designing a perennial garden and also identifies the most important parameters to consider when choosing the players for a garden symphony. Part III introduces the concept of the Garden Symphony Charts as a design tool to keep the garden symphony playing bright and clear all season long. Part IV walks the reader through the step-by-step design of five garden symphonies using the charts as a guide for choosing the players. Part V consists of four chapters with additional supporting information. The first, Chapter 21, is easy-to-access, in-depth descriptions of all of the plants listed on the charts. The last three chapters provide guidance on planting, supplementing color and structure, and maintenance in a perennial garden from season to season.

As one member of the garden symphony fades (opposite top and top), another bursts into bloom and takes its place. The part of this garden to the right of the sidewalk is only one year post-planting in a once asphalt-covered parking lot.

PART I

Making Sure We Are All in the Same Garden

Lychnis 'Vesuvius' in the foreground against the backdrop of an OT lily that is waiting to play its part and a *Nepeta siberica* in full bloom.

CHAPTER 1

Before We Begin

Why be a gardener and why a perennial gardener?

Gardening combines science, art, exercise, and time in the outdoors in touch with nature. One of the many joys of sharing your life with a dog is that walking it each day gives you a purpose and a schedule for getting outdoors. A garden also gives purpose, physical exercise, and time in the outdoors as you plant, deadhead, weed, or cut flowers for a bouquet. You can view your garden as the plant version of having a dog companion. I cannot count the number of times I have passed through my garden on my way indoors and stopped briefly to pluck a spent flower or to dig up a dandelion. An hour passes in a flash and with no deadheads or weeds left in sight, I forget about whatever I was going to do indoors, and instead sit on a bench in the garden or in the grass under a tree, a cat by my side, to marvel at the beauty of my surroundings. The added advantage of a perennial garden is that it returns each year, forever encouraging you to be involved with plants and the earth.

Garden benches and secluded spaces have a devious way of encouraging the gardener to spend time maintaining the garden (below).

Whether in a greenhouse in May (top left), an annual garden in July (top center) or a garden in August (top right), flower color in the north is flamboyant, intense, and iridescent.

Super sweet Fairbanks-grown carrots (opposite, top left).

Broccoli loves Interior Alaska's growing conditions. This variety is 'Arcadia' but I have not met a broccoli cultivar that does not thrive in Fairbanks (opposite, top right).

Why garden in the north—in a place like Fairbanks, Alaska on the northern edge of the range of most plants—and especially perennial plants?

There are many myths and truths about growing plants where the sun shines nearly all night long during the summer, and then hides much further south during the winter leaving us and our gardens in the dark.

When I attend horticultural conferences in the warmer forty-nine states and I mention operating a greenhouse-nursery in Alaska, the first question I am often asked is, "Can you really grow anything up there?" My perspective may be biased, but I truly believe that the northern growing climate has some great advantages.

The long daylight hours (just under twenty-two hours on the summer solstice in Fairbanks), low humidity, and lack of intense heat provide growing conditions like nowhere else. It's true that avocadoes, *Plumeria*, and citrus are not in our repertoire, but we excel at growing huge and vibrant tuberous begonias, pest-free broccoli, the sweetest carrots, stunning Himalayan blue poppies, giant cabbages, and stubbornly hardy perennials.

Summer's long daylight and the cool temperatures coupled with the low angle of the sun allow for a more vibrant expression of colors in flowers. Visitors to the state often comment on the intensity of the flower color, mistakenly assuming that we get our seeds and tubers from special supply sources.

The long daylight hours through the growing season mean that even a north exposure receives adequate light to sustain plants that might be considered sun-lovers. The cooler temperatures and low angle of the sun allow traditionally shade-loving plants to flourish in south exposures. This north-south flexibility adds innumerable possibilities to plant combinations and garden designs.

Another great advantage that we northern gardeners enjoy is fewer insect pests than in more temperate climate gardens. Cool, short summers and long, cold winters serve to hold pest populations in check.

Two people, a large knife, and a heavy-duty wagon are required to harvest an OS-Cross cabbage at The Plant Kingdom. The key to success growing cabbage in Fairbanks is the long daylight hours, lots of water, and plenty of plant food (above and left).

But even with all these advantages, isn't the season terribly short?
Is it worth the effort for a few months of garden time?

The gardening season in the north is admittedly short but it is intense and highly productive. In Fairbanks, some years actually have five months of frost-free weather or at least five months that are friendly to hardened-off plants (this would include perennials in an established garden). Although numerous perennials may be at their prime from late August into September, many of us start selectively cutting back our herbaceous perennials at the beginning of September to avoid the possibility of doing it in freezing temperatures and/or snow. In a sense, we lose several weeks of beauty in our gardens because we can't forget the few times the snow has arrived in mid-September and stayed until spring. There are also many microclimates in the Fairbanks area where

The Himalayan blue poppy is at the northern edge of its range in Interior Alaska. The totally unique blue of the flower is more than ample reward for any gardener who manages to coax these plants through the first few years until they are established.

the frost-free season is only late May to late August. It is also true that, historically, there has been a killing frost every month of the summer. However, the ephemeral nature of gardens in northern climates is actually crucial for gardeners. We literally can be in our gardens twenty-four hours a day for the summer. The rate of growth of both ornamentals and vegetables is unequalled and the time to enjoy, maintain, and harvest is short. The gardening season in the north is breathtaking, awe-inspiring, and exhausting. We need winter, without our gardens, to re-charge for the hectic pace of the next summer's growing season.

Now that you are convinced that, yes, of course you want to be a *Northern* perennial gardener, I invite you to come with me through the pages that follow and learn how to create your own *Garden Symphony*.

Interior Alaska and more southern parts of the state provide growing conditions for tuberous begonias like no other location in the United States.

FIGURE 1

Interior Alaska *(map by UA Press)*

CHAPTER 2

What is a Northern Garden?

When I speak of a northern perennial garden, I am considering gardens that roughly span USDA climate zone 2A (with an average annual minimum temperature of -50 to -45 degrees Fahrenheit) to 4B (-25 to -20 degrees Fahrenheit). Keep in mind that the actual minimum temperature a perennial experiences may be modified in the warmer direction by microclimates that are (1) natural, such as those created by snow cover, or (2) provided by the gardener, such as row crop fabric or organic mulch. Similarly, areas within a climate zone may be colder than expected due to factors like wind exposure or the absence of snow insulation in the shadow of a roof overhang.

Geographically, I visualize a northern garden to be one that is situated roughly between latitudes 62 and 66 degrees north. In Alaska this is the area referred to as the Interior (see Figure 1), one of six loosely defined regions of the state. The Interior is the central part of the state, lying between the Alaska Range to the south and the Brooks Range to the north. Measuring 175,000 square miles, the Interior represents 30% of the state's landmass. A large share of this lies north of the sixty-third parallel and south of the Arctic Circle. It is this region, Interior Alaska, that I am considering the heartland of the northern garden. Often I will refer to gardens in and around Fairbanks, the largest population center in Interior Alaska and the part of this north with which I am most familiar from a gardening standpoint.

None of these are exact boundaries to the northern garden, but hopefully they help place the reader. Do not be limited by this geographic placement, however. Many of the concepts laid out ahead apply to perennial gardens no matter the address.

CHAPTER 3

Perennial, Annual, Herbaceous, Woody— What Does it All Mean?

The focus of this book is perennials, and primarily herbaceous perennials. However, we will discuss the use of annuals as another way to add color to the perennial landscape. We will also look at ways to use woody plants as a means of adding structure to a garden year around. Defining some terms will add clarity to the pages ahead.

Annuals are defined botanically as plants that complete their life cycle, going from seed to seed production, in one growing season. In a northern garden, the completion of this life cycle may be prevented by the onset of freezing temperatures. Annuals may be direct-seeded in the garden, but in northern climates with a short growing season, most are started indoors or purchased from local nurseries in cell packs. The seedlings are planted outdoors in late spring, and they bloom their hearts out all season until the first frost of fall, when they melt in a heap and compost in place. There are annuals grown primarily for their foliage, such as coleus, but most are given space in the garden because of their floral displays. Some annuals may appear in your garden the following spring. These are not the original plants, but instead came from seed that remained viable all winter after being dropped by the previous season's plant.

Perennials are plants that live multiple years unless destroyed by unfriendly events such as serious weather, disease, or that hopefully unlikely scenario, neglect or abuse at the hands of a gardener. In addition to this difference in length of life cycle, another giant distinction (especially from the design standpoint) is that each perennial has a finite period of the growing season during which it blooms. This contrasts with the non-stop-bloom-all-season habit of annuals. One classification within the larger group of perennials is short-lived perennials, and these are varieties that characteristically survive for a few years rather than many, even when conditions are to their liking.

Zinnias and marigolds are sun-loving annuals that add intense color all summer long (above left).

A garden of primarily annual *Phlox* planted in June and still blooming profusely in early September (above right).

Biennials are plants that complete their life cycle in two seasons. Growth during the first season is vegetative, primarily leaves and stems. In the second season flowers are produced, and if season length and fall temperatures permit, seed is also produced. Familiar biennials include cabbage and carrots. Some natural biennials, such as foxglove, have been manipulated by plant breeders to produce cultivars (e.g. 'Foxy', 'Dalmation') which are annual in behavior and so they produce flowers the first year when grown from seed. Biennials are often included in perennial gardens, especially if they are prolific producers of viable seed. This means they return each season as second year flowering plants or first year vegetative growth from self-sown seed. *Hesperis matronali*s, often called dame's rocket or sweet rocket, would be an example.

We also need to distinguish herbaceous from woody. Herbaceous plants are ones that have no woody structure above ground. In the case of herbaceous annuals, the plant produces flowers and seed and then dies at the end of its growing season. The life cycle starts again from another seed. Herbaceous perennials also have above-ground parts that die at the end of the growing season, but unlike herbaceous annuals, parts of the plant below the ground's surface, roots or underground stems (e.g., bulbs, tubers, and rhizomes), survive and produce new growth the following season. In contrast to herbaceous plants, woody plants have an above-ground woody structure that persists and grows each year. The lignin and cellulose of the vascular cell walls provide the resilient structure of woody plants. This hard stem supports buds that survive above ground through the cold winter months.

Woody plants are usually grouped as shrubs or trees. The distinction between the two is not one based solely on size, as is commonly thought. Shrubs are woody perennial plants that have *multiple stems*, usually produced near the soil line of the plants. They are generally considered to be less than twelve feet in height and they often have a rounded or "bushy" form. Trees are perennial woody plants that have a *single central* stem topped with a distinct head or crown of branches. In Interior Alaska, ornamental trees may be "pruned" by moose that chew out the main leader. If this is all that is eaten, another branch may take over as the leader and therefore the tree form is maintained. If the main stem of a young tree is chewed low enough, multiple shoots may emerge at ground level, giving a shrub-like growth form to the original tree. If it is a grafted tree and it is chewed off below the graft, the new shoots will be the rootstock plant rather than the tree that was grafted on to it. Selective pruning by the gardener of the many stems of a shrub to a single stem or just a few stems can achieve a tree-like form. Some woody plants, such as *Prunus virginiana* (Canada red chokecherry or Schubert chokecherry) and *Acer ginnala* (Amur maple), are routinely available at nurseries in both shrub and tree growth forms.

Then there is the often-misunderstood concept of whether a plant is hardy or not. Hardiness of a plant most commonly refers to its ability to survive the winter temperatures of the area in which it is being cultivated. This suggests that the USDA hardiness zone designations would be a good predictor of hardiness. While this is true to an extent, there are many microclimates within any given USDA zone. These microclimates may be only a few hundred feet or a few miles apart but temperatures may

South exposure perennial border in late June. Participating in the garden symphony at this time in the western end of the border are *Nepeta* 'Dropmore Blue;' *Achillea* 'The Pearl' and 'Terra Cotta;' *Lychnis* 'Vesuvius;' *Ligularia przewalskii*; and yellow and orange Asiatic lilies. The ribbon grass in the foreground and the snow on the mountain in front of the 'Terra Cotta' add foliage interest all season (below left).

A mixed perennial garden at The Plant Kingdom in late June. Both herbaceous and woody perennials are playing in this symphony (below right).

vary widely between them. In Fairbanks on a cold, clear January day, the temperature inversion between a south exposure hillside and the valley floor may create a temperature differential of as much as twenty degrees Fahrenheit within a distance of a few miles. Microclimates are also created by differences in wind exposure, sun exposure, soil drainage, surrounding vegetation and amount of snow cover, as well as by human intervention such as mulching. All of these can be reasons that a plant is or is not hardy in a garden.

When a plant is described as being hardy (or not), the designation is always in reference to a location, climate, or growing condition. For example, it is "hardy in zone 4" or it is "hardy in Interior Alaska" or it is "hardy above five hundred feet elevation in the Tanana Valley." A plant is not simply hardy—it is hardy with respect to certain conditions that affect its viability, whether spoken or unspoken.

Digitalis 'Foxy' in the entrance garden at The Plant Kingdom. This is a biennial plant that has been bred to behave as an annual. It begins blooming in early to mid July from an early June plant-out date and continues until hard frost.

Hesperis matronalis displayed next to *Elaeagnus commutata*, a woody shrub with soft gray leaves and silver berries (hence the common name silverberry). This *Hesperis* is a biennial (top left).

Woody plants go into the fall and through the winter with the woody structure and its buds persisting above ground (top right).

In the background on the right and in the far background are native trees, but all the other woody plants in this photo are non-native ornamental shrubs including the large lilac at the far end of the house (middle left).

A border of shrubs in the foreground with three trees in the background. The trees are from left to right: *Pyrus ussuriensis*, *Pyrus* 'Mountain Frost,' and *Malus* 'Pink Spires' (middle right).

Here in the foreground are small shrubs. The three *Prunus virginiana* (upper right of photo), with their burgundy leaves, are shrub forms even though they are the same height as the tree forms of the *Prunus maackii* at the far back center and of the *Sorbus decora* (upper left of photo) at the back corner of the house (bottom).

Here I must mention that there are many beautiful *perennials* that are not *hardy perennials* in Fairbanks because they do not survive the winter. However, they thrive during our summer growing season and so are used extensively in annual gardens. *Rudbeckia* and lupine are two examples. They are perennials (repeat their life cycle year after year in the right conditions) but they are not *hardy* perennials in Interior Alaska (having ground-level or underground plant parts that can survive our winter conditions). These plants and others are used as annuals in Fairbanks even though, as their plant tags will indicate, they are perennials. The disclaimer is: returning year after year *in the right conditions*. Therefore, being a perennial does not necessarily mean that a plant will survive the winter in your garden, but it may well function as a stunning annual. Perennials that perform well as annuals and bloom all summer are often ones that have received much attention from plant breeders with emphasis on selection for long bloom time.

The bright yellow *Rudbeckia* and the red lupine are both perennial plants that are not winter-hardy in Interior Alaska, but they function beautifully as annuals.

Hardy perennials are plants that not only survive the winter, but also then flaunt their success, performing a spectacular color dance in the endless summer light of a northern garden.

It is not surprising that one objective of perennial plant breeders is to increase the hardiness of plants in a variety of climatic zones and growing conditions. The more widely adaptable and disease-free a plant is, the more gardens in which it will thrive and be hardy. Perennial plant breeding has received a lot of attention in the last few decades. Advances in propagation techniques and disease control have created cultivars of plants such as *Phlox* and *Veronica* that are more resistant to powdery mildew, for example. Plants not weakened by powdery mildew have more energy to put into surviving other environmental challenges and are therefore hardy in more gardens.

If at this point you are feeling overwhelmed with definitions, you may relax. I think it is important to have this framework I have presented; however, for the remainder of this book, I will use the word "perennial" to refer to herbaceous perennials that are generally hardy in Interior Alaska and specifically in gardens in the Fairbanks area. Any time I stray from this interpretation, I will clarify the change.

CHAPTER 4

Native Plants versus Non-Natives

At perennial plant conferences I have attended and in perennial gardens I have visited outside of Alaska, interest in native plants in the landscape is high. The use of native plants in perennial gardens is a frequent subject in gardening literature.

In Interior Alaska as compared to other parts of the United States, it seems there is somewhat less interest in landscapes consisting of primarily native plants. I can only attribute that to where we live and with what we live. Many gardeners in this part of the north have gardens and yards surrounded by native vegetation. Much of Alaska is quite rural, out in the country, and pretty close to nature and the wild. Even those who live in more urban areas are only minutes away from open land, native vegetation, and the possibility of moose wandering through their gardens. This may explain the emphasis

There are constant reminders that ornamentals are just a human thing.

A native birch is the focal point in
this yard that is otherwise all
non-native ornamentals.

A native birch is the focal point in this yard that is otherwise all non-native ornamentals.

on non-native ornamentals. The native plants are a front-and-center part of our land-scape already. We are attracted to the contrast offered by non-native ornamentals, or at least to a garden that includes a mix of both.

Here I want to consider the terms native and non-native. Be warned that these terms are only a human attempt to give black-and-white definition to quite a gray area. Native plants are considered by some to be the plant species that evolved within a defined geological time frame in a given area and are reproducing and growing there. Some are satisfied with an even looser definition, considering native plants to be those that grow and reproduce locally. Native plants are frequently propagated by seed but may be clonally propagated as well. Non-native plants (also called exotic, alien, non-indigenous, or introduced) are plants that have been carried to an area outside their native distribution through the action of humans, purposefully or accidentally. Plant breeders select from both native and non-native plants for certain traits that are desirable in ornamental gardens. These cultivated selections, or cultivars, often have larger flower size, longer bloom time, wider flower color range, and more compact or controlled growth. Being adaptable to a broader habitat range and having very predictable expression of desired traits are also focuses in breeding new ornamental perennial cultivars. Once a cultivar has been selected and stabilized, it is vegetatively

propagated, assuring very stable and uniform expression of its traits. To clarify here, varieties and cultivars are both groupings within a species, but varieties occur naturally whereas cultivars are varieties that were selectively cultivated through human intervention. In more recent discussions, you may also see the term "nativar," which was introduced by Allan Armitage as a way for specifically designating cultivars of native plants. Hybrids, or crosses of two different varieties, can occur in nature or through human efforts. Genetic changes are ongoing in any species and they can occur at a slow rate in response to the natural environment or at a much faster rate in response to the plant breeder's goals. Plant breeders are essentially speeding up natural selection, as driven by the perennial gardener's agenda.

The backdrop for this garden is entirely native vegetation (top left).

Alaska gardens incorporate native vegetation somewhat by default (top right).

Native species may be highly adapted to very specific niches. They have the competitive advantage in their native environment, but this niche may be very narrow. There are also native plants that are generalists in terms of habitat requirements, which makes them highly successful in a variety of habitats. Many ornamental cultivars have been bred specifically to thrive in a variety of climates, which of course increases the extent of their use and their accompanying economic value. When you incorporate native plants into your perennial garden, be sure you can offer them the possibly narrow range of habitat conditions that they require, and that they can tolerate conditions strange to them such as fertilizer-rich garden soil. Our native dwarf dogwood (*Cornus canadensis*) is beautiful and thrives under a forest canopy. A south exposure perennial garden may not provide these conditions.

My focus here will be on cultivars and varieties of ornamental herbaceous perennials. However, the design principles apply to native plants as well. Native perennials can play quite effectively in your garden symphony. I think this is especially true when they are planted with their non-native and selectively bred relatives.

CHAPTER 5

Some Thoughts About Varieties and Cultivars

As I have shown customers through the perennials at The Plant Kingdom, I have been asked more than once why we sell so many more perennial varieties than patrons remember seeing in the past in Fairbanks. Just a few decades ago, a perennial garden in Interior Alaska was delphiniums, *Lychnis* Maltese Cross, Asiatic lilies, and columbine. Even today there are gardeners and commercial installers who have not ventured out from this plant palette. However, there is so much more available.

Over the last several decades, perennials have received much more attention from plant breeders. The resulting jump in the supply of new introductions has served to

A perennial garden at The Plant Kingdom displaying a colorful garden symphony in mid summer. This bed has since been converted to junipers because the native trees and shrubs to the west encroached severely and very destructively on the root zone of the herbaceous perennials.

increase the demand and add excitement to the horticulture industry and to perennial gardens.

Improved propagation methods, such as the extensive use of virus testing and tissue culture, have produced virus-free and genetically consistent cultivars. Today's plant introductions are often superior to the ones grown twenty or thirty years ago. Modern plant-breeding techniques have also sped up the process of releasing new cultivars. Showcasing these each season is reminiscent of the clothing fashion industry and the ongoing demand for something new and better.

And then there is climate change. Over the last century the growing season in Fairbanks has increased from 85 to 123 days. The growing season is measured from

The "Nose Bed" at The Plant Kingdom features a wide variety of perennials.

the last frost in spring to the first frost in fall, so for hardened-off and very frost–tolerant perennials, the growing season is even more than 123 days. The average annual temperature has increased 2.5 degrees Fahrenheit and the climate is about 11% drier. All of these statistics are real-life parameters to the resident plants. These changes have helped drive the increase in hardy perennial varieties here in Interior Alaska. Should this trend continue, it may ultimately change the makeup of the perennial palette even more. For example, there is some concern that the changing climate with accompanying increase in pests and diseases and habitat change may, for at least some native trees, result in their being replaced by more widely adapted non-native ornamentals in a relatively short time.

PART II

Setting the Stage and Preparing to Audition the Players

Lilium 'Fata Morgana,'
Nepeta siberica, Lychnis 'Molten
Lava,' and *Lilium* 'Peach Pixie'
singing out in bold color
in mid to late summer.

CHAPTER 6

Begin with a Plan

It is true that sometimes the most spontaneous unplanned gardens turn out beautiful. Generally though, the success and beauty of a planting is directly proportional to the amount of planning before planting. Free-form, naturalistic gardens that may look like they just happened most likely required some quite mechanical planning to achieve that ambiance and visual effect. Planning can range from formal sketches showing exact placement of plants to more of a design-as-you-plant method during which you are considering colors, textures, heights of plants, and bloom time on the spot, as you combine the plants in your garden.

When you stroll through this garden, gridded paper, straight pencil lines, and rectangular pieces of geotextile fabric are not what come to mind. However, they were all integral to the planning process that created the visually happy, free-form feel of the garden (below).

Two plants that add both foliage and flowers to the garden symphony are the dark-leafed *Actaea* 'Black Negligee' and *Lamium* 'Silver Beacon' with its white leaves edged in green (opposite, top left).

'Blizzard' mock orange and white flowered peonies both add white to a garden at the same time, but the flower shapes and sizes make them visually different (opposite, top center).

This garden has a combination of spiky, fluffy, sprawling, and mounded growth forms. A passerby simply cannot walk by without stopping to enjoy its beauty (opposite, top right).

When you browse through a book about perennials on a cold January day, or study seed catalogs in March, or wander through a local nursery in June, you may be overwhelmed with the number of different ornamental perennials. You may decide this is where the term "mind boggling" was coined. It will be clear to you immediately that you need a plan.

For some it works best to look at the plants and get a plan in their minds. For others, it is crucial to formulate the plan before looking at the plants. It is somewhat like the choice of going to the grocery store to get inspiration for a dinner recipe or going to the grocery store with the recipe in hand and buying the ingredients. However it works best for you, there are some primary considerations. We will discuss all of these in detail in Chapter 7, but I will list them here so that you can better understand the planning process:

1) Shade-loving plant or sun-loving plant? What are the light conditions in the garden where I am planting it?

2) What are the specific cultural requirements of this plant with respect to water, soil characteristics (such as temperature, pH, drainage, etc.), and nutrients?

3) What is the potential mature height of the plant?

4) What sort of form and texture does this plant have? Is the overall growth form spiky or fluffy, sprawling or mounded?

5) Does the foliage add color other than green?

6) What physical size and shape is the flower?

7) What color is the flower, assuming it has one?

> *Let me pause here and say that the seven preceding considerations apply to all gardens wherever they may be and whether they are annual or perennial. For perennial gardens there is an eighth very important consideration.*

8) What is the bloom time of this plant?

These are the eight major considerations to keep in mind as you begin the planning process. There are other minor considerations as well, some of which can become major if they are ignored. For example, you might ask whether the plant is fragrant, an important question if your garden's theme is fragrance.

And then there is the question, "Do I like this plant?" Tolerance is desirable but personal preference does exist. Some gardeners hate marigolds—period. Others dislike yarrow and may even describe its tall rangy habit as "weedy" (not desirable). As baffling as it is to a serious cat aficionado like myself, some gardeners won't plant catmint (*Nepeta*), because they don't want to attract cats to their yard. My advice here: Don't use a plant you hate, but try not to hate very many plants.

The variety and quantity of plant choices available in Alaska nurseries may seem like information overload when you first begin perennial gardening (center).

A mid summer perennial display at The Plant Kingdom full of blooming perennials. These plants have probably been blooming for two weeks and will continue to do so for a couple more weeks. If you choose any of these for your garden, you would need also to choose an equal number of earlier blooming plants and an equal number of later blooming plants (bottom).

The Importance of Having a Map

When growing an annual garden, you only have to endure a design error, such as the tall marigold planted in front of the short zinnia, for one season. In the case of perennial gardens, a mistake in plant placement literally becomes a perennial problem, returning year after year. Sometimes the problem is solved by the death of the plant. This does occasionally happen, either due to natural causes or in extreme cases, due to murder at the hands of the gardener.

Before you resort to extreme measures, let me interject here—you are allowed to move plants in a perennial garden. For the best chance of success in moving a perennial, cut it back to fall cutback level (see "Fall Cleanup and Preparation for Winter" in Chapter 24), dig it up with the root ball attached, and move it somewhere else. The ideal time to do this is either in early spring, or even better, in late fall. In the spirit of transparency, I will admit that once, to make way for a minimum egress window installation, I had to dig up all the perennials in a twenty-by-four-foot perennial garden in late June. I stored them with root balls exposed but crowded together in two wheelbarrows parked in a shady spot. I kept them quite wet but not in standing water in the wheelbarrows. When I moved the perennials out of the wheelbarrows into the garden a month or more later, I kept them well-watered for the rest of the season, and

A second year perennial garden in mid to late June (top left).

The same perennial garden shown on the left but in mid to late July. Now the early bloomers, including the mock orange and the *Thalictrum*, are resting quietly while the yarrows and the lilies are tuned and playing strong (top right).

An island bed of perennials in mid-July. The *Campanula* and the *Meconopsis* are at peak bloom while the *Lythrum* and the lilies are just beginning (bottom left).

This same island bed a few weeks later. The *Campanula* and the *Meconopsis* are fading but the *Lythrum* and the lilies are now major players (bottom right).

watched them grow and thrive. Mid-growing season is not the ideal time to dig and move established perennials, but in this case it was my only option.

So you can move perennials, but it takes time for them to re-establish, and there will be some rare cases when the plant does not forgive you for moving it. The best way to avoid digging and moving perennials in your garden is to start your planting project with a well thought-out plan—a map to your garden. There are several ways to do this, so let's take a closer look at our options.

The Paper Map

One way to select and place plants in a perennial garden is to draw out a plan on paper. It is easier to erase on paper than dig up plants in a garden. This may sound sterile and boring and mechanical, but it's amazing how it can stimulate your creative juices and raise your heart rate. In my own case, planning on paper was not always something I'd choose to do. I didn't plan ahead enough to create a paper plan. Suddenly, I would have a free hour to plant, and I wanted to get right to the dirt outdoors rather than spending time indoors on paper. Fortunately, as part of my life in the greenhouse/nursery

A plan that leads to a map that leads to a garden.

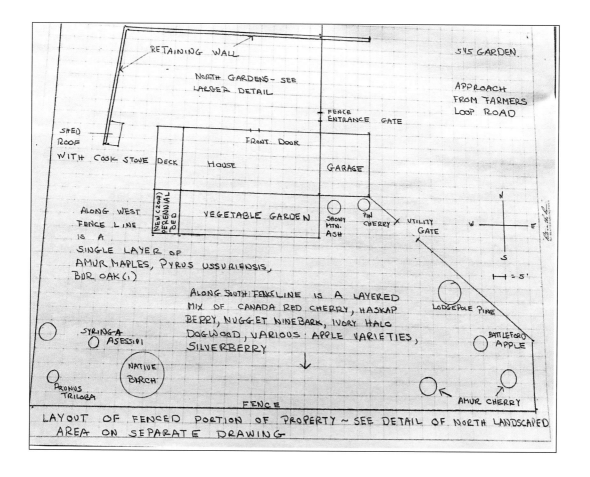

LAYOUT OF FENCED PORTION OF PROPERTY ~ SEE DETAIL OF NORTH LANDSCAPED AREA ON SEPARATE DRAWING

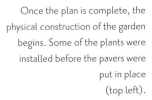

Once the plan is complete, the physical construction of the garden begins. Some of the plants were installed before the pavers were put in place (top left).

It's more fun to install plants, but the center paver area had to be completed in order to avoid carrying pavers through and over new plantings (below left).

The completed garden, a result of the plan in Figure 2 (above right).

business, I could not physically be at all of our planting projects, so I was forced to somehow transfer my vision for a garden into the hands of the actual planters. This required me to begin planning on paper, and it gave me an appreciation for the value of a map, the term my planting crew gave to our sketched plans.

Not only is the end result more predictable and pleasing, but a paper plan also allows you to know exactly which plants and how many of them you need, before starting to plant. How many of us have gone to the grocery store, bought a cart full of ingredients for our favorite recipes, and returned home to find that when we actually look at the recipes, we have some of the ingredients for quite a few of the dishes, but not all of the ingredients for any of them? The message here: have your map in hand when you go plant shopping for your perennial garden.

The first step in drawing a plan is to measure your proposed garden site, and then to transfer its configuration and dimensions to the paper, as shown in the drawing on the previous page. Gridded paper works well for keeping the measurements of the garden and the chosen plants easy to visualize. In order to keep in mind your sun exposure, it is useful to designate north and south on your drawing. It's also helpful to sketch in buildings, resident trees, utility poles and any other existing plants or structures that may figure into the exposure or growing conditions of your garden.

There are several methods for designating plant material on your sketch. One way is to draw circles whose diameter is proportional to the mature size of the plant. This circular feel to the drawing may seem more in keeping with the somewhat rounded growth form of plants. Figure 2 is an example of this type of plan, and the garden generated from this plan is the one shown in the photos above.

FIGURE 2

The Paper Map

This paper map uses proportionally sized circles to designate
plant material and soften the edges of a rectangular garden bed.

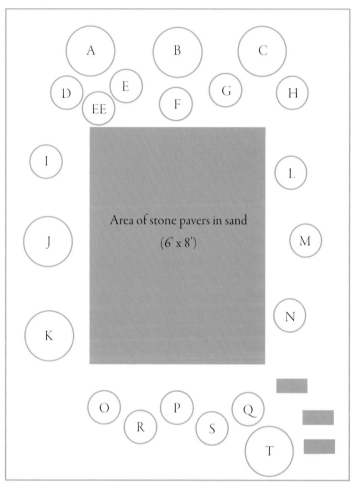

A = *Philapelphius lewisii* 'Blizzard'

B = *Physocarpus* 'Nugget'

C = *Thuja occidentalis* 'Woodwardii'

D = *Achillea* 'Pomegranate'

E = *Achillea* 'Saucy Seduction'

EE = *Achillea* 'The Pearl'

F = *Draba siberica*

G = *Achillea* 'Terra Cotta'

H = *Hemerocallis* 'Flava'

I = *Paeonia* 'Sorbet'

J = *Prunus* 'Carmine Jewell'

K = *Ribes josta*

L = *Polemonium* 'Touch of Class'

M = *Paeonia* 'Buckeye Belle'

N = *Hemerocallis* 'Stella de Oro'

O = *Meconopsis* 'Lingholm'

P = *Aquilegia sp.*

Q = *Lilium* 'Apricot Fudge'

R = *Thalictrum* 'Black Stockings'

S = *Tanacetum* 'Crispum'

T = *Physocarpus* 'Amber Jubilee'

A second way to denote plant material on a sketch is to draw it in block or linear form. I used the block method to design a perennial garden five feet deep and one hundred thirty-five feet in length along the top of a retaining wall. This very non-organic feeling plan was completed in winter and then translated to garden form the following spring. I divided the full length into five by four-feet sections, and then divided each section into twenty twelve-inch square planting blocks in four rows—all on gridded paper. See Figure 3.

This is a very dense spacing for most perennials, but the desired end result was a very full planting the first growing season. This spacing was also a response to my concern about the exposure of the garden on the edge that bordered the retaining wall. This would not have snow cover until several feet of snow had fallen, setting the stage for the possibility of greater than normal winter mortality.

To keep continuity and at the same time a transitional flow on this long border, each row was symmetrical from end to end. In the first and third rows (numbered from the front edge of the retaining wall toward the back), the center three plants changed from section to section, but the end plants remained the same for two sections. In the second and fourth row, the center three plants remained the same for two sections but the end plants changed with each section. All the blocks were populated with plants with different bloom times. The stark image of pencil on gridded paper was transferred to live plants in real soil in the spring. Even that first season it was a vibrant, freewheeling and naturalistic display. The crucial supporting member of this end result was the dedicated gardener, who put his resources and energy into the translation from paper to garden and then followed through with maintenance.

Still another way to designate plants on your paper plan is a method I call wedging. A bit more free form than circles or squares, this method designates loosely curved, triangular, or wedge-shaped areas that represent a mass planting of one variety or even several varieties similar in growth form or color. This works especially well with annuals but I have also used it with perennials. See Figure 4.

The wedging method was used to draw the plans for an annual garden on the same property as the retaining wall garden I described previously. See Figure 5.

Plan it in Place

A second way to plan a perennial garden is a method we use in the Garden-to-Go program that we developed at The Plant Kingdom. Customers provide us with a few pieces of critical information about their proposed perennial garden: dimensions, sun exposure, position with respect to surrounding buildings and yard, the color palette they

FIGURE 3

The Paper Map

This paper map uses a linear block format to designate plant material in a long border bed.

Lychnis Maltese Cross	*Delphinium* 'Magic Fountains Sky Blue'	*Thalictrum* 'Black Stockings'	*Delphinium* 'Magic Fountains Sky Blue'	*Lychnis* Maltese Cross

Achillia 'Terra Cotta'	*Ligularia* 'The Rocket'	*Aquilegia* 'Rocky Mountain Blue'	*Aquilegia* 'Songbird Robin'	*Ligularia* 'The Rocket'	*Achillia* 'Terra Cotta'

Phalaris 'Feesey's Form'	*Trollius ledebourii*	*Achilea* 'The Pearl'	*Lilium* 'Buff Pixie'	*Phalaris* 'Feesey's Form'

Polemoniom 'Bressingham Purple'	*Nepeta* 'Dropmore Blue'	*Artemesia* 'Silver Mound'	*Aegopodium* 'Variegata'	*Nepeta* 'Dropmore Blue'	*Polemoniom* 'Bressingham Purple'

Several sections of the retaining wall bed two months after installation. Each five-foot section was based on a map like the one shown in Figure 3 (bottom left).

A view of part of the retaining wall bed in its first season (bottom right).

A vignette from the retaining wall border bed (top right).

FIGURE 4

The Paper Map

In this paper map the wedging method of drawing works well to fit plant groupings into the rounded contours of the garden.

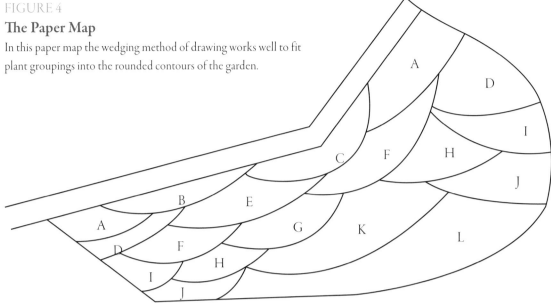

A = Lupine Gallery Red

B = *Salvia* Victoria White

C = *Salvia* Rhea

D = Marigold Lulu

E = Snapdragon Sonnet Yellow

F = *Zinnia* Orange Profusion

G = *Zinnia* Cherry Profusion

H = *Dianthus* Ideal Crimson

I = *Aster* Milady Blue

J = *Dianthus* Ideal Coral

K = *Dianthus* Floral Lace Violet

L = *Rudbeckia* Toto Lemon

The annual garden that grew from the plan in Figure 4.

FIGURE 5

The Paper Map

This map uses the wedging method of drawing as a way to translate a relaxed flow to a very linear garden bed.

BACK

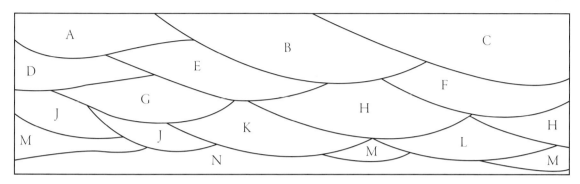

FRONT

A = *Rudbeckia* Goldilocks

B = Lupine Gallery Red

C = *Rudbeckia* Indian Summer

D = *Salvia* Rhea

E = Snapdragon Sonnet Yellow

F = Snapdragon Sonnet Crimson

G = Marigold Tangerine Gem

H = Marigold Lulu

I = *Rudbeckia* Toto Lemon

K = *Dianthus* Ideal Crimson

L = *Zinna* Orange Profusion

M = *Verbena* Quartz Scarlet

N = *Alyssum* Easter Bonnet
      Deep Violet

The garden that grew from the plan in Figure 5.

A mixed perennial and annual garden that grew from a complex map which used both the wedging and circle notation methods.

want, and the names of plant varieties that they especially love or hate. We then cut a piece of biodegradable paper mulch or a piece of woven geotextile fabric that fits the proposed garden footprint, position it on the pavement along the side of a greenhouse, and set out our chosen potted perennials (based on the customer's stated parameters) on the mulch in the exact arrangement that they will be planted. The customer then returns to look at the design and to decide whether it does or doesn't require adjustment. Once the design meets the customer's approval, we use an indelible marker to mark the spot of each pot on the mulch with a number and then create a written key matching the number on the mulch with the corresponding plant variety name.

You can do this yourself. Lay out your cut-to-fit mulch on the site or on any flat area. Place your plants, chosen using the eight criteria mentioned earlier. Allow yourself hours or days or a week to decide if you like the plan. Depending on the size of your garden, you could even take the mulch to a nursery and position it in a secluded flat area. Then experiment with the layout using potted plants from the nursery's perennial displays. There are several advantages of doing this at a nursery. One is that you will have knowledgeable staff available to answer questions and give advice. This also allows you to get a feel for the whole garden design, even if you do not have the time or resources to purchase all the plants at once. Once you have the key made

The geotextile fabric was laid on the planting area for this garden and then perennials were placed on it, using the design considerations as well as knowledge of the garden owner's preferences. Adjustments were made as needed to meet the owner's approval. At that point, holes were cut in the fabric and the plants were installed.

The same section of this garden a year later.

The section of garden along the fence right after planting.

The section along the fence one year after planting.

and each plant's space marked, you can plant all of the garden or only part of it. The spots for adding remaining plants will wait, labeled and weed-free, until you plant the rest of the garden.

Two cautions about how long you wait to finish the garden, if you choose not to plant all of it initially. Be certain about the longevity of the marker ink when exposed to sun and water. Also, happy perennials increase in size and vigor each year, so don't wait more than one growing season or so, as the established plants may shade and out-compete smaller, newer ones.

The garden shown in the photographs on the previous page was planted using this method. The geotextile fabric was cut to fit the site and put in place. I transported an assortment of perennials to the site and placed them in a design that I chose, but that was guided by the parameters specified by the client. I took more plants to the site than we actually used, but this gave me (and the client) choices for modifying the design.

Plan as You Plant

Finally, there is what might be called the plan-as-you-plant method, or what I sometimes refer to as the design-plant method of planning your perennial garden. Here you are starting with a collection of plants and improvising as you plant. The main requirement for this to be successful is that you are very familiar with the traits and growing

The focus of this project was to create a visual barrier from the road, and so it included both herbaceous and woody material. Once the geotextile fabric was anchored on the planting surface, a preliminary placement of plants gave time for everyone to reflect on the layout before the plants were installed.

The view of my house from the entrance off the main highway prior to the garden project.

requirements of your plants. In choosing your plants, you will have thought about at least some of the eight primary considerations so that when you get to the garden, you already have some parameters fixed with respect to color, texture, height, and bloom time. With this framework in mind and your innate knowledge of the plants in your collection, you are ready to start planting. You are a seasoned composer who, given a collection of instruments and players and some rules of composition, can create a symphony. This ability, in gardening or music, comes with experience and practice.

This is the method I used to plant the gardens on the north side of my own home (see photos on the next page). When I moved there, the entire area from the front of the house to the retaining wall on the north and to the highway on the east was pavement. After living in this parking lot environment for ten years, I hired a contractor to remove the approximately forty by seventy-feet area of pavement between the house and the retaining wall. We brought the area back up to grade with river loess that was left over from a nearby building project. We built a six-feet-tall cedar fence to separate this new garden area from the view toward the garage and the highway. The rest of the garden, as well as the entire yard surrounding the house on the west and the south, was enclosed with six-feet-tall farm fencing. The cedar portion of the fence provides privacy from the highway, and the fence as a whole serves to keep moose out and cats in.

A sidewalk divides the new garden area from a six-feet-wide perennial garden already in place along the whole north length of the house. The retaining wall along the north and west boundaries of this new garden area is about three feet in height, so it essentially creates a sunken garden ambiance. The wall was repaired in a few areas and then washed with tones of green on the north wall and tones of blue-gray on the west wall. A large brick barbeque was removed from the south end of the west wall and replaced with a wood-burning cook stove protected by a shed roof structure.

The first step in the installation of the garden itself was to cover the entire 2,800-square-feet planting surface with woven geotextile fabric. Next, garden hoses were used to visualize and lay out curved paths and to designate the position of rock

The entire area of the future garden was covered with geotextile fabric, and then a flexible garden hose was used to lay out the lines for one of the main paths leading through the garden (top left).

Looking from the west end of the parking lot (future garden) toward the highway (top right).

A built-in barbeque was removed and the retaining wall was extended as part of the project and a wood cook stove was installed in its place (center left).

This shows the method used to install the paver paths (center right).

The first season after the initial installation.

walls. These walls were built on top of the geotextile fabric with stacked landscape rock from a local quarry. The geotextile fabric was cut out in the area where the paths were to be built but the piece of fabric was kept intact when it was removed. The path area was excavated to a depth of about eight to ten inches and the piece of geotextile fabric that had been cut out was repositioned at the bottom of the excavation. Six inches of paving sand was used to fill the excavation, and then pavers were bedded to bring the path up to grade. Sand was brushed over the top to fill in the spaces between the pavers.

At this point, I began to draw with chalk on the geotextile fabric to designate the borders of individual gardens. I positioned shrubs along the cedar fence for added highway noise abatement and to soften the feel of the fence. I also placed shrubs to define garden rooms. By now I had shrubs in place and had designated the shapes and borders of both the perennial and annual gardens within the whole forty by seventy-feet space. Next I cut out the geotextile fabric in all the spaces not set aside for gardens and planted clover mixed with lawn seed. This lawn area now serves as paths and a connecting backdrop for all the gardens.

Several years after the project was completed (top left).

A view of the garden looking north six years after the original installation (top center).

Current view (twelve years after the garden was built) to the northeast in the garden (top right).

Annual and perennial beds within the whole garden (bottom).

Once I had reached this point, I did not have to make the herbaceous perennial planting decisions in one season, because the geotextile fabric kept all the planting areas free of weeds and ready to plant for whenever I decided what to plant. My choice of plants over the next two seasons was a very fluid and evolving process, guided by my knowledge of the plants and their parameters. For each new area I planted, I gathered a collection of perennials and set them in place on the fabric, always considering the eight design criteria. Sometimes I installed all the perennials in a given garden bed; other times, I planted a sort of skeletal structure that had a theme and design but which had room for additional plants as I acquired the right players. I left one large central bed unplanted for several seasons, and actually temporarily covered the exposed fabric in that area with decorative cedar bark and pots of annuals. As the rest of the total garden area grew and established, I had a better idea of what plants thrived in my conditions, how I was using the whole garden, and ultimately, what part I wanted this large bed to play in the garden as a whole.

A rainy day in the present garden, looking northwest (opposite, top).

Looking northeast from the kitchen area (opposite, bottom left).

The outdoor kitchen centered around the wood cook stove (opposite, bottom right).

CHAPTER 7

Designing a Perennial Garden

The basic elements of design hold true whether we are creating a painting, arranging an interior space in our home, or planting a garden. If you look at a painting or a piece of architecture or a garden and jot down what draws you to it, you will have defined the elements of design that created it.

Design is a heavy-sounding word when considering a perennial garden. Don't be frightened. It basically denotes the process of putting together a workable plan for a result that is both pleasing to the eye and pleasing to the mind. To accomplish this, plants for your garden must be vetted with respect to the eight primary considerations introduced in Chapter 6.

We will first address:

    1) light requirements and

    2) cultural requirements

Once you have chosen a palette that meets the growing conditions of your space, we will next focus on:

    3) bloom time

    4) height

    5) plant form and texture

    6) foliage characteristics and color

    7) flower shape and size

    8) flower color

With these eight considerations in mind you have the tools to move into the realm of design. We will discuss them more fully in the pages that follow.

Hydrangea 'Pink Diamond" is one of several cultivars of this genus that are hardy in Interior Alaska.

The principles of design are a framework, but from there on it's a matter of personal taste. You can do this. There is no right or wrong. It is your own personal taste being expressed through the plant choices you make within this framework that makes your garden unique and a reflection of you.

Where new perennial gardeners often feel most insecure in the beginning stages is in their limited knowledge of the medium, which is to say a lack of familiarity with the plants themselves. In a paint store you can look at the colors, in a quilt shop you can feel the fabric, in a home improvement store you can see wallpaper and carpet and tile samples. You may have trouble visualizing the mature height and color and form of a 'Patty's Plum' poppy when you are looking at it as a young green plant in a 6-inch pot in a nursery in May.

An extensive introduction to at least a sampling of the medium, the garden symphony players, follows later in this book in Chapter 21. However, there are a variety of additional sources to help build your familiarity with the constantly expanding list of

perennials that thrive even in the north. First, treat yourself to some reading time with the multitude of books on perennial plants and gardens, including *There's a Moose in My Garden* and *Cool Plants for Cold Climates* both by Alaska author Brenda Adams. A common lament I hear is that many gardening books feature and picture plants that do not survive in our northern climate. This is true, but oftentimes there is a northern-hardy relative. In the case of *Hydrangea*, choose 'Pink Diamond,' 'Peegee,' and 'Limelight' which are all Fairbanks-hardy even though many other *Hydrangea* are not. For roses, the Explorer roses and the *Rosa rugosa* hybrids can substitute for tea roses. In cases where there is no same-species variety that is hardy, there is almost always a look-alike perennial that is northern-hardy and that fills the same design niche. You simply get the look of the design with a different plant. The *Nepeta siberica* in my garden gives me the height and color of *Agapanthus*. A tall violet *Veronica* can stand in for less hardy *Liatris*. A *Phlomis tuberosa* grows on the north side of my house. I remove all the flower stalks as soon as they poke out from under the foliage. The result is a large, lush,

Rosa 'Therese Bugnet' is a hardy, quite double, long bloom season rose that thrives in Interior Alaska.

mounded foliage plant reminiscent of *Acanthus*, a species not hardy in my northern garden. When you see a design in a book or a magazine or on Pinterest, make it your own, and start substituting look-alikes for the non-hardy (in your zone) components.

Another valuable source of information on the medium is local nurseries. Walk through their perennial displays every week or two during the summer to get a real-life feel for how these plants grow and bloom during the season. What you see in May will be very different from what you see a month or two or three later.

And finally, spend time in gardens: those of friends, of commercial properties, and in public spaces such as parks and botanical gardens. The more exposure you have to live plants in different parts of the season and in different locations, the more comfortable and successful you will be with your medium.

Nepeta siberica threading its way up through the shrubs in a north exposure garden and providing a visual similarity to *Agapanthus* (opposite).

Phlomis tuberosa (back center in photo) providing a strong foliage presence similar to *Acanthus* (left).

CHAPTER 8

Design at the Macro Level

Before we zero in on the choice and placement of plants in our garden, there are a few macro-level aspects to address and some "big picture" questions to ask.

How are you going to view and use your garden?

If this is a drive-by garden, one that is a border along an edge of your property and is seen mostly from a street or highway, then you may want to consider big plants, large flowers, and bold colors. This is an ideal situation for mass plantings, large patches of the same variety in one color, rather than a few each of many different plant varieties and colors. These are all characteristics that are effective from a distance and at driving speed. Contrast this with a garden by your front door, one that is viewed close up and frequently. Here you may want to use fragrances and subtle textures.

This perennial garden at The Plant Kingdom is known as the "Nose Bed." This garden is one that visitors drive by and see as they round the curve of the lawn to reach the main entrance. This calls for big, bold plants including woody shrubs.

This border bed in Dublin, Ireland is seen only from the pathway and so plant heights grade from short in front to tall in back. This is a long border bed, so tall and wide-spreading plants have been used often. Notice also how rhythm and continuity are created with repeating heights, repeating colors (even though the colors come from different species), and by varying but repeating growth forms and textures (center).

This border bed of annuals at The Plant Kingdom is primarily seen by visitors through the windows of their vehicles, as they arrive and leave. The garden uses bold color to grab attention from a distance (bottom left).

This large garden area has border beds (both annual and perennial) that are viewed from the path and are one-sided. It also has an island bed (annuals) in the center left of the walkway, which is viewed from all sides so it has a spine of tall plants with shorter ones on either side (bottom right).

I once was helping a family with an overall yard design that involved a fairly large area surrounding their house. I laid out all my ideas and was particularly excited about one area that I thought would be perfect for a perennial display viewed front and center from their living room. What I had failed to ask at the onset was how they used their yard and what was important to them in their outdoor space. The family included several elementary-school-aged children and one of the primary considerations in the use of their yard was their sledding hill. It was the very spot that I thought was perfect for a perennial garden. Sledding on top of a perennial garden all winter was not going to work.

Is your garden one-sided or two-sided?

It might be the border up against a building and so it is viewed from only one side or it might be a rectangular garden in the middle of a lawn that is viewed from all sides. A border along a walkway may be viewed from the walkway only or it may also be seen from across a lawn that is separated from the walkway by the border. In a one-sided garden, the plants usually grade from tall in the back down to short on the side from which the garden is viewed. In a two-sided garden, there may be a central spine of tall plants grading down to shorter plants on each side. Because it is viewed from the two separate sides, the plants on one side do not necessarily need to be the same varieties as on the other side, as long as they coordinate in a design sense with the central spine.

How is balance achieved in your garden?

Is your garden asymmetrical or symmetrical? If it is circular, will the design radiate out from the center in concentric arcs or in triangular wedges or in intersecting waves? Or possibly it will instead be viewed from one point, so the tall plants are in the back and grade down to shorter plants along the front edge. If your garden is a border bed, will the same plant varieties and colors repeat periodically or will they gradually change, morphing into a new look as the border progresses but with enough variety and color repetition to achieve continuity, a form of balance? In all of these situations, the balance can be driven by size, color, and texture of the plants. For example, a color balance based on repeating blue plants does not always have to use the same variety or the same shade of blue. Similarly, repeating a noticeable plant such as yarrow in different colors can create height and texture balance, even though the color changes.

This is a circular annual garden that is viewed primarily from one half of the circumference so the tall plants at the back and short ones at the front fit the point of view.

The viewer's desire to walk this balanced path is driven by repeating colors, repeating heights, and varied but repeating textures and forms (top left).

In this annual garden (on the left in the photo), the yellows are positioned to zigzag through the space and keep the viewer's eye in the garden. The contrasting reds and oranges in the border are also eye magnets. They vary in shade and intensity and are echoed through the depth of the garden. The textures and heights are part of the excitement here but the primary driver is color. On the right in this photo, in the perennial garden, color repetition is provided by the subtle peaches of the foxglove and yarrow, the yellow foliage of the Hosta and the bleeding heart, and the hot pink of the Lythrum and the Geranium (top right).

How will you create eye movement in your garden?

How will your design catch a viewer's attention and keep it?

A successful garden design pulls us visually into the garden, through it, back out, and then back in, without our ever physically stepping into the garden. One design concept that accomplishes this is the triangle concept. Arrange the showpieces of your garden, whether created by color, height and texture, or contrast, in a visual triangle. For example, contrast attracts the eye, however it is created. Yellow is a color that grabs the viewer's attention, especially when it is starkly contrasted with other colors. Consider the implications of this: a border bed of reds and oranges with tall yellow flowers at the back does not work because the viewer's eye is drawn to the yellow at the back, exits the garden, and leaves. If there is a spot of yellow at the front corners of the bed, and maybe a few clusters of yellow in the middle as well as at the back, the viewer's eye bounces from front to middle to back and is drawn in again by the yellow at the front. Different textures, heights, and contrasting colors can all be used effectively to move viewers through the garden visually and to keep them returning to it.

If the garden is large enough for visitors to stroll through, walking paths should curve and wind so as to continually expose new vistas. This also serves to slow the viewer's pace and to maximize enjoyable time in the garden.

How are you going to create contrast in your garden, and what kind and how much will you use?

Eye movement is not the only aspect of a garden that is affected by contrast. The amount of contrast, whether introduced by color, texture, size, or any other plant characteristic, can determine much about the ambiance and character of a garden. Colors opposite each other on the color wheel can create high energy, an "espresso coffee" mood, whereas combining pastel colors serves to have a calming effect, or a "chamomile tea" feel. When attempting to create contrast, be careful not to design a garden that is too busy or disconnected. Repetition is one way to create cohesion without creating boredom. Repeat or echo colors, textures, and plant varieties (as mentioned in the case of the border bed earlier). In attempting to create a contrasting or high energy ambiance, avoid the one-of-everything concept, which makes your garden chaotic rather than exciting. And if you are planting a garden with many different varieties, be sure you have some type of unifying concept, such as a border of only one variety. This can bring some rest and calm to the storm of contrast and variation.

There are no two plants the same in this vignette of a border garden but the blues of the columbine, the *Campanula* and the monkshood give it unity. The intense blues contrasted with the bright salmon creates an ambiance of excitement. By the time these have finished blooming, the *Hydrangea* will have started. The pink of this woody plant's blossoms will be echoed in the salmon pink of the long-blooming yarrow and in the rose pink of the snapdragons in the annual bed on its north side.

In this border bed rhythm and movement are accomplished by the repetition of the same color provided by different species as in the case of the purple blue provided by two different varieties of *Nepeta* and in the distance by a *Campanula* and a *Veronica*. The repetition of white starts with *Phalaris*, then moves to *Achillea* 'The Pearl' ending with *Aegopodium*. Orange Asiatic lilies, *Lychnis* and *Achillea* provide a unifying repetition of orange. The voice of the yellow Asiatic lily is repeated by the yellow spikes of *Ligularia*. In this bed the varying textures and plant species are unified by the repetition of color and only slightly by the repetition of species (opposite).

These foxglove function as annuals in Fairbanks. This 'Dalmation Mix' display is an assortment of colors but they are all the same variety and that provides a fair amount of cohesion. However to bring a unifying concept to the whole garden of random colors we surrounded it with *Lobularia* 'Snow Princess' (left).

What is the scale of the setting into which you are adding a garden?
A perennial garden backed by a multistory building, a tall fence, or a high retaining wall may require plants with some height, such as *Thalictrum, Delphinium, Ligularia,* or tall Asiatic lilies. With such backdrops, a garden may even be most successful with some shrubs installed behind it. Short perennials will look lost and out of scale in these situations. On the opposite side of the spectrum, a rock garden is one where the plants are often very small, low-growing, and viewed on an individual basis at a close distance. In between these extremes is the scale of a border design along a narrow walkway to a front door. This is a place that calls for medium-height plants.

CHAPTER 9

Design at the Medium Level

Now let's focus on which players will be in our symphony. We have our stage, the garden space, waiting for us. We have formulated a macro plan so that we have a feel for how we are going to view and use the garden and what sort of ambiance we want it to have.

The next (and most fun) step is making our choices at the medium level, the instrument level, the plant level. Stop here for a moment and familiarize yourself with the physical characteristics of your site—sun exposure, soil chemistry, water availability, soil temperature—and then choose plants whose sunlight and cultural requirements are compatible.

As we discussed in Chapter 1, sun and shade are not always distinct in our northern climate. A definite example of sun exposure is a garden positioned against a highly reflective siding material and facing directly south with no shrubs, trees, or other shading elements to its south. An exposure that should be considered true shade is a garden on the north side of a building, surrounded and shaded by shrubs, trees, another building, or some other structural element to its north. In between these extremes is the wonderful gray area provided by northern climates where most plants, sun-loving or shade-loving, will thrive in the long hours of warm, low-angle sunlight. And so, even using the same plant palette, with the same number of plant varieties, the sun and shade choices are nearly double in the north as compared to more temperate climates.

Sun exposure can also be modified by where in the garden a plant is placed. Planting tall, bushy, sun-loving perennials at the southern-most sun-exposed side of the garden will serve to provide shade to the plants north of them, and hence a suitable habitat for more shade-loving perennials.

One aspect of cultural requirements is soil temperature. This is especially important for certain shade-loving perennials. It has been my experience that *Hosta*, *Astilbe*,

Here are *Hosta* and *Ligularia* in their second season in what could be considered a true shade location. It is an east exposure but there are tall trees about fifty feet east of this border garden, which is positioned in the shadow of the roof overhang. The soil is fairly warm here because the lawn receives a lot of south sun (top left).

Hosta 'Guacamole' growing in a south-facing garden that has shrubs and large herbaceous perennials. These provide shade for the *Hosta* (top right).

and the Himalayan blue poppies, for example, are traditionally shade-loving plants that seem to have a higher survival rate in our northern climate when they are grown in a southern exposure with warm soil, but with sun protection from surrounding plants. My conclusion, not scientifically proven, is that they prefer shade but not the colder soil temperatures associated with true shade in the north.

An added challenge around Fairbanks and much of Interior Alaska is gardening in areas that are underlain by permafrost and that have the often-accompanying conditions of poor drainage, low soil pH, low soil temperatures, and possibly a shorter frost-free growing season. You must vet your plant palette according to these parameters before considering anything else.

If you plan on enhancing your perennial garden with fall bulbs for early spring blooms, you should think about soil temperature and sun exposure when choosing your planting spot. See "Supplementing the Color in Your Perennial Garden" in Chapter 23.

Aside from the permafrost situation, I don't feel that other cultural requirements such as soil pH, soil fertility, and decent soil drainage are strongly species-specific within the perennial palette available to us in a northern climate like that of Fairbanks. Information gained from a soil test is always useful so that amendments such as limestone, compost, and other nutrients can be applied accordingly. Varietal tweaking for these cultural conditions would be nice in a perfect world or in lab conditions, but it will not mean life-or-death consequences in most perennial garden settings. My point is that the cultural conditions that work for *Achillea* will probably also be just fine for an Asiatic lily.

With macro decisions made and the physical parameters of the garden site established, we are ready to consider the characteristics of the plants themselves. Elements that will figure into the design process include bloom time; plant height; plant texture, form, and foliage; and flower color and form.

A Himalayan blue poppy showing its unusual color in a south exposure garden where it is surrounded and protected from the sun by a mixture of sun-tolerant perennials (left).

Astilbe 'Peach Blossom' enjoying a south exposure garden where taller plants shield it from the direct rays of the sun (right).

Bloom Time

Bloom time, as you are now aware, is the main design parameter that differentiates annual and perennial gardens. It is the big challenge of perennial design that may seem overwhelming on first glance. In fact, this challenge is the very reason that perennial garden design is so much fun.

The majority of perennial plants bloom for a relatively short portion of the growing season compared to annuals. The average duration of bloom time in herbaceous perennials is about a month, and in our northern climate, that could be in May or in August or somewhere in between. The challenge that this presents is to put all the other design considerations together and to do it in a way that assures at least something in your garden is blooming at any given time. To accomplish this, you must be familiar with the bloom time constraints of all of your component plants.

Spare yourself the experience of going to a garden center in mid-June and choosing the perennials that are in bloom simply because they catch your eye. If you follow this strategy, then in the following year (and years), your perennial garden will be glorious for a week or two on either side of mid-June, but the rest of the season it will be green and flowerless.

Bloom time boundaries are not black and white, but the relative positions of bloom times are fairly predictable. For example, Snowdrop Anemone will always complete its main bloom period before the *Ligularia* in your garden start blooming. This is where books on perennials can be useful no matter what the hardiness zone. There are many influencing factors that can jog the bloom time of a given plant earlier or later, but a spring blooming perennial will always bloom before a late summer blooming perennial.

Perennial wildflower mixes are great examples of the successful manipulation of bloom time. The varieties in these mixes have been chosen so that about the time one group has reached its bloom peak, another group is kicking in, and so there is a stunning display of color from spring to fall.

Sun, shade, and other factors creating microclimates can stall or hasten bloom time. Asiatic lilies on the north side of my house bloom several weeks later than those in the gardens on the south side. The later bloom time of herbaceous peonies in Alaska as compared to more temperate climates has been the basis for the development of our peony cut flower industry. Microclimates within the state have further separated the bloom times of peonies, another marketing plus.

Weather differences from season to season can move bloom times forward or back. Extremes such as the heat of the summer of 2013 and the heavy rainfall of 2014 in Interior Alaska make these shifts very noticeable. It is not only summer weather that affects bloom time end points. How spring happens, how fall happens, and what winter weather brings can not only shift the bloom season, but can also determine whether the perennial survives.

Paeonia 'Sarah Bernhardt' blossoming on the north side of a house in the shadow of the roof overhang. This sun-loving plant does not receive direct sunlight but it receives many hours of light at this time of year. Note that it is thriving in conditions that are also suitable for the shade-loving begonia on the right.

A gradual, steady temperature increase in the spring and decrease in the fall is conducive to consistent bloom times and good plant survival. A quick, early spring warm up may bring perennials out of dormancy early and so bloom time shifts earlier. A sudden, early fall can shorten or erase the bloom time of late fall bloomers.

Snow cover is crucial to the survival of many perennials because of the protective insulation it provides. Adequate snow cover ensures that perennials emerge strong in the spring and ready to bloom on time or maybe even early, depending on how spring arrives. However, very heavy snowfall may mean that it takes longer to melt and all perennials, especially those in shady areas, may emerge late and begin blooming later than they normally do.

Early fall weather that prevents adequate nutrient build-up and storage may weaken perennials and, in extreme cases, delay or even prevent bloom time entirely the next season. Freeze-thaw cycles in fall and spring can have a similar weakening effect, altering or delaying bloom time for a season.

Even activities of the gardener can change bloom time. Removing spent flowers, or deadheading, not only makes perennials look better, but also can extend the bloom season. Watering, fertilizing, enhancing soil nutrients, and weeding are all ways to grow a healthier plant and maximize bloom time length and bloom quality. Stressed plants tend to bloom early and briefly.

Using bloom time as a design tool is a basic of perennial design. Once you have mastered the concept and are having fun, you can take it to another level to showcase the power of bloom time. Imagine the Chameleon Garden, in which the garden color shifts through the season. For example, in early summer, the principal flower colors might be white and yellow, then shift to orange and red mid season, and end the summer in predominantly shades of blue and purple. Another version of this power of bloom time manipulation is one in which a consistent color palette is maintained through the season, but with a constantly changing plant palette as bloom times end and begin.

Ahhh! The challenge of micro-managing your perennial garden.

Plant Height

Consider also **plant height.** In any garden, our goal is to have tall plants behind shorter ones. Occasionally plants do not grow the height we expect. A plant growing taller than planned and blocking a shorter one in a perennial garden detracts from the visual order for more than just one season.

Varying heights, textures, forms, and foliage are all working together in this perennial garden vignette.

Plant tags and plant books are some places to look for information about plant height. However, there are variables that affect plant height from season to season. Growing conditions, including weather, can modify potential plant height seasonally. The distribution of water and fertilizer will also determine the height of a perennial from season to season, or of the height of the same variety at different spots in the same garden and the same season. Care given by the gardener can be a factor here, but changes such as growth in nearby native or ornamental shrubs and trees can also serve to decrease available water and nutrients. Sun exposure may affect plant height. In my own garden, Asiatic lilies that grow in the shade are not only later blooming but also taller than their counterparts in my south exposure garden. Depending on the plant, sun exposure can have the opposite effect on plant height. A sun-loving plant may thrive and reach its mature height a season or two sooner than the same plant in a shade location. The best way to deal with this uncertainty and variability in height is to avoid planting perennials exactly in front of each other. Instead, position each to one side of the plant immediately behind it in a zigzag fashion.

Texture, Form, and Foliage

Texture, form, and foliage are also parts of the plant choice decision. One way to add excitement to any garden is by using plants with different growth forms, textures and foliage. A combination of linear plants such as *Delphinium*, iris, and *Veronica* may give a "row of fenceposts" look; add the fluff of yarrow or columbine and immediately the balance and visual appeal improve. A variety of growth forms and leaf sizes keeps

the viewer's eye moving around in the garden. Equally effective is the practice of using just one or a few noticeable growth structures—such as Altai onion—to create a focal point within a collection of contrasting growth forms. Juxtaposing dramatically different growth forms, such as Snow on the Mountain (*Aegopodium variegatum*) with Asiatic lilies, creates pleasing contrast and excitement.

Plants that primarily add texture (such as *Artemesia* 'Silver Mound') and foliage (such as hostas) do not produce flowers as a major part of their function in the garden. Instead, they serve to showcase and provide contrasting background for their floriferous neighbors. They create calm and unity in the sea of color. Plants known for texture and foliage can also serve to unify a visually busy perennial planting if they are repeated strategically throughout the garden. The great strength of these plants is that they are always at their best, because blooms are not a necessary part of their contribution. Of course, plants known both for their foliage and their blooms are especially nice. Examples include *Polemonium* 'Touch of Class' with lavender blue flowers and variegated green and white foliage, and *Dicentra* 'Gold Heart' with chartreuse foliage and pink blooms. Others have dramatic form as well as flowers. such as many of the *Thalictrum* hybrids and cultivars.

The blue gray foliage of the Blue Globe Spruce and the Red Leaf Rose and the soft silvery leaves of the Silverberry add eye catching foliage and texture as they showcase the rose blossoms and tie in with the lilacs a few feet away (top right).

Lots of color in this small section of a garden but only one third of it is coming from flowers. The rest is foliage (top left).

Texture, form, foliage, and blossoms all working together to create this garden (bottom left).

The white of the 'The Pearl' is picked up in the foliage of the *Aegopodium* and both contrast with the other bright colored *Achillea* (right).

The elegant and unifying foliage of the *Hosta* and the *Aegopodium* are the reason these lilies stand out in the garden symphony (far right).

Flower Color, Shape, and Size

The characteristics of flowers—**their color, their shape, and their size**—all figure heavily in the design of a perennial garden. Any garden is more visually pleasing if
it includes a variety of flower sizes and shapes. Think of tiny, delicate forget-me-nots
sharing the stage with large, bold Asiatic lily blossoms and stately spikes of speedwell.
Of course, flower color is what we probably notice most in any garden, but especially
in a northern garden. Here the quality of ambient light intensifies all flower colors.
The many months of snow-covered gardens give us all a hunger and great appreciation
for the summer abundance of color.

It is the yellow green foliage of *Tanacetum* 'Isla Gold' providing the stunning backdrop and the contrast that makes the flowers in this garden sing out clearly (opposite bottom).

Pastel colors, an undulating flow created by different heights and growth forms, and the clear white of the variegated dogwood make this a peaceful garden (top left).

Cheerful soft colors, a mix of growth forms, and touches of white give this garden a chamomile tea feel (top right).

Complementary colors add excitement to this garden (bottom left).

Contrasting colors charge this garden with energy (bottom right).

June 6 (back side)

July 6 (front side)

July 22 (front side)

July 22 (backside)

August 1 (front side)

August 22 (front side)

In a perennial garden, as in any landscape, flowers in warm color tones such as red, yellow, and orange move visually forward in a garden whereas the cooler colors, including blue, violet, and green, recede. You can use this trait of color to guide your viewer's eye in the garden. Complementary colors (those opposite each other on the color wheel) serve to create contrast and excitement when placed together in a garden. Think of *Trollius* 'Golden Queen,' Asiatic lily 'Fata Morgana,' *Veronica* 'Purpleicious,' and *Lychnis* 'Molten Lava.' When combined in a perennial garden, these produce what I like to think of as an Espresso Garden. Perennial garden designs that combine shades and hues of the same color will have a soothing effect. Picture Asiatic lily 'Elodie,' *Campanula* 'Pink Octopus,' *Veronica* 'Pink Damask,' and *Achillea* 'Appleblossom,' with some *Achillea* 'The Pearl' added for fluff. This to me is a Chamomile Tea Garden, calming and quiet. Color catches your eye, creates an ambiance, and holds the position of a major player in the garden symphony.

Now it is time to make the plant choices appropriate to our specific garden. We will make those choices within the framework of parameters outlined in this chapter. To assure that our plant choices create a garden symphony that has at least some plants adding color all through the season, we will refer to the Garden Symphony Charts in Chapters 11 through 14 of Part III, always considering bloom time as we choose heights, colors, and foliage.

June 6. Foliage is adding dependable color in this garden where *Centaurea montana*, a blue columbine, Snowdrop Anemone and *Paeonia* 'Jana' (far right end of garden) are the only blooming plants.

July 6. Yellow bedstraw, two cultivars of *Lychnis*, *Valerian*, and yarrow have all now chimed in.

July 22. In this photo of the front of the bed we see the blue of *Nepeta* in two areas and also of *Clematis integrifolia*.

July 22. In this photo of the back side of the bed on the same date, a white *Veronica* and *Ligularia* 'The Rocket' are now serious players. We can see also that the seedpods of the Altai onion have already formed.

August 1. The plants chiming in now are *Veronica* 'Ulster Blue' and a yellow daylily.

August 22. Note that many perennials have received their fall cutback in this photo. The new bloomers are the salmon colored flowers of the daylily and the low-growing gentian to the right of the yellow daylily.

A glorious wildflower mix in full bloom in mid to late summer at The Plant Kingdom. These mixes are built on the concept of sequential bloom of perennials (left).

PART III

The Charts

Achillea 'The Pearl,'
Veronica 'Charlotte,'
Filipendula sp., and
Nepeta siberica
in the background with
Verbascum 'Southern Charm'
in the foreground.

CHAPTER 10

A Guide to the Charts

What I want to introduce to you now are the Garden Symphony Charts—lists of perennials categorized by specific design parameters. These parameters are crucial to the mechanical process of choosing the players for your garden symphony. For an alphabetical listing and more complete description of each of the perennials referenced in the Garden Symphony Charts, see Chapter 21: "The Symphony Players."

The Master Chart lists approximately two hundred fifty perennials by genus and common name and then by species or cultivar. It includes the bloom time, height, and color category for each plant and notes foliage or fragrance when these apply. A second set of three charts assorts the perennials according to Early, Mid, and Late Bloom Time. The Bloom Time Charts provide a temporal arrangement to the garden and are crucial to the creation of a garden symphony that truly sings with color all season long. Three more charts organize the perennials according to Short, Medium, or Tall height and provide spatial guidance for the garden. The remaining six charts assort the perennial flowers according to color groups. These are blue or purple, pink or lavender, orange or peach, red, yellow, and white. These flower color charts and the foliage designations facilitate the finely-tuned expression of the gardener's color sensibilities. The overlap of information across the charts and the assortment by specific parameters, means the ones you will find most useful in designing a specific garden will be determined by the most dominant theme of your garden.

These charts have all the information you need to make the plant choices for a perennial garden that is full of music all summer long. First, let's look a little more closely at the parameters presented in the Garden Symphony Charts.

Bloom Time

The three bloom time categories are broken down as follows:

> Early: May-June
>
> Mid: June-July
>
> Late: July-August

These are fluid boundaries. The Bloom Time classification shows the relative position of the bloom cycle. As was discussed in Chapter 9, the actual dates may be skewed earlier or later by the growing conditions offered by a particular growing season or by a particular garden habitat. If a plant begins blooming in early June and has completed most of its bloom by the first week in July, I would consider it part of the Early category. If it begins blooming in mid June and continues until mid July, I would consider it a Mid season bloomer. For purposes of the garden symphony, the exact dates of a plant's bloom time are not crucial. Its bloom time in relation to the bloom times of others in the symphony is what determines the success and flow of the music. In timing the garden symphony, the phrase "it's all relative" truly applies

Many perennials span two or even three of the bloom time categories. All of the species or cultivars that start blooming in May or in June are listed as Early, but they may also be listed as Mid and even Late if the bloom time continues on through July or August. This means that their names will appear on the Mid and Late Charts as well. Similarly, plants listed on the Mid Chart may begin blooming in mid season and continue through August or later, and so their names will also appear on the Late Chart.

Height Charts

The purpose of these charts is to give the relative heights of the plants that are being incorporated in the design.

I have chosen three height designations as follows:

> Short – 12" or less
>
> Medium – 12"-24"
>
> Tall – 24" or more

There is overlap among the three height categories because there is always some variation in height, even within a given species or cultivar. For example, when choosing the height designation for a given cultivar, if most of the individuals are not taller than 12 inches, I would classify it as Short for purposes of design. If the majority of the individuals in the cultivar are 12 inches or taller but less than 24 inches, I would categorize it as a Medium height plant. Following the height category designation for each species or cultivar, I have listed in parentheses either a numerical range of heights or a single maximum height specific to this plant group (in inches, unless otherwise noted).

As we discussed earlier, there is always the possibility of height variation related to factors such as weather, nutrients, moisture, and sun exposure. This is the reason that it is wise to stagger plants when positioning them in the garden so that no plant is directly in front of or behind a plant in the next row.

Color

I have classified flower color into six different color groups. Within each of these six groups there are many shades, hues, intensities, and expressions of that color. As you fine-tune the color palette of your garden, you will become more familiar with the subtle color differences between flowers and the way they are expressed in the garden. You will also become more discerning of specific color shades that blend or contrast with the colors of other flowers that are blooming at the same time. It won't be long before you know what plants produce blooms that are the exact hue that you need in your garden.

For picotee or bicolor flowers I have either listed them under the predominant color, or in a few cases where the picotee aspect is evenly split between two colors, I have listed that plant under two different color categories.

Remember also that when you are choosing plants based on the color charts, it is equally important to check the bloom time. If, for example, you want to create a garden where intense dark blue and lemon yellow flowers are blooming at the same time, you will not achieve this by planting *Gentiana septemfida* next to *Trollius* 'Earliest of All.' The colors are right but the bloom times are not, and the *Trollius* will have finished blooming some time in June while the gentian will not start until late July.

Foliage

I have made what may seem like arbitrary decisions about whether the Foliage column on the charts is checked. After all, the foliage of almost all perennials is a useful design feature. I have checked this column for plants with unusual foliage (color, variegation, texture) or for plants whose main contribution to the garden is their foliage as opposed to their flowers.

Fragrance

I have checked the Fragrance column if the fragrance of flowers and/or foliage is a noticeable part of the plant's contribution to the garden symphony. Almost any plant in the perennial garden has its own scent, especially in high humidity conditions, but there are certain plants whose scent is their signature. Consider a peony, a sweet rocket, or a rose.

Plant Names

The Garden Symphony Charts show the genus or scientific name of the plant and next to that, the common name is in parentheses. In the case of some plants, gardeners may be more familiar with the scientific name than the common name, but the opposite may be true as well. I find myself more comfortable with *Thalictrum* than meadow rue but on the other hand, I am much more likely to refer to yarrow rather than *Achillea*. Hence, I feel it is useful to show both and I will use them interchangeably as we continue.

The second column in each chart lists "species or cultivar", terms which are not at the same level in the taxonomic hierarchy. However, from a design standpoint I consider them equivalent because the plants we are using are, for the most part, either species or cultivars of a species.

A Final Note

I mentioned earlier but must remind you again that the list of plants in the charts that follow is not exhaustive. There are many perennials that you may have grown yourself or that are most certainly hardy but which none of us have trialed. Add to this the complication that availability and popularity of perennial plant cultivars is constantly changing. Old ones may be dropped from commercial production and new ones are constantly being added by plant breeders. So even if my lists were all-inclusive at this moment, the names of the players will change over time.

What my plant lists are intended to do is to provide you with a manageable palette of perennials with known parameters, so that you can practice the mechanics of fitting together the players in the garden symphony. Once you have the system in place, you can add new plants to the Garden Symphony Charts as they become available and as they prove to be hardy.

CHAPTER 11

Master Chart

Genus	Species or Cultivar	Bloom Time	Height (inches)	Color	Foliage	Fragrance
Achillea (Yarrow)	Appleblossom	Early, Mid, Late	Tall (18-30)	Pink or Lavender		x
Achillea (Yarrow)	Laura	Early, Mid, Late	Tall (24)	Red		x
Achillea (Yarrow)	Love Parade	Early, Mid, Late	Tall (18-30)	Pink or Lavender		x
Achillea (Yarrow)	Paprika	Early, Mid, Late	Medium (18-24)	Red		x
Achillea (Yarrow)	Saucy Seduction	Early, Mid, Late	Tall (27)	Pink or Lavender		x
Achillea (Yarrow)	Sunny Seduction	Early, Mid, Late	Tall (27)	Yellow		x
Achillea (Yarrow)	Terra Cotta	Early, Mid, Late	Tall (30-36)	Orange or Peach		x
Achillea (Yarrow)	The Pearl	Early, Mid, Late	Medium (24)	White		
Aconitum (Monkshood)	*arendsii*	Late	Tall (40)	Blue or Purple		
Aconitum (Monkshood)	Blue and White Bicolor	Late	Tall (48)	Blue or Purple		
Aconitum (Monkshood)	Blue Lagoon	Late	Short (10-12)	Blue or Purple		

Genus	Species or Cultivar	Bloom Time	Height (inches)	Color	Foliage	Fragrance
Aconitum (Monkshood)	Bressingham Spire	Late	Tall (30-36)	Blue or Purple		
Aconitum (Monkshood)	Pink Sensation	Late	Tall (40-48)	Pink or Lavender		
Aconitum (Monkshood)	Stainless Steel	Late	Tall (40)	Blue or Purple		
Actaea (Bugbane)	Black Negligee	Late	Tall (42-60)	White	x	
Actaea (Bugbane)	Pink Spike	Late	Tall (42-60)	Pink or Lavender	x	
Aegopodium (Bishop's Weed)	Variegata	Early, Mid	Medium (16)	White	x	
Allium (Ornamental Onion)	*altaicum*	Mid	Tall (24-36)	White		x
Allium (Ornamental Onion)	Millenium	Late	Medium (12-18)	Pink or Lavender		x
Allium (Ornamental Onion)	Purple Sensation	Early	Tall (24-36)	Blue or Purple		x
Allium (Ornamental Onion)	*senescens*	Mid	Short (6-12)	Pink or Lavender		x
Anemone (Windflower)	Snowdrop	Early	Medium (12-15)	White		
Anemone (Windflower)	Robustissima	Late	Tall (32)	Pink or Lavender		
Aquilegia (Columbine)	Cameo Blue-White	Early	Short (6-8)	Blue or Purple		
Aquilegia (Columbine)	Cameo Pink-White	Early	Short (6-8)	Pink or Lavender		
Aquilegia (Columbine)	Colorado Violet and White	Early, Mid	Tall (24-28)	Blue or Purple		
Aquilegia (Columbine)	Nora Barlow	Early, Mid	Tall (30)	Pink or Lavender		
Aquilegia (Columbine)	Rocky Mountain Blue	Early, Mid	Medium (24)	Blue or Purple		
Aquilegia (Columbine)	Songbird Cardinal	Early, Mid	Medium (16-24)	Red		

Genus	Species or Cultivar	Bloom Time	Height (inches)	Color	Foliage	Fragrance
Aquilegia (Columbine)	Songbird Robin	Early, Mid	Medium (16-24)	Pink or Lavender		
Aquilegia (Columbine)	Swan Yellow	Early, Mid	Medium (20-24)	Yellow		
Aquilegia (Columbine)	Swan Pink and Yellow	Early, Mid	Medium (20-24)	Pink or Lavender, Yellow		
Aquilegia (Columbine)	Winky Double Dark Blue-White	Early, Mid	Short (12)	Blue or Purple		
Aquilegia (Columbine)	Winky Double Rose-White	Early, Mid	Short (12)	Pink or Lavender		
Aquilegia (Columbine)	Woodside Gold	Early, Mid	Medium (18-24)	Blue or Purple	x	
Artemesia (Wormwood)	Silver Brocade	Mid	Short (6-12)	Yellow	x	
Artemesia (Wormwood)	Silver Mound	Mid	Short (10)	Yellow	x	
Artemesia (Wormwood)	Valerie Finnis	Mid	Medium (15-18)	Yellow	x	
Aruncus (Goat's Beard)	*aethusifolius*	Mid	Short (10)	White	x	
Aruncus (Goat's Beard)	*dioicus*	Mid	Tall (60)	White	x	
Aruncus (Goat's Beard)	Horatio	Mid	Tall (48)	White	x	
Aruncus (Goat's Beard)	Kneiffii	Mid	Tall (24-36)	White	x	
Astilbe (False Spirea)	Chocolate Shogun	Mid, Late	Medium (18-24)	Pink or Lavender	x	
Astilbe (False Spirea)	Colorflash	Late	Medium (20)	Pink or Lavender	x	
Astilbe (False Spirea)	Fanal	Mid, Late	Medium (24)	Red		
Astilbe (False Spirea)	Maggie Daley	Late	Tall (28)	Pink or Lavender		
Astilbe (False Spirea)	Peach Blossom	Mid, late	Medium (24)	Pink or Lavender		
Astilbe (False Spirea)	Rhythm and Blues	Late	Tall (26)	Pink or Lavender		

Genus	Species or Cultivar	Bloom Time	Height (inches)	Color	Foliage	Fragrance
Bergenia (Pigsqueak)	Winterglow	Early	Medium (12-15)	Pink or Lavender	x	
Brunnera (Siberian Bugloss)	Alexander's Great	Early	Medium (16)	Blue or Purple	x	
Brunnera (Siberian Bugloss)	Jack Frost	Early	Medium (16)	Blue or Purple	x	
Campanula (Bell Flower)	Campbell	Mid, Late	Medium (16-18)	Blue or Purple		
Campanula (Bell Flower)	Cherry Bells	Mid, Late	Medium (16-18)	Red		
Campanula (Bell Flower)	Genti Twisterbell	Mid, Late	Medium (16-18)	Blue or Purple		
Campanula (Bell Flower)	Kent Belle	Mid, Late	Tall (18-28)	Blue or Purple		
Campanula (Bell Flower)	Olympia	Mid, Late	Short (6-12)	Blue or Purple		
Campanula (Bell Flower)	Pink Octopus	Mid, Late	Short (12)	Pink or Lavender		
Campanula (Bell Flower)	Silver Bells	Mid, Late	Medium (15)	Pink or Lavender	x	x
Campanula (Bell Flower)	*superba*	Mid, Late	Tall (24-30)	Blue or Purple		
Campanula (Bell Flower)	*takesimana*	Mid, Late	Medium (24)	Pink or Lavender		
Centaurea (Bachelor's Button)	Amethyst in Snow	Early, Mid, Late	Medium (14-16)	White		
Centaurea (Bachelor's Button)	Black Sprite	Early, Mid, Late	Medium (16)	Blue or Purple		
Centaurea (Bachelor's Button)	John Coutts	Early, Mid, Late	Medium (20)	Pink or Lavender		
Centaurea (Bachelor's Button)	Mountain Bluet	Early, Mid, Late	Tall (24-30)	Blue or Purple		
Cerastium (Snow-in-Summer)	*tomentosum*	Early	Short (6)	White	x	

Genus	Species or Cultivar	Bloom Time	Height (inches)	Color	Foliage	Fragrance
Chelone (Turtlehead)	Alba	Late	Tall (36)	White		
Chelone (Turtlehead)	*rosea*	Late	Tall (24-36)	Pink or Lavender		
Chelone (Turtlehead)	Tiny Tortuga	Late	Medium (14-16)	Pink or Lavender		
Clematis (Clematis)	Blue Bird	Early, Mid	Tall (10 feet)	Blue or Purple		
Clematis (Clematis)	*integrifolia*	Early, Mid, Late	Tall (18-36)	Blue or Purple		
Clematis (Clematis)	Alba	Early, Mid, Late	Tall (18-36)	White		
Clematis (Clematis)	Rosea	Early, Mid, Late	Tall (18-36)	Pink or Lavender		
Clematis (Clematis)	Purpurea	Early, Mid	Tall (30)	White	x	
Clematis (Clematis)	Radar Love	Early, Mid	Tall (12-15 feet)	Yellow		x
Delphinium (Delphinium)	Blue Butterfly	Mid	Medium (16)	Blue or Purple		
Delphinium (Delphinium)	Magic Fountains Dark Blue-Dark Bee	Mid	Tall (24-40)	Blue or Purple		
Delphinium (Delphinium)	Magic Fountains Lilac Pink-White Bee	Mid	Tall (24-40)	Pink or Lavender		
Delphinium (Delphinium)	Magic Fountains Pure White	Mid	Tall (24-40)	White		
Delphinium (Delphinium)	Magic Fountains Sky Blue-White Bee	Mid	Tall (24-40)	Blue or Purple		
Delphinium (Delphinium)	Summer Blues	Mid	Short (12)	Blue or Purple		

Genus	Species or Cultivar	Bloom Time	Height (inches)	Color	Foliage	Fragrance
Delphinium (Delphinium)	Summer Morning	Mid	Short (12)	Pink or Lavender		
Delphinium (Delphinium)	Summer Nights	Mid	Short (12)	Blue or Purple		
Dianthus (Pinks)	Arctic Fire	Mid, Late	Short (6-8)	Red, White		
Dianthus (Pinks)	Pink Maiden	Mid, Late	Short (6-8)	Pink or Lavender		
Dianthus (Pinks)	Red Maiden	Mid, Late	Short (6-8)	Pink or Lavender		
Dicentra (Bleeding Heart)	Burning Hearts	Mid	Short (10-12)	Red	x	
Dicentra (Bleeding Heart)	Candy Hearts	Mid	Short (10-12)	Pink or Lavender	x	
Dicentra (Bleeding Heart)	Gold Heart	Mid	Tall (24-30)	Pink or Lavender	x	
Dicentra (Bleeding Heart)	*spectabilis*	Mid	Tall (30)	Pink or Lavender		
Dicentra (Bleeding Heart)	Alba	Mid	Tall (30)	White		
Dicentra (Bleeding Heart)	Valentine	Mid	Tall (30)	Red		
Dodecatheon (Shooting Star)	*meadia*	Early	Short (6-12)	Pink or Lavender		
Dodecatheon (Shooting Star)	Aphrodite	Early	Medium (18)	Pink or Lavender		
Draba (Whitlow-grass)	*siberica*	Early, Late	Short (6)	Yellow		
Filipendula (Meadowsweet)	Kahome	Early	Short (12)	Pink or Lavender	x	
Filipendula (Meadowsweet)	Elegans	Early	Tall (28)	Pink or Lavender	x	
Filipendula (Meadowsweet)	Venusta	Early	Tall (60)	Pink or Lavender	x	
Filipendula (Meadowsweet)	Variegata	Early	Tall (36-48)	White	x	
Galium (Bedstraw)	*verum*	Early, Late	Medium (10-24)	Yellow		

Genus	Species or Cultivar	Bloom Time	Height (inches)	Color	Foliage	Fragrance
Gentiana (Gentian)	*septemfida*	Late	Short (8-12)	Blue or Purple		
Gentiana (Gentian)	True Blue	Late	Tall (30)	Blue or Purple		
Geranium (Cranesbill)	Birch Double	Mid	Short (10-12)	Pink or Lavender		
Geranium (Cranesbill)	Double Jewel	Mid	Short (12)	White		
Geranium (Cranesbill)	Lakwijk Star	Mid, Late	Medium (12-18)	Pink or Lavender	x	
Geranium (Cranesbill)	Nimbus	Mid, Late	Medium (16-24)	Blue or Purple		
Hemerocallis (Day Lily)	Flava	Early, Mid	Tall (30)	Yellow	x	x
Hemerocallis (Day Lily)	Fragrant Returns	Mid, Late	Medium (18)	Yellow	x	x
Hemerocallis (Day Lily)	Little Grapette	Mid	Short (12)	Blue or Purple	x	
Hemerocallis (Day Lily)	Hyperion	Late	Tall (36-42)	Yellow	x	x
Hemerocallis (Day Lily)	Mauna Loa	Late	Medium (22)	Orange or Peach	x	
Hemerocallis (Day Lily)	Stella de Oro	Early, Mid, Late	Medium (12-18)	Yellow		
Hesperis (Rocket)	*matronalis*	Early	Tall (36)	Pink or Lavender		x
Hosta (Plantain Lily)	Guacamole	Mid	Medium (12-24)	Blue or Purple	x	x
Hosta (Plantain Lily)	True Blue	Mid	Tall (24-30)	White	x	
Iris (Iris)	Butter and Sugar	Mid	Tall (24-30)	Yellow	x	
Iris (Iris)	Caesar's Brother	Mid	Tall (24-39)	Blue or Purple	x	
Iris (Iris)	Ruffled Velvet	Mid	Tall (30)	Blue or Purple	x	
Iris (Iris)	*setosa*	Early	Medium (12-24)	Blue or Purple		

Genus	Species or Cultivar	Bloom Time	Height (inches)	Color	Foliage	Fragrance
Iris (Iris)	Snow Queen	Mid	Tall (24-30)	White	x	
Lamium (Dead Nettle)	Beacon Silver	Early, Mid, Late	Short (6-8)	Pink or Lavender	x	
Lamium (Dead Nettle)	Pink Pewter	Early, Mid, Late	Short (6-8)	Pink or Lavender	x	
Lamium (Dead Nettle)	White Nancy	Early, Mid, Late	Short (6-8)	White	x	
Lewisia (Bitterroot)	Little Peach	Mid, Late	Short (6)	Orange or Peach		
Lewisia (Bitterroot)	Little Plum	Mid, Late	Short (6)	Pink or Lavender		
Leymus (Wild Rye)	*arenarius*	Mid	Tall (24-36)	Yellow	x	
Ligularia (Ligularia)	Britt-Marie Crawford	Late	Tall (36-40)	Yellow	x	
Ligularia (Ligularia)	Desdemona	Mid, Late	Tall (30-36)	Yellow		
Ligularia (Ligularia)	Little Rocket	Mid	Tall (30)	Yellow		
Ligularia (Ligularia)	Othello	Late	Tall (36)	Yellow	x	
Ligularia (Ligularia)	The Rocket	Mid	Tall (72)	Yellow		
Lilium (Lily)	Apricot Fudge	Mid, late	Tall (24-36)	Orange or Peach		
Lilium (Lily)	Blackout	Mid, Late	Tall (48)	Red		
Lilium (Lily)	Citronelle	Late	Tall (48)	Yellow		
Lilium (Lily)	Conca d'Or	Mid, late	Tall (36-60)	Yellow		
Lilium (Lily)	Elodie	Mid, Late	Tall (48)	Pink or Lavender		
Lilium (Lily)	Fata Morgana	Mid, Late	Tall (36-48)	Yellow		
Lilium (Lily)	Golden Matrix	Mid, Late	Medium (16)	Yellow		
Lilium (Lily)	Landini	Mid, Late	Tall (42)	Red		
Lilium (Lily)	Lily Looks™ Tiny Moon	Mid, Late	Medium (12-14)	Orange or Peach		
Lilium (Lily)	Matrix	Mid, Late	Medium (16)	Orange or Peach		
Lilium (Lily)	Pink Tiger	Late	Tall (48)	Pink or Lavender		

Genus	Species or Cultivar	Bloom Time	Height (inches)	Color	Foliage	Fragrance
Lilium (Lily)	Splendens	Late	Tall (48)	Orange or Peach		
Lilium (Lily)	Tango Passions	Mid, Late	Medium (14-16)	Pink or Lavender		
Lychnis (Campion)	Dusky Salmon	Mid, Late	Tall (48)	Orange or Peach		
Lychnis (Campion)	Lumina Salmon Shades	Mid, late	Medium (12-15)	Orange or Peach		
Lychnis (Campion)	Maltese Cross	Mid	Tall (48)	Red		
Lychnis (Campion)	Molten Lava	Mid, Late	Medium (12-15)	Red		
Lychnis (Campion)	Orange Gnome	Mid, Late	Medium (12-15)	Orange or Peach		
Lychnis (Campion)	Vesuvius	Mid, Late	Medium (12-15)	Red		
Lysimachia (Loosestrife)	Alexander	Mid, Late	Medium (12-24)	Yellow		
Lysimachia (Loosestrife)	Firecracker	Mid, Late	Medium (12-24)	Yellow		
Lythrum (Purple Loosestrife)	Rosy Gem	Late	Tall (48-60)	Pink or Lavender		
Meconopsis (Himalayan Blue Poppy)	*betonicifolia*	Mid, Late	Tall (30-48)	Blue or Purple		
Meconopsis (Himalayan Blue Poppy)	Lingholm	Mid, Late	Tall (36-48)	Blue or Purple		
Myosotis (Forget-Me-Not)	*alpestris*	Mid	Short (6-10)	Blue or Purple		
Nepeta (Nepeta)	Blue Dreams	Mid, Late	Tall (24-36)	Blue or Purple		x
Nepeta (Nepeta)	Dropmore Blue	Mid, Late	Medium (24)	Blue or Purple		x
Nepeta (Nepeta)	Pink Dreams	Mid, Late	Tall (24-36)	Pink or Lavender		x

Genus	Species or Cultivar	Bloom Time	Height (inches)	Color	Foliage	Fragrance
Nepeta (Nepeta)	*siberica*	Mid, Late	Tall (36)	Blue or Purple		x
Nepeta (Nepeta)	Souvenir D' Andre Chaudrón	Mid, Late	Tall (36)	Blue or Purple		x
Nepeta (Nepeta)	Walker's Low	Mid, Late	Medium (24)	Blue or Purple		x
Paeonia (Peony)	Bartzella	Mid	Tall (34)	Yellow		x
Paeonia (Peony)	Buckeye Belle	Mid	Tall (34)	Red		x
Paeonia (Peony)	Coral Charm	Mid	Tall (36)	Orange or Peach		x
Paeonia (Peony)	Festiva Maxima	Mid	Tall (40)	White		x
Paeonia (Peony)	Jana	Early	Tall (36)	Pink or Lavender		
Paeonia (Peony)	Karl Rosenfeld	Mid	Tall (38)	Red		x
Paeonia (Peony)	Kopper Kettle	Mid	Tall (32)	Orange or Peach		x
Paeonia (Peony)	Sorbet	Mid	Tall (28)	Pink or Lavender		x
Papaver (Poppy)	Allegro	Mid	Short (10-12)	Red		
Papaver (Poppy)	Brilliant	Mid	Tall (32-36)	Orange or Peach		
Papaver (Poppy)	Little Patty's Plum	Mid	Medium (20)	Pink or Lavender		
Papaver (Poppy)	Patty's Plum	Mid	Tall (28-32)	Pink or Lavender		
Papaver (Poppy)	Princess Louise	Mid	Tall (24)	Orange or Peach		
Phalaris (Ribbon Grass)	Dwarf Garters	Late	Short ((10-15)	White	x	
Phalaris (Ribbon Grass)	Picta	Late	Medium (24)	White	x	
Phalaris (Ribbon Grass)	Strawberries and Cream	Late	Medium (24)	White	x	
Phlomis (Phlomis)	*tuberosa*	Mid	Tall (36-48)	Pink or Lavender		

Genus	Species or Cultivar	Bloom Time	Height (inches)	Color	Foliage	Fragrance
Phlox (Phlox)	Blue Emerald	Early.Mid	Short (6)	Blue or Purple		
Phlox (Phlox)	North Hills	Early, Mid	Short (4-8)	Blue or Purple, White		
Phlox (Phlox)	Sherwood Purple	Mid, late	Short (6-10)	Blue or Purple		x
Polemonium (Jacob's Ladder)	Bressingham Purple	Early, Mid	Medium (15)	Blue or Purple		x
Polemonium (Jacob's Ladder)	Touch of Class	Early, Mid	Medium (15-18)	Blue or Purple	x	x
Physostegia (Obedient Plant)	Crystal Peak White	Late	Medium (16)	White		
Physostegia (Obedient Plant)	Bouquet Rose	Late	Medium (24)	Pink or Lavender		
Physostegia (Obedient Plant)	Variegata	Late	Tall (24-36)	Pink or Lavender	x	
Polygonatum (Solomon's Seal)	Variegatum	Mid	Medium (18-24)	White	x	
Potentilla (Cinquefoil)	Monarch's Velvet	Mid, Late	Medium (10-15)	Red		
Potentilla (Cinquefoil)	William Rollinson	Mid, Late	Medium (16)	Orange or Peach		
Primula (Primrose)	*florindae*	Early, Mid	Medium (20)	Yellow		x
Primula (Primrose)	*matthioli*	Early	Short (10)	Pink or Lavender		
Primula (Primrose)	*sikkimensis*	Early, Mid	Medium (20)	Yellow		x
Pulsatilla (Pasque Flower)	Alba	Early	Short (10)	White		
Pulsatilla (Pasque Flower)	Rubra	Mid	Short (10)	Red		
Pulsatilla (Pasque Flower)	*vulgaris*	Early	Short (10)	Blue or Purple		
Sedum (Stonecrop)	Tricolor	Mid, Late	Short (4)	Red	x	
Sedum (Stonecrop)	Variegatum	Mid, Late	Short (5)	Orange or Peach	x	

Genus	Species or Cultivar	Bloom Time	Height (inches)	Color	Foliage	Fragrance
Solidago (Goldenrod)	Little Lemon	Late	Short (12)	Yellow		
Tanacetum (Tansy)	Crispum	Mid, Late	Tall (24-36)	Yellow	x	
Tanacetum (Tansy)	Isla Gold	Mid, Late	Tall (36-48)	Yellow	x	
Tanacetum (Tansy)	Robinson's Pink	Mid, Late	Medium (18-24)	Pink or Lavender		
Tanacetum (Tansy)	Robinson's Red	Mid, Late	Medium (18-24)	Pink or Lavender		
Tanacetum (Tansy)	*vulgare*	Mid, Late	Tall (36-48)	Yellow		
Thalictrum (Meadow Rue)	Anne	Mid	Tall (84)	Pink or Lavender	x	
Thalictrum (Meadow Rue)	*aquilegifolium*	Mid	Tall (48)	Pink or Lavender	x	
Thalictrum (Meadow Rue)	Black Stockings	Mid	Tall (48)	Pink or Lavender	x	
Thalictrum (Meadow Rue)	Flavum	Mid, Late	Tall (48)	Yellow	x	
Thalictrum (Meadow Rue)	Hewitt's Double	Mid, Late	Tall (48)	Blue or Purple	x	
Thalictrum (Meadow Rue)	Splendide	Mid, Late	Tall (48-72)	Pink or Lavender	x	
Trollius (Globeflower)	Alabaster	Mid	Medium (24)	White		
Trollius (Globeflower)	Earliest of All	Early	Medium (24)	Yellow		
Trollius (Globeflower)	*europaeus*	Early	Medium (24)	Yellow		
Trollius (Globeflower)	Golden Queen	Late	Tall (36)	Orange or Peach		
Trollius (Globeflower)	*ledebourii*	Mid, Late	Medium (18-24)	Orange or Peach		
Trollius (Globeflower)	Lemon Queen	Mid	Tall (18-36)	Yellow		
Trollius (Globeflower)	*pumilus*	Early	Short (6-8)	Yellow		
Trollius (Globeflower)	Superbus	Mid	Medium (24)	Yellow		
Veronica (Speedwell)	Bicolor Explosion	Mid, Late	Medium (15-18)	Blue or Purple		
Veronica (Speedwell)	Blue Bomb	Mid, late	Medium (15-18)	Blue or Purple		
Veronica (Speedwell)	Charlotte	Mid, Late	Tall (30)	White		
Veronica (Speedwell)	*gentianoides*	Early	Medium (18-20)	Blue or Purple		

Genus	Species or Cultivar	Bloom Time	Height (inches)	Color	Foliage	Fragrance
Veronica (Speedwell)	Giles van Hees	Mid	Short (6-8)	Pink or Lavender		
Veronica (Speedwell)	Icicle White	Mid, Late	Medium (18)	White		
Veronica (Speedwell)	Pink Bomb	Mid, Late	Medium (15-18)	Pink or Lavender		
Veronica (Speedwell)	Pink Damask	Mid, Late	Tall (24-36)	Pink or Lavender		
Veronica (Speedwell)	Purpleicious	Mid, Late	Medium (20)	Blue or Purple		
Veronica (Speedwell)	Red Fox	Mid	Medium (18)	Pink or Lavender		
Veronica (Speedwell)	Royal Candles	Mid, Late	Medium (16-18)	Blue or Purple		
Veronica (Speedwell)	Spicata Blue	Mid	Medium (18-24)	Blue or Purple		
Veronica (Speedwell)	Spicata Rose	Mid	Medium (18-24)	Pink or Lavender		
Veronica (Speedwell)	Ulster Blue	Mid	Short (6-8)	Blue or Purple		
Veronica (Speedwell)	Waterperry Blue	Early	Short (6-8)	Blue or Purple		
Veronicastrum (Culver Root)	Apollo	Late	Tall (59)	Blue or Purple		
Veronicastrum (Culver Root)	Erica	Late	Tall (59)	Pink or Lavender		
Veronicastrum (Culver Root)	Fascination	Late	Tall (59)	Blue or Purple		
Veronicastrum (Culver Root)	Red Arrow	Late	Tall (49)	Pink or Lavender		

List your own species and cultivars here:

Genus	Species or Cultivar	Bloom Time	Height (inches)	Color	Foliage	Fragrance

CHAPTER 12

Bloom Time Charts

Early-Season Bloomers

Genus	Species or Cultivar	Bloom Time	Height (inches)	Color	Foliage	Fragrance
Achillea (Yarrow)	Appleblossom	Early, Mid, Late	Tall (18-30)	Pink or Lavender		x
Achillea (Yarrow)	Laura	Early, Mid, Late	Tall (24)	Red		x
Achillea (Yarrow)	Love Parade	Early, Mid, Late	Tall (18-30)	Pink or Lavender		x
Achillea (Yarrow)	Paprika	Early, Mid, Late	Medium (18-24)	Red		x
Achillea (Yarrow)	Saucy Seduction	Early, Mid, Late	Tall (27)	Pink or Lavender		x
Achillea (Yarrow)	Sunny Seduction	Early, Mid, Late	Tall (27)	Yellow		x
Achillea (Yarrow)	Terra Cotta	Early, Mid, Late	Tall (30-36)	Orange or Peach		x
Achillea (Yarrow)	The Pearl	Early, Mid, Late	Medium (24)	White		
Aegopodium (Bishop's Weed)	Variegata	Early, Mid	Medium (16)	White	x	
Allium (Ornamental Onion)	Purple Sensation	Early	Tall (24-36)	Blue or Purple		
Anemone (Windflower)	Snowdrop	Early	Medium (12-15)	White		

Genus	Species or Cultivar	Bloom Time	Height (inches)	Color	Foliage	Fragrance
Aquilegia (Columbine)	Cameo Blue-White	Early	Short (6-8)	Blue or Purple		
Aquilegia (Columbine)	Cameo Pink-White	Early	Short (6-8)	Pink or Lavender		
Aquilegia (Columbine)	Colorado Violet and White	Early, Mid	Tall (24-28)	Blue or Purple		
Aquilegia (Columbine)	Nora Barlow	Early, Mid	Tall (30)	Pink or Lavender		
Aquilegia (Columbine)	Rocky Mountain Blue	Early, Mid	Medium (24)	Blue or Purple		
Aquilegia (Columbine)	Songbird Cardinal	Early, Mid	Medium (16-24)	Red		
Aquilegia (Columbine)	Songbird Robin	Early, Mid	Medium (16-24)	Pink or Lavender		
Aquilegia (Columbine)	Swan Pink and Yellow	Early, Mid	Medium (20-24)	Pink or Lavender, Yellow		
Aquilegia (Columbine)	Swan Yellow	Early, Mid	Medium (20-24)	Yellow		
Aquilegia (Columbine)	Winky Double Dark Blue-White	Early, Mid	Short (12)	Blue or Purple		
Aquilegia (Columbine)	Winky Double Rose-White	Early, Mid	Short (12)	Pink or Lavender		
Aquilegia (Columbine)	Woodside Gold	Early, Mid	Medium (18-24)	Blue or Purple	x	
Bergenia (Pigsqueak)	Winterglow	Early	Medium (12-15)	Pink or Lavender	x	
Brunnera (Siberian Bugloss)	Alexander's Great	Early	Medium (16)	Blue or Purple	x	
Brunnera (Siberian Bugloss)	Jack Frost	Early	Medium (16)	Blue or Purple	x	
Centaurea (Bachelor's Button)	Amethyst in Snow	Early, Mid, Late	Medium (14-16)	White		

Genus	Species or Cultivar	Bloom Time	Height (inches)	Color	Foliage	Fragrance
Centaurea (Bachelor's Button)	Black Sprite	Early, Mid, Late	Medium (16)	Blue or Purple		
Centaurea (Bachelor's Button)	John Coutts	Early, Mid, Late	Medium (20)	Pink or Lavender		
Centaurea (Bachelor's Button)	Mountain Bluet	Early, Mid, Late	Tall (24-30)	Blue or Purple		
Cerastium (Snow-in-Summer)	*tomentosum*	Early	Short (6)	White	x	
Clematis (Clematis)	Blue Bird	Early, Mid	Tall (10 feet)	Blue or Purple		
Clematis (Clematis)	Purpurea	Early, Mid	Tall (30)	White	x	
Clematis (Clematis)	Radar Love	Early, Mid	Tall (12-15 feet)	Yellow		
Clematis (Clematis)	*integrifolia*	Early, Mid, Late	Tall (18-36)	Blue or Purple		
Clematis (Clematis)	Alba	Early, Mid, Late	Tall (18-36)	White		
Clematis (Clematis)	Rosea	Early, Mid, Late	Tall (18-36)	Pink or Lavender		
Dodecatheon (Shooting Star)	*meadia*	Early	Short (6-12)	Pink or Lavender		
Dodecatheon (Shooting Star)	Aphrodite	Early	Medium (18)	Pink or Lavender		
Draba (Whitlow-grass)	*siberica*	Early, Late	Short (6)	Yellow		
Filipendula (Meadowsweet)	Kahome	Early	Short (12)	Pink or Lavender	x	
Filipendula (Meadowsweet)	Elegans	Early	Tall (28)	Pink or Lavender	x	
Filipendula (Meadowsweet)	Venusta	Early	Tall (60)	Pink or Lavender	x	
Filipendula (Meadowsweet)	Variegata	Early	Tall (36-48)	White	x	
Galium (Bedstraw)	*verum*	Early, Late	Medium (10-24)	Yellow		
Hemerocallis (Day Lily)	Flava	Early, Mid	Tall (30)	Yellow	x	
Hemerocallis (Day Lily)	Stella de Oro	Early, Mid, Late	Medium (12-18)	Yellow		

Genus	Species or Cultivar	Bloom Time	Height (inches)	Color	Foliage	Fragrance
Hesperis (Rocket)	*matronalis*	Early	Tall (36)	Pink or Lavender		
Iris (Iris)	*setosa*	Early	Medium (12-24)	Blue or Purple		
Lamium (Dead Nettle)	Beacon Silver	Early, Mid, Late	Short (6-8)	Pink or Lavender	x	
Lamium (Dead Nettle)	Pink Pewter	Early, Mid, Late	Short (6-8)	Pink or Lavender	x	
Lamium (Dead Nettle)	White Nancy	Early, Mid, Late	Short (6-8)	White	x	
Paeonia (Peony)	Jana	Early	Tall (36)	Pink or Lavender		
Phlox (Phlox)	Blue Emerald	Early, Mid	Short (6)	Blue or Purple		
Phlox (Phlox)	North Hills	Early, Mid	Short (4-8)	Blue or Purple, White		
Polemonium (Jacob's Ladder)	Bressingham Purple	Early, Mid	Medium (15)	Blue or Purple		x
Polemonium (Jacob's Ladder)	Touch of Class	Early, Mid	Medium (15-18)	Blue or Purple	x	x
Primula (Primrose)	*florindae*	Early, Mid	Medium (20)	Yellow		
Primula (Primrose)	*matthioli*	Early	Short (10)	Pink or Lavender		
Primula (Primrose)	*sikkimensis*	Early, Mid	Medium (20)	Yellow		
Pulsatilla (Pasque Flower)	Alba	Early	Short (10)	White		
Pulsatilla (Pasque Flower)	*vulgaris*	Early	Short (10)	Blue or Purple		
Trollius (Globeflower)	Earliest of All	Early	Medium (24)	Yellow		
Trollius (Globeflower)	*europaeus*	Early	Medium (24)	Yellow		
Trollius (Globeflower)	*pumilus*	Early	Short (6-8)	Yellow		
Veronica (Speedwell)	*gentianoides*	Early	Medium (18-20)	Blue or Purple		
Veronica (Speedwell)	Waterperry Blue	Early	Short (6-8)	Blue or Purple		

List your own species and cultivars here:

Genus	Species or Cultivar	Bloom Time	Height (inches)	Color	Foliage	Fragrance

Mid-Season Bloomers

Genus	Species or Cultivar	Bloom Time	Height (inches)	Color	Foliage	Fragrance
Achillea (Yarrow)	Appleblossom	Early, Mid, Late	Tall (18-30)	Pink or Lavender		x
Achillea (Yarrow)	Laura	Early, Mid, Late	Tall (24)	Red		x
Achillea (Yarrow)	Love Parade	Early, Mid, Late	Tall (18-30)	Pink or Lavender		x
Achillea (Yarrow)	Paprika	Early, Mid, Late	Medium (18-24)	Red		x
Achillea (Yarrow)	Saucy Seduction	Early, Mid, Late	Tall (27)	Pink or Lavender		x
Achillea (Yarrow)	Sunny Seduction	Early, Mid, Late	Tall (27)	Yellow		x
Achillea (Yarrow)	Terra Cotta	Early, Mid, Late	Tall (30-36)	Orange or Peach		x
Achillea (Yarrow)	The Pearl	Early, Mid, Late	Medium (24)	White		
Aegopodium (Bishop's Weed)	Variegata	Early, Mid	Medium (16)	White	x	
Allium (Ornamental Onion)	*altaicum*	Mid	Tall (24-36)	White		
Allium (Ornamental Onion)	*senescens*	Mid	Short (6-12)	Pink or Lavender		
Aquilegia (Columbine)	Colorado Violet and White	Early, Mid	Tall (24-28)	Blue or Purple		
Aquilegia (Columbine)	Nora Barlow	Early, Mid	Tall (30)	Pink or Lavender		
Aquilegia (Columbine)	Rocky Mountain Blue	Early, Mid	Medium (24)	Blue or Purple		
Aquilegia (Columbine)	Songbird Cardinal	Early, Mid	Medium (16-24)	Red		
Aquilegia (Columbine)	Songbird Robin	Early, Mid	Medium (16-24)	Pink or Lavender		
Aquilegia (Columbine)	Swan Pink and Yellow	Early, Mid	Medium (20-24)	Pink or Lavender, Yellow		

Genus	Species or Cultivar	Bloom Time	Height (inches)	Color	Foliage	Fragrance
Aquilegia (Columbine)	Swan Yellow	Early, Mid	Medium (20-24)	Yellow		
Aquilegia (Columbine)	Winky Double Dark Blue-White	Early, Mid	Short (12)	Blue or Purple		
Aquilegia (Columbine)	Winky Double Rose-White	Early, Mid	Short (12)	Pink or Lavender		
Aquilegia (Columbine)	Woodside Gold	Early, Mid	Medium (18-24)	Blue or Purple	x	
Artemesia (Wormwood)	Silver Brocade	Mid	Short (6-12)	Yellow	x	
Artemesia (Wormwood)	Silver Mound	Mid	Short (10)	Yellow	x	
Artemesia (Wormwood)	Valerie Finnis	Mid	Medium (15-18)	Yellow	x	
Aruncus (Goat's Beard)	*aethusifolius*	Mid	Short (10)	White	x	
Aruncus (Goat's Beard)	*dioicus*	Mid	Tall (60)	White	x	
Aruncus (Goat's Beard)	Horatio	Mid	Tall (48)	White	x	
Aruncus (Goat's Beard)	Kneiffii	Mid	Tall (24-36)	White	x	
Astilbe (False Spirea)	Chocolate Shogun	Mid, Late	Medium (18-24)	Pink or Lavender	x	
Astilbe (False Spirea)	Fanal	Mid, Late	Medium (24)	Red		
Astilbe (False Spirea)	Peach Blossom	Mid, late	Medium (24)	Pink or Lavender		
Campanula (Bell Flower)	Campbell	Mid, Late	Medium (16-18)	Blue or Purple		
Campanula (Bell Flower)	Cherry Bells	Mid, Late	Medium (16-18)	Red		
Campanula (Bell Flower)	Genti Twisterbell	Mid, Late	Medium (16-18)	Blue or Purple		
Campanula (Bell Flower)	Kent Belle	Mid, Late	Tall (18-28)	Blue or Purple		
Campanula (Bell Flower)	Olympia	Mid, Late	Short (6-12)	Blue or Purple		
Campanula (Bell Flower)	Pink Octopus	Mid, Late	Short (12)	Pink or Lavender		

Genus	Species or Cultivar	Bloom Time	Height (inches)	Color	Foliage	Fragrance
Campanula (Bell Flower)	Silver Bells	Mid, Late	Medium (15)	Pink or Lavender	x	x
Campanula (Bell Flower)	Superba	Mid, Late	Tall (24-30)	Blue or Purple		
Campanula (Bell Flower)	*takesimana*	Mid, Late	Medium (24)	Pink or Lavender		
Centaurea (Bachelor's Button)	Amethyst in Snow	Early, Mid, Late	Medium (14-16)	White		
Centaurea (Bachelor's Button)	Black Sprite	Early, Mid, Late	Medium (16)	Blue or Purple		
Centaurea (Bachelor's Button)	John Coutts	Early, Mid, Late	Medium (20)	Pink or Lavender		
Centaurea (Bachelor's Button)	Mountain Bluet	Early, Mid, Late	Tall (24-30)	Blue or Purple		
Clematis (Clematis)	Blue Bird	Early, Mid	Tall (10 feet)	Blue or Purple		
Clematis (Clematis)	Purpurea	Early, Mid	Tall (30)	White	x	
Clematis (Clematis)	Radar Love	Early, Mid	Tall (12-15 feet)	Yellow		x
Clematis (Clematis)	*integrifolia*	Early, Mid, Late	Tall (18-36)	Blue or Purple		
Clematis (Clematis)	Alba	Early, Mid, Late	Tall (18-36)	White		
Clematis (Clematis)	Rosea	Early, Mid, Late	Tall (18-36)	Pink or Lavender		
Delphinium (Delphinium)	Blue Butterfly	Mid	Medium (16)	Blue or Purple		
Delphinium (Delphinium)	Magic Fountains Dark Blue-Dark Bee	Mid	Tall (24-40)	Blue or Purple		
Delphinium (Delphinium)	Magic Fountains Lilac Pink-White Bee	Mid	Tall (24-40)	Pink or Lavender		

Genus	Species or Cultivar	Bloom Time	Height (inches)	Color	Foliage	Fragrance
Delphinium (Delphinium)	Magic Fountains Pure White	Mid	Tall (24-40)	White		
Delphinium (Delphinium)	Magic Fountains Sky Blue-White Bee	Mid	Tall (24-40)	Blue or Purple		
Delphinium (Delphinium)	Summer Blues	Mid	Short (12)	Blue or Purple		
Delphinium (Delphinium)	Summer Morning	Mid	Short (12)	Pink or Lavender		
Delphinium (Delphinium)	Summer Nights	Mid	Short (12)	Blue or Purple		
Dianthus (Pinks)	Arctic Fire	Mid, Late	Short (6-8)	Red, White		
Dianthus (Pinks)	Pink Maiden	Mid, Late	Short (6-8)	Pink or Lavender		
Dianthus (Pinks)	Red Maiden	Mid, Late	Short (6-8)	Pink or Lavender		
Dicentra (Bleeding Heart)	Burning Hearts	Mid	Short (10-12	Red	x	
Dicentra (Bleeding Heart)	Candy Hearts	Mid	Short (10-12)	Pink or Lavender	x	
Dicentra (Bleeding Heart)	Gold Heart	Mid	Tall (24-30)	Pink or Lavender	x	
Dicentra (Bleeding Heart)	*spectabilis*	Mid	Tall (30)	Pink or Lavender		
Dicentra (Bleeding Heart)	Alba	Mid	Tall (30)	White		
Dicentra (Bleeding Heart)	Valentine	Mid	Tall (30)	Red		
Geranium (Cranesbill)	Birch Double	Mid	Short (10-12)	Pink or Lavender		
Geranium (Cranesbill)	Double Jewel	Mid	Short (12)	White		
Geranium (Cranesbill)	Lakwijk Star	Mid, Late	Medium (12-18)	Pink or Lavender	x	

Genus	Species or Cultivar	Bloom Time	Height (inches)	Color	Foliage	Fragrance
Geranium (Cranesbill)	Nimbus	Mid, Late	Medium (16-24)	Blue or Purple		
Hemerocallis (Day Lily)	Little Grapette	Mid	Short (12)	Blue or Purple	x	
Hemerocallis (Day Lily)	Flava	Early, Mid	Tall (30)	Yellow	x	x
Hemerocallis (Day Lily)	Stella de Oro	Early, Mid, Late	Medium (12-18)	Yellow		
Hemerocallis (Day Lily)	Fragrant Returns	Mid, Late	Medium (18)	Yellow	x	x
Hosta (Plantain Lily)	Guacamole	Mid	Medium (12-24)	Blue or Purple	x	
Hosta (Plantain Lily)	True Blue	Mid	Tall (24-30)	White	x	
Iris (Iris)	Butter and Sugar	Mid	Tall (24-30)	Yellow	x	
Iris (Iris)	Caesar's Brother	Mid	Tall (24-39)	Blue or Purple	x	
Iris (Iris)	Ruffled Velvet	Mid	Tall (30)	Blue or Purple	x	
Iris (Iris)	Snow Queen	Mid	Tall (24-30)	White	x	
Lamium (Dead Nettle)	Beacon Silver	Early, Mid, Late	Short (6-8)	Pink or Lavender	x	
Lamium (Dead Nettle)	Pink Pewter	Early, Mid, Late	Short (6-8)	Pink or Lavender	x	
Lamium (Dead Nettle)	White Nancy	Early, Mid, Late	Short (6-8)	White	x	
Lewisia (Bitteerroot)	Little Peach	Mid, Late	Short (6)	Orange or Peach		
Lewisia (Bitteerroot)	Little Plum	Mid, Late	Short (6)	Pink or Lavender		
Leymus (Wild Rye)	*arenarius*	Mid	Tall (24-36)	Yellow	x	
Ligularia (Ligularia)	Little Rocket	Mid	Tall (30)	Yellow		
Ligularia (Ligularia)	The Rocket	Mid	Tall (72)	Yellow		
Ligularia (Ligularia)	Desdemona	Mid, Late	Tall (30-36)	Yellow		
Lilium (Lily)	Tango Passions	Mid, Late	Medium (14-16)	Pink or Lavender		

Genus	Species or Cultivar	Bloom Time	Height (inches)	Color	Foliage	Fragrance
Lilium (Lily)	Apricot Fudge	Mid, late	Tall (24-36)	Orange or Peach		
Lilium (Lily)	Blackout	Mid, Late	Tall (48)	Red		
Lilium (Lily)	Conca d'Or	Mid, late	Tall (36-60)	Yellow		
Lilium (Lily)	Elodie	Mid, Late	Tall (48)	Pink or Lavender		
Lilium (Lily)	Fata Morgana	Mid, Late	Tall (36-48)	Yellow		
Lilium (Lily)	Golden Matrix	Mid, Late	Medium (16)	Yellow		
Lilium (Lily)	Landini	Mid, Late	Tall (42)	Red		
Lilium (Lily)	Lily Looks™ Tiny Moon	Mid, Late	Medium (12-14)	Orange or Peach		
Lilium (Lily)	Matrix	Mid, Late	Medium (16)	Orange or Peach		
Lychnis (Campion)	Maltese Cross	Mid	Tall (48)	Red		
Lychnis (Campion)	Dusky Salmon	Mid, Late	Tall (48)	Orange or Peach		
Lychnis (Campion)	Lumina Salmon Shades	Mid, late	Medium (12-15)	Orange or Peach		
Lychnis (Campion)	Molten Lava	Mid, Late	Medium (12-15)	Red		
Lychnis (Campion)	Orange Gnome	Mid, Late	Medium (12-15)	Orange or Peach		
Lychnis (Campion)	Vesuvius	Mid, Late	Medium (12-15)	Red		
Lysimachia (Loosestrife)	Alexander	Mid, Late	Medium (12-24)	Yellow		
Lysimachia (Loosestrife)	Firecracker	Mid, Late	Medium (12-24)	Yellow		
Meconopsis (Himalayan Blue Poppy)	*betonicifolia*	Mid, Late	Tall (30-48)	Blue or Purple		
Meconopsis (Himalayan Blue Poppy)	Lingholm	Mid, Late	Tall (36-48)	Blue or Purple		
Myosotis (Forget-Me-Not)	*alpestris*	Mid	Short (6-10)	Blue or Purple		

Genus	Species or Cultivar	Bloom Time	Height (inches)	Color	Foliage	Fragrance
Nepeta (Nepeta)	Blue Dreams	Mid, Late	Tall (24-36)	Blue or Purple		x
Nepeta (Nepeta)	Dropmore Blue	Mid, Late	Medium (24)	Blue or Purple		x
Nepeta (Nepeta)	Pink Dreams	Mid, Late	Tall (24-36)	Pink or Lavender		x
Nepeta (Nepeta)	*siberica*	Mid, Late	Tall (36)	Blue or Purple		x
Nepeta (Nepeta)	Souvenir D' Andre Chaudrón	Mid, Late	Tall (36)	Blue or Purple		x
Nepeta (Nepeta)	Walker's Low	Mid, Late	Medium (24)	Blue or Purple		x
Paeonia (Peony)	Bartzella	Mid	Tall (34)	Yellow		
Paeonia (Peony)	Buckeye Belle	Mid	Tall (34)	Red		
Paeonia (Peony)	Coral Charm	Mid	Tall (36)	Orange or Peach		
Paeonia (Peony)	Festiva Maxima	Mid	Tall (40)	White		
Paeonia (Peony)	Karl Rosenfeld	Mid	Tall (38)	Red		
Paeonia (Peony)	Kopper Kettle	Mid	Tall (32)	Orange or Peach		
Paeonia (Peony)	Sorbet	Mid	Tall (28)	Pink or Lavender		
Papaver (Poppy)	Allegro	Mid	Short (10-12)	Red		
Papaver (Poppy)	Brilliant	Mid	Tall (32-36)	Orange or Peach		
Papaver (Poppy)	Little Patty's Plum	Mid	Medium (20)	Pink or Lavender		
Papaver (Poppy)	Patty's Plum	Mid	Tall (28-32)	Pink or Lavender		
Papaver (Poppy)	Princess Louise	Mid	Tall (24)	Orange or Peach		
Phlomis (Phlomis)	*tuberosa*	Mid	Tall (36-48)	Pink or Lavender		

Genus	Species or Cultivar	Bloom Time	Height (inches)	Color	Foliage	Fragrance
Phlox (Phlox)	Blue Emerald	Early, Mid	Short (6)	Blue or Purple		
Phlox (Phlox)	North Hills	Early, Mid	Short (4-8)	Blue or Purple, White		
Phlox (Phlox)	Sherwood Purple	Mid, late	Short (6-10)	Blue or Purple		x
Polemonium (Jacob's Ladder)	Bressingham Purple	Early, Mid	Medium (15)	Blue or Purple		x
Polemonium (Jacob's Ladder)	Touch of Class	Early, Mid	Medium (15-18)	Blue or Purple	x	x
Polygonatum (Solomon's Seal)	Variegatum	Mid	Medium (18-24)	White	x	
Potentilla (Cinquefoil)	Monarch's Velvet	Mid, Late	Medium (10-15)	Red		
Potentilla (Cinquefoil)	William Rollinson	Mid, Late	Medium (16)	Orange or Peach		
Primula (Primrose)	*florindae*	Early, Mid	Medium (20)	Yellow		x
Primula (Primrose)	*sikkimensis*	Early, Mid	Medium (20)	Yellow		x
Pulsatilla (Pasque Flower)	Rubra	Mid	Short (10)	Red		
Sedum (Stonecrop)	Tricolor	Mid, Late	Short (4)	Red	x	
Sedum (Stonecrop)	Variegatum	Mid, Late	Short (5)	Orange or Peach	x	
Tanacetum (Tansy)	Crispum	Mid, Late	Tall (24-36)	Yellow	x	
Tanacetum (Tansy)	Isla Gold	Mid, Late	Tall (36-48)	Yellow	x	
Tanacetum (Tansy)	Robinson's Pink	Mid, Late	Medium (18-24)	Pink or Lavender		
Tanacetum (Tansy)	Robinson's Red	Mid, Late	Medium (18-24)	Pink or Lavender		
Tanacetum (Tansy)	*vulgare*	Mid, Late	Tall (36-48)	Yellow		
Thalictrum (Meadow Rue)	Anne	Mid	Tall (84)	Pink or Lavender	x	
Thalictrum (Meadow Rue)	*aquilegifolium*	Mid	Tall (48)	Pink or Lavender	x	
Thalictrum (Meadow Rue)	Black Stockings	Mid	Tall (48)	Pink or Lavender	x	

Genus	Species or Cultivar	Bloom Time	Height (inches)	Color	Foliage	Fragrance
Thalictrum (Meadow Rue)	Flavum	Mid, Late	Tall (48)	Yellow	x	
Thalictrum (Meadow Rue)	Hewitt's Double	Mid, Late	Tall (48)	Blue or Purple	x	
Thalictrum (Meadow Rue)	Splendide	Mid, Late	Tall (48-72)	Pink or Lavender	x	
Trollius (Globeflower)	Alabaster	Mid	Medium (24)	White		
Trollius (Globeflower)	Lemon Queen	Mid	Tall (18-36)	Yellow		
Trollius (Globeflower)	Superbus	Mid	Medium (24)	Yellow		
Trollius (Globeflower)	ledebourii	Mid, Late	Medium (18-24)	Orange or Peach		
Veronica (Speedwell)	Giles van Hees	Mid	Short (6-8)	Pink or Lavender		
Veronica (Speedwell)	Red Fox	Mid	Medium (18)	Pink or Lavender		
Veronica (Speedwell)	Spicata Blue	Mid	Medium (18-24)	Blue or Purple		
Veronica (Speedwell)	Spicata Rose	Mid	Medium (18-24)	Pink or Lavender		
Veronica (Speedwell)	Bicolor Explosion	Mid, Late	Medium (15-18)	Blue or Purple		
Veronica (Speedwell)	Blue Bomb	Mid, late	Medium (15-18)	Blue or Purple		
Veronica (Speedwell)	Charlotte	Mid, Late	Tall (30)	White		
Veronica (Speedwell)	Icicle White	Mid, Late	Medium (18)	White		
Veronica (Speedwell)	Pink Bomb	Mid, Late	Medium (15-18)	Pink or Lavender		
Veronica (Speedwell)	Pink Damask	Mid, Late	Tall (24-36)	Pink or Lavender		
Veronica (Speedwell)	Purpleicious	Mid, Late	Medium (20)	Blue or Purple		
Veronica (Speedwell)	Royal Candles	Mid, Late	Medium (16-18)	Blue or Purple		

List your own species and cultivars here:

Genus	Species or Cultivar	Bloom Time	Height (inches)	Color	Foliage	Fragrance

Late-Season Bloomers

Genus	Species or Cultivar	Bloom Time	Height (inches)	Color	Foliage	Fragrance
Achillea (Yarrow)	Appleblossom	Early, Mid, Late	Tall (18-30)	Pink or Lavender		x
Achillea (Yarrow)	Laura	Early, Mid, Late	Tall (24)	Red		x
Achillea (Yarrow)	Love Parade	Early, Mid, Late	Tall (18-30)	Pink or Lavender		x
Achillea (Yarrow)	Paprika	Early, Mid, Late	Medium (18-24)	Red		x
Achillea (Yarrow)	Saucy Seduction	Early, Mid, Late	Tall (27)	Pink or Lavender		x
Achillea (Yarrow)	Sunny Seduction	Early, Mid, Late	Tall (27)	Yellow		x
Achillea (Yarrow)	Terra Cotta	Early, Mid, Late	Tall (30-36)	Orange or Peach		x
Achillea (Yarrow)	The Pearl	Early, Mid, Late	Medium (24)	White		
Aconitum (Monkshood)	Arendsii	Late	Tall (40)	Blue or Purple		
Aconitum (Monkshood)	Blue and White Bicolor	Late	Tall (48)	Blue or Purple		
Aconitum (Monkshood)	Blue Lagoon	Late	Short (10-12)	Blue or Purple		
Aconitum (Monkshood)	Bressingham Spire	Late	Tall (30-36)	Blue or Purple		
Aconitum (Monkshood)	Pink Sensation	Late	Tall (40-48)	Pink or Lavender		
Aconitum (Monkshood)	Stainless Steel	Late	Tall (40)	Blue or Purple		
Actaea (Bugbane)	Black Negligee	Late	Tall (42-60)	White	x	
Actaea (Bugbane)	Pink Spike	Late	Tall (42-60)	Pink or Lavender	x	
Allium (Ornamental Onion)	Millenium	Late	Medium (12-18)	Pink or Lavender		x

Genus	Species or Cultivar	Bloom Time	Height (inches)	Color	Foliage	Fragrance
Anemone (Windflower)	Robustissima	Late	Tall (32)	Pink or Lavender		
Astilbe (False Spirea)	Colorflash	Late	Medium (20)	Pink or Lavender	x	
Astilbe (False Spirea)	Maggie Daley	Late	Tall (28)	Pink or Lavender		
Astilbe (False Spirea)	Rhythm and Blues	Late	Tall (26)	Pink or Lavender		
Astilbe (False Spirea)	Chocolate Shogun	Mid, Late	Medium (18-24)	Pink or Lavender	x	
Astilbe (False Spirea)	Fanal	Mid, Late	Medium (24)	Red		
Astilbe (False Spirea)	Peach Blossom	Mid, late	Medium (24)	Pink or Lavender		
Campanula (Bell Flower)	Campbell	Mid, Late	Medium (16-18)	Blue or Purple		
Campanula (Bell Flower)	Cherry Bells	Mid, Late	Medium (16-18)	Red		
Campanula (Bell Flower)	Genti Twisterbell	Mid, Late	Medium (16-18)	Blue or Purple		
Campanula (Bell Flower)	Kent Belle	Mid, Late	Tall (18-28)	Blue or Purple		
Campanula (Bell Flower)	Olympia	Mid, Late	Short (6-12)	Blue or Purple		
Campanula (Bell Flower)	Pink Octopus	Mid, Late	Short (12)	Pink or Lavender		
Campanula (Bell Flower)	Silver Bells	Mid, Late	Medium (15)	Pink or Lavender	x	x
Campanula (Bell Flower)	Superba	Mid, Late	Tall (24-30)	Blue or Purple		
Campanula (Bell Flower)	*takesimana*	Mid, Late	Medium (24)	Pink or Lavender		
Centaurea (Bachelor's Button)	Amethyst in Snow	Early, Mid, Late	Medium (14-16)	White		
Centaurea (Bachelor's Button)	Black Sprite	Early, Mid, Late	Medium (16)	Blue or Purple		

Genus	Species or Cultivar	Bloom Time	Height (inches)	Color	Foliage	Fragrance
Centaurea (Bachelor's Button)	John Coutts	Early, Mid, Late	Medium (20)	Pink or Lavender		
Centaurea (Bachelor's Button)	Mountain Bluet	Early, Mid, Late	Tall (24-30)	Blue or Purple		
Chelone (Turtlehead)	Alba	Late	Tall (36)	White		
Chelone (Turtlehead)	Rosea	Late	Tall (24-36)	Pink or Lavender		
Chelone (Turtlehead)	Tiny Tortuga	Late	Medium (14-16)	Pink or Lavender		
Clematis (Clematis)	*integrifolia*	Early, Mid, Late	Tall (18-36)	Blue or Purple		
Clematis (Clematis)	Alba	Early, Mid, Late	Tall (18-36)	White		
Clematis (Clematis)	Rosea	Early, Mid, Late	Tall (18-36)	Pink or Lavender		
Dianthus (Pinks)	Arctic Fire	Mid, Late	Short (6-8)	Red, White		
Dianthus (Pinks)	Pink Maiden	Mid, Late	Short (6-8)	Pink or Lavender		
Dianthus (Pinks)	Red Maiden	Mid, Late	Short (6-8)	Pink or Lavender		
Draba (Whitlow-grass)	*siberica*	Early, Late	Short (6)	Yellow		
Galium (Bedstraw)	*verum*	Early, Late	Medium (10-24)	Yellow		
Gentiana (Gentian)	*septemfida*	Late	Short (8-12)	Blue or Purple		
Gentiana (Gentian)	True Blue	Late	Tall (30)	Blue or Purple		
Geranium (Cranesbill)	Lakwijk Star	Mid, Late	Medium (12-18)	Pink or Lavender	x	
Geranium (Cranesbill)	Nimbus	Mid, Late	Medium (16-24)	Blue or Purple		
Hemerocallis (Day Lily)	Hyperion	Late	Tall (36-42)	Yellow	x	x
Hemerocallis (Day Lily)	Mauna Loa	Late	Medium (22)	Orange or Peach	x	
Hemerocallis (Day Lily)	Stella de Oro	Early, Mid, Late	Medium (12-18)	Yellow		

Genus	Species or Cultivar	Bloom Time	Height (inches)	Color	Foliage	Fragrance
Hemerocallis (Day Lily)	Fragrant Returns	Mid, Late	Medium (18)	Yellow	x	x
Lamium (Dead Nettle)	Beacon Silver	Early, Mid, Late	Short (6-8)	Pink or Lavender	x	
Lamium (Dead Nettle)	Pink Pewter	Early, Mid, Late	Short (6-8)	Pink or Lavender	x	
Lamium (Dead Nettle)	White Nancy	Early, Mid, Late	Short (6-8)	White	x	
Lewisia (Bitterroot)	Little Peach	Mid, Late	Short (6)	Orange or Peach		
Lewisia (Bitterroot)	Little Plum	Mid, Late	Short (6)	Pink or Lavender		
Ligularia (Ligularia)	Britt-Marie Crawford	Late	Tall (36-40)	Yellow	x	
Ligularia (Ligularia)	Othello	Late	Tall (36)	Yellow	x	
Ligularia (Ligularia)	Desdemona	Mid, Late	Tall (30-36)	Yellow		
Lilium (Lily)	Citronelle	Late	Tall (48)	Yellow		
Lilium (Lily)	Pink Tiger	Late	Tall (48)	Pink or Lavender		
Lilium (Lily)	Splendens	Late	Tall (48)	Orange or Peach		
Lilium (Lily)	Tango Passions	Mid, Late	Medium (14-16)	Pink or Lavender		
Lilium (Lily)	Apricot Fudge	Mid, late	Tall (24-36)	Orange or Peach		
Lilium (Lily)	Blackout	Mid, Late	Tall (48)	Red		
Lilium (Lily)	Conca d 'Or	Mid, late	Tall (36-60)	Yellow		
Lilium (Lily)	Elodie	Mid, Late	Tall (48)	Pink or Lavender		
Lilium (Lily)	Fata Morgana	Mid, Late	Tall (36-48)	Yellow		
Lilium (Lily)	Golden Matrix	Mid, Late	Medium (16)	Yellow		
Lilium (Lily)	Landini	Mid, Late	Tall (42)	Red		
Lilium (Lily)	Lily Looks™ Tiny Moon	Mid, Late	Medium (12-14)	Orange or Peach		

Genus	Species or Cultivar	Bloom Time	Height (inches)	Color	Foliage	Fragrance
Lilium (Lily)	Matrix	Mid, Late	Medium (16)	Orange or Peach		
Lychnis (Campion)	Dusky Salmon	Mid, Late	Tall (48)	Orange or Peach		
Lychnis (Campion)	Lumina Salmon Shades	Mid, late	Medium (12-15)	Orange or Peach		
Lychnis (Campion)	Molten Lava	Mid, Late	Medium (12-15)	Red		
Lychnis (Campion)	Orange Gnome	Mid, Late	Medium (12-15)	Orange or Peach		
Lychnis (Campion)	Vesuvius	Mid, Late	Medium (12-15)	Red		
Lysimachia (Loosestrife)	Alexander	Mid, Late	Medium (12-24)	Yellow		
Lysimachia (Loosestrife)	Firecracker	Mid, Late	Medium (12-24)	Yellow		
Lythrum (Purple Loosestrife)	Rosy Gem	Late	Tall (48-60)	Pink or Lavender		
Meconopsis (Himalayan Blue Poppy)	*betonicifolia*	Mid, Late	Tall (30-48)	Blue or Purple		
Meconopsis (Himalayan Blue Poppy)	Lingholm	Mid, Late	Tall (36-48)	Blue or Purple		
Nepeta (Nepeta)	Blue Dreams	Mid, Late	Tall (24-36)	Blue or Purple		x
Nepeta (Nepeta)	Dropmore Blue	Mid, Late	Medium (24)	Blue or Purple		x
Nepeta (Nepeta)	Pink Dreams	Mid, Late	Tall (24-36)	Pink or Lavender		x
Nepeta (Nepeta)	*siberica*	Mid, Late	Tall (36)	Blue or Purple		x
Nepeta (Nepeta)	Souvenir D' Andre Chaudrón	Mid, Late	Tall (36)	Blue or Purple		x
Nepeta (Nepeta)	Walker's Low	Mid, Late	Medium (24)	Blue or Purple		x

Genus	Species or Cultivar	Bloom Time	Height (inches)	Color	Foliage	Fragrance
Phalaris (Ribbon Grass)	Dwarf Garters	Late	Short (10-15)	White	x	
Phalaris (Ribbon Grass)	Picta	Late	Medium (24)	White	x	
Phalaris (Ribbon Grass)	Strawberries and Cream	Late	Medium (24)	White	x	
Phlox (Phlox)	Sherwood Purple	Mid, late	Short (6-10)	Blue or Purple		x
Physostegia (Obedient Plant)	Crystal Peak White	Late	Medium (16)	White		
Physostegia (Obedient Plant)	Bouquet Rose	Late	Medium (24)	Pink or Lavender		
Physostegia (Obedient Plant)	Variegata	Late	Tall (24-36)	Pink or Lavender	x	
Potentilla (Cinquefoil)	Monarch's Velvet	Mid, Late	Medium (10-15)	Red		
Potentilla (Cinquefoil)	William Rollinson	Mid, Late	Medium (16)	Orange or Peach		
Sedum (Stonecrop)	Tricolor	Mid, Late	Short (4)	Red	x	
Sedum (Stonecrop)	Variegatum	Mid, Late	Short (5)	Orange or Peach	x	
Solidago (Goldenrod)	Little Lemon	Late	Short (12)	Yellow		
Tanacetum (Tansy)	Crispum	Mid, Late	Tall (24-36)	Yellow	x	
Tanacetum (Tansy)	Isla Gold	Mid, Late	Tall (36-48)	Yellow	x	
Tanacetum (Tansy)	Robinson's Pink	Mid, Late	Medium (18-24)	Pink or Lavender		
Tanacetum (Tansy)	Robinson's Red	Mid, Late	Medium (18-24)	Pink or Lavender		
Tanacetum (Tansy)	*vulgare*	Mid, Late	Tall (36-48)	Yellow		
Thalictrum (Meadow Rue)	Flavum	Mid, Late	Tall (48)	Yellow	x	
Thalictrum (Meadow Rue)	Hewitt's Double	Mid, Late	Tall (48)	Blue or Purple	x	
Thalictrum (Meadow Rue)	Splendide	Mid, Late	Tall (48-72)	Pink or Lavender	x	
Trollius (Globeflower)	*ledebourii*	Mid, Late	Medium (18-24)	Orange or Peach		
Trollius (Globeflower)	Golden Queen	Late	Tall (36)	Orange or Peach		

Genus	Species or Cultivar	Bloom Time	Height (inches)	Color	Foliage	Fragrance
Veronica (Speedwell)	Bicolor Explosion	Mid, Late	Medium (15-18)	Blue or Purple		
Veronica (Speedwell)	Blue Bomb	Mid, late	Medium (15-18)	Blue or Purple		
Veronica (Speedwell)	Charlotte	Mid, Late	Tall (30)	White		
Veronica (Speedwell)	Icicle White	Mid, Late	Medium (18)	White		
Veronica (Speedwell)	Pink Bomb	Mid, Late	Medium (15-18)	Pink or Lavender		
Veronica (Speedwell)	Pink Damask	Mid, Late	Tall (24-36)	Pink or Lavender		
Veronica (Speedwell)	Purpleicious	Mid, Late	Medium (20)	Blue or Purple		
Veronica (Speedwell)	Royal Candles	Mid, Late	Medium (16-18)	Blue or Purple		
Veronicastrum (Culver Root)	Apollo	Late	Tall (59)	Blue or Purple		
Veronicastrum (Culver Root)	Erica	Late	Tall (59)	Pink or Lavender		
Veronicastrum (Culver Root)	Fascination	Late	Tall (59)	Blue or Purple		
Veronicastrum (Culver Root)	Red Arrow	Late	Tall (49)	Pink or Lavender		

List your own species and cultivars here:

Genus	Species or Cultivar	Bloom Time	Height (inches)	Color	Foliage	Fragrance

List your own species and cultivars here:

Genus	Species or Cultivar	Bloom Time	Height (inches)	Color	Foliage	Fragrance

CHAPTER 13

Height Charts

Short Plants

Genus	Species or Cultivar	Bloom Time	Height (inches)	Color	Foliage	Fragrance
Aconitum (Monkshood)	Blue Lagoon	Late	Short (10-12)	Blue or Purple		
Allium (Ornamental Onion)	*senescens*	Mid	Short (6-12)	Pink or Lavender		x
Aquilegia (Columbine)	Winky Double Dark Blue-White	Early, Mid	Short (12)	Blue or Purple		
Aquilegia (Columbine)	Winky Double Rose-White	Early, Mid	Short (12)	Pink or Lavender		
Aquilegia (Columbine)	Cameo Blue-White	Early	Short (6-8)	Blue or Purple		
Aquilegia (Columbine)	Cameo Pink-White	Early	Short (6-8)	Pink or Lavender		
Artemesia (Wormwood)	Silver Mound	Mid	Short (10)	Yellow	x	
Artemesia (Wormwood)	Silver Brocade	Mid	Short (6-12)	Yellow	x	
Aruncus (Goat's Beard)	*aethusifolius*	Mid	Short (10)	White	x	
Campanula (Bell Flower)	Pink Octopus	Mid, Late	Short (12)	Pink or Lavender		
Campanula (Bell Flower)	Olympia	Mid, Late	Short (6-12)	Blue or Purple		

Genus	Species or Cultivar	Bloom Time	Height (inches)	Color	Foliage	Fragrance
Cerastium (Snow-in-Summer)	*tomentosum*	Early	Short (6)	White	x	
Delphinium (Delphinium)	Summer Blues	Mid	Short (12)	Blue or Purple		
Delphinium (Delphinium)	Summer Morning	Mid	Short (12)	Pink or Lavender		
Delphinium (Delphinium)	Summer Nights	Mid	Short (12)	Blue or Purple		
Dianthus (Pinks)	Arctic Fire	Mid, Late	Short (6-8)	Red, White		
Dianthus (Pinks)	Pink Maiden	Mid, Late	Short (6-8)	Pink or Lavender		
Dianthus (Pinks)	Red Maiden	Mid, Late	Short (6-8)	Pink or Lavender		
Dicentra (Bleeding Heart)	Burning Hearts	Mid	Short (10-12)	Red	x	
Dicentra (Bleeding Heart)	Candy Hearts	Mid	Short (10-12)	Pink or Lavender	x	
Dodecatheon (Shooting Star)	*meadia*	Early	Short (6-12)	Pink or Lavender		
Draba (Whitlow-grass)	*siberica*	Early, Late	Short (6)	Yellow		
Filipendula (Meadowsweet)	Kahome	Early	Short (12)	Pink or Lavender	x	
Gentiana (Gentian)	*septemfida*	Late	Short (8-12)	Blue or Purple		
Geranium (Cranesbill)	Birch Double	Mid	Short (10-12)	Pink or Lavender		
Geranium (Cranesbill)	Double Jewel	Mid	Short (12)	White		
Hemerocallis (Day Lily)	Little Grapette	Mid	Short (12)	Blue or Purple	x	
Lamium (Dead Nettle)	Beacon Silver	Early, Mid, Late	Short (6-8)	Pink or Lavender	x	
Lamium (Dead Nettle)	Pink Pewter	Early, Mid, Late	Short (6-8)	Pink or Lavender	x	
Lamium (Dead Nettle)	White Nancy	Early, Mid, Late	Short (6-8)	White	x	

Genus	Species or Cultivar	Bloom Time	Height (inches)	Color	Foliage	Fragrance
Lewisia (Bitterroot)	Little Peach	Mid, Late	Short (6)	Orange or Peach		
Lewisia (Bitterroot)	Little Plum	Mid, Late	Short (6)	Pink or Lavender		
Myosotis (Forget-Me-Not)	*alpestris*	Mid	Short (6-10)	Blue or Purple		
Papaver (Poppy)	Allegro	Mid	Short (10-12)	Red		
Phalaris (Ribbon Grass)	Dwarf Garters	Late	Short (10-15)	White	x	
Phlox (Phlox)	Blue Emerald	Early, Mid	Short (6)	Blue or Purple		
Phlox (Phlox)	North Hills	Early, Mid	Short (4-8)	Blue or Purple, White		
Phlox (Phlox)	Sherwood Purple	Mid, late	Short (6-10)	Blue or Purple		x
Primula (Primrose)	*matthioli*	Early	Short (10)	Pink or Lavender		
Pulsatilla (Pasque Flower)	Alba	Early	Short (10)	White		
Pulsatilla (Pasque Flower)	Rubra	Mid	Short (10)	Red		
Pulsatilla (Pasque Flower)	*vulgaris*	Early	Short (10)	Blue Purple		
Sedum (Stonecrop)	Tricolor	Mid, Late	Short (4)	Pink	x	
Sedum (Stonecrop)	Variegatum	Mid, Late	Short (5)	Orange or Peach	x	
Solidago (Goldenrod)	Little Lemon	Late	Short (12)	Yellow		
Trollius (Globeflower)	*pumilus*	Early	Short (6-8)	Yellow		
Veronica (Speedwell)	Waterperry Blue	Early	Short (6-8)	Blue or Purple		
Veronica (Speedwell)	Giles van Hees	Mid	Short (6-8)	Pink or Lavender		
Veronica (Speedwell)	Ulster Blue	Mid	Short (6-8)	Blue or Purple		

List your own species and cultivars here:

Genus	Species or Cultivar	Bloom Time	Height (inches)	Color	Foliage	Fragrance

Medium Plants

Genus	Species or Cultivar	Bloom Time	Height (inches)	Color	Foliage	Fragrance
Achillea (Yarrow)	Paprika	Early, Mid, Late	Medium (18-24)	Red		x
Achillea (Yarrow)	The Pearl	Early, Mid, Late	Medium (24)	White		
Aegopodium (Bishop's Weed)	Variegata	Early, Mid	Medium (16)	White	x	
Allium (Ornamental Onion)	Millenium	Late	Medium (12-18)	Pink or Lavender		x
Anemone (Windflower)	Snowdrop	Early	Medium (12-15)	White		
Aquilegia (Columbine)	Songbird Cardinal	Early, Mid	Medium (16-24)	Red		
Aquilegia (Columbine)	Songbird Robin	Early, Mid	Medium (16-24)	Pink or Lavender		
Aquilegia (Columbine)	Woodside Gold	Early, Mid	Medium (18-24)	Blue or Purple	x	
Aquilegia (Columbine)	Swan Yellow	Early, Mid	Medium (20-24)	Yellow		
Aquilegia (Columbine)	Swan Pink and Yellow	Early, Mid	Medium (20-24)	Pink or Lavender, Yellow		
Aquilegia (Columbine)	Rocky Mountain Blue	Early, Mid	Medium (24)	Blue or Purple		
Artemesia (Wormwood)	Valerie Finnis	Mid	Medium (15-18)	Yellow	x	
Astilbe (False Spirea)	Chocolate Shogun	Mid, Late	Medium (18-24)	Pink or Lavender	x	
Astilbe (False Spirea)	Colorflash	Late	Medium (20)	Pink or Lavender	x	
Astilbe (False Spirea)	Fanal	Mid, Late	Medium (24)	Red		
Astilbe (False Spirea)	Peach Blossom	Mid, late	Medium (24)	Pink or Lavender		
Bergenia (Pigsqueak)	Winterglow	Early	Medium (12-15)	Pink or Lavender	x	
Brunnera (Siberian Bugloss)	Alexander's Great	Early	Medium (16)	Blue or Purple	x	

Genus	Species or Cultivar	Bloom Time	Height (inches)	Color	Foliage	Fragrance
Brunnera (Siberian Bugloss)	Jack Frost	Early	Medium (16)	Blue or Purple	x	
Campanula (Bell Flower)	Silver Bells	Mid, Late	Medium (15)	Pink or Lavender	x	x
Campanula (Bell Flower)	Campbell	Mid, Late	Medium (16-18)	Blue or Purple		
Campanula (Bell Flower)	Cherry Bells	Mid, Late	Medium (16-18)	Red		
Campanula (Bell Flower)	Genti Twisterbell	Mid, Late	Medium (16-18)	Blue or Purple		
Campanula (Bell Flower)	*takesimana*	Mid, Late	Medium (24)	Pink or Lavender		
Centaurea (Bachelor's Button)	Amethyst in Snow	Early, Mid, Late	Medium (14-16)	White		
Centaurea (Bachelor's Button)	Black Sprite	Early, Mid, Late	Medium (16)	Blue or Purple		
Centaurea (Bachelor's Button)	John Coutts	Early, Mid, Late	Medium (20)	Pink or Lavender		
Chelone (Turtlehead)	Tiny Tortuga	Late	Medium (14-16)	Pink or Lavender		
Delphinium (Delphinium)	Blue Butterfly	Mid	Medium (16)	Blue or Purple		
Dodecatheon (Shooting Star)	Aphrodite	Early	Medium (18)	Pink or Lavender		
Galium (Bedstraw)	*verum*	Early, Late	Medium (10-24)	Yellow		
Geranium (Cranesbill)	Lakwijk Star	Mid, Late	Medium (12-18)	Pink or Lavender	x	
Geranium (Cranesbill)	Nimbus	Mid, Late	Medium (16-24)	Blue or Purple		
Hemerocallis (Day Lily)	Stella de Oro	Early, Mid, Late	Medium (12-18)	Yellow		
Hemerocallis (Day Lily)	Fragrant Returns	Mid, Late	Medium (18)	Yellow	x	x
Hemerocallis (Day Lily)	Mauna Loa	Late	Medium (22)	Orange or Peach	x	

Genus	Species or Cultivar	Bloom Time	Height (inches)	Color	Foliage	Fragrance
Hosta (Plantain Lily)	Guacamole	Mid	Medium (12-24)	Blue or Purple	x	x
Iris (Iris)	*setosa*	Early	Medium (12-24)	Blue or Purple		
Lilium (Lily)	Lily Looks™· Tiny Moon	Mid, Late	Medium (12-14)	Orange or Peach		
Lilium (Lily)	Tango Passions	Mid, Late	Medium (14-16)	Pink or Lavender		
Lilium (Lily)	Golden Matrix	Mid, Late	Medium (16)	Yellow		
Lilium (Lily)	Matrix	Mid, Late	Medium (16)	Orange or Peach		
Lychnis (Campion)	Lumoina Salmon Shades	Mid, late	Medium (12-15)	Orange or Peach		
Lychnis (Campion)	Molten Lava	Mid, Late	Medium (12-15)	Red		
Lychnis (Campion)	Orange Gnome	Mid, Late	Medium (12-15)	Orange or Peach		
Lychnis (Campion)	Vesuvius	Mid, Late	Medium (12-15)	Red		
Lysimachia (Loosestrife)	Alexander	Mid, Late	Medium (12-24)	Yellow		
Lysimachia (Loosestrife)	Firecracker	Mid, Late	Medium (12-24)	Yellow		
Nepeta (Nepeta)	Dropmore Blue	Mid, Late	Medium (24)	Blue or Purple		
Nepeta (Nepeta)	Walker's Low	Mid, Late	Medium (24)	Blue or Purple		
Papaver (Poppy)	Little Patty's Plum	Mid	Medium (20)	Pink or Lavender		
Phalaris (Ribbon Grass)	Picta	Late	Medium (24)	White	x	
Phalaris (Ribbon Grass)	Strawberries and Cream	Late	Medium (24)	White	x	
Physostegia (Obedient Plant)	Crystal Peak White	Late	Medium (16)	White		

Genus	Species or Cultivar	Bloom Time	Height (inches)	Color	Foliage	Fragrance
Physostegia (Obedient Plant)	Bouquet Rose	Late	Medium (24)	Pink or Lavender		
Polemonium (Jacob's Ladder)	Touch of Class	Early, Mid	Medium (15-18)	Blue or Purple	x	x
Polemonium (Jacob's Ladder)	Bressingham Purple	Early, Mid	Medium (15)	Blue or Purple		x
Polygonatum (Solomon's Seal)	Variegatum	Mid	Medium (18-24)	White	x	
Potentilla (Cinquefoil)	Monarch's Velvet	Mid, Late	Medium (10-15)	Red		
Potentilla (Cinquefoil)	William Rollinson	Mid, Late	Medium (16)	Orange or Peach		
Primula (Primrose)	*florindae*	Early, Mid	Medium (20)	Yellow		x
Primula (Primrose)	*sikkimensis*	Early, Mid	Medium (20)	Yellow		x
Tanacetum (Tansy)	Robinson's Pink	Mid, Late	Medium (18-24)	Pink or Lavender		
Tanacetum (Tansy)	Robinson's Red	Mid, Late	Medium (18-24)	Pink or Lavender		
Trollius (Globeflower)	*ledebourii*	Mid, Late	Medium (18-24)	Orange or Peach		
Trollius (Globeflower)	Alabaster	Mid	Medium (24)	White		
Trollius (Globeflower)	Earliest of All	Early	Medium (24)	Yellow		
Trollius (Globeflower)	*europaeus*	Early	Medium (24)	Yellow		
Trollius (Globeflower)	Superbus	Mid	Medium (24)	Yellow		
Veronica (Speedwell)	Bicolor Explosion	Mid, Late	Medium (15-18)	Blue or Purple		
Veronica (Speedwell)	Blue Bomb	Mid, late	Medium (15-18)	Blue or Purple		
Veronica (Speedwell)	Pink Bomb	Mid, Late	Medium (15-18)	Pink or Lavender		
Veronica (Speedwell)	Royal Candles	Mid, Late	Medium (16-18)	Blue or Purple		
Veronica (Speedwell)	*gentianoides*	Early	Medium (18-20)	Blue or Purple		
Veronica (Speedwell)	Spicata Blue	Mid	Medium (18-24)	Blue or Purple		

Genus	Species or Cultivar	Bloom Time	Height (inches)	Color	Foliage	Fragrance
Veronica (Speedwell)	Spicata Rose	Mid	Medium (18-24)	Pink or Lavender		
Veronica (Speedwell)	Red Fox	Mid	Medium (18)	Pink or Lavender		
Veronica (Speedwell)	Icicle White	Mid, Late	Medium (18)	White		
Veronica (Speedwell)	Purpleicious	Mid, Late	Medium (20)	Blue or Purple		

List your own species and cultivars here:

Genus	Species or Cultivar	Bloom Time	Height (inches)	Color	Foliage	Fragrance

Tall Plants

Genus	Species or Cultivar	Bloom Time	Height (inches)	Color	Foliage	Fragrance
Achillea (Yarrow)	Appleblossom	Early, Mid, Late	Tall (18-30)	Pink or Lavender		x
Achillea (Yarrow)	Love Parade	Early, Mid, Late	Tall (18-30)	Pink or Lavender		x
Achillea (Yarrow)	Laura	Early, Mid, Late	Tall (24)	Red		x
Achillea (Yarrow)	Saucy Seduction	Early, Mid, Late	Tall (27)	Pink or Lavender		x
Achillea (Yarrow)	Sunny Seduction	Early, Mid, Late	Tall (27)	Yellow		x
Achillea (Yarrow)	Terra Cotta	Early, Mid, Late	Tall (30-36)	Orange or Peach		x
Aconitum (Monkshood)	Bressingham Spire	Late	Tall (30-36)	Blue or Purple		
Aconitum (Monkshood)	Pink Sensation	Late	Tall (40-48)	Pink or Lavender		
Aconitum (Monkshood)	Stainless Steel	Late	Tall (40)	Blue or Purple		
Aconitum (Monkshood)	Arendsii	Late	Tall (40)	Blue or Purple		
Aconitum (Monkshood)	Blue and White Bicolor	Late	Tall (48)	Blue or Purple		
Actaea (Bugbane)	Black Negligee	Late	Tall (42-60)	White	x	
Actaea (Bugbane)	Pink Spike	Late	Tall (42-60)	Pink or Lavender	x	
Allium (Ornamental Onion)	Altai Onion	Mid	Tall (24-36)	White		x
Allium (Ornamental Onion)	Purple Sensation	Early	Tall (24-36)	Blue or Purple		x
Anemone (Windflower)	Robustissima	Late	Tall (32)	Pink or Lavender		
Aquilegia (Columbine)	Colorado Violet and White	Early, Mid	Tall (24-28)	Blue or Purple		

Genus	Species or Cultivar	Bloom Time	Height (inches)	Color	Foliage	Fragrance
Aquilegia (Columbine)	Nora Barlow	Early, Mid	Tall (30)	Pink or Lavender		
Aruncus (Goat's Beard)	Kneiffii	Mid	Tall (24-36)	White	x	
Aruncus (Goat's Beard)	Horatio	Mid	Tall (48)	White	x	
Aruncus (Goat's Beard)	*dioicus*	Mid	Tall (60)	White	x	
Astilbe (False Spirea)	Rhythm and Blues	Late	Tall (26)	Pink or Lavender		
Astilbe (False Spirea)	Maggie Daley	Late	Tall (28)	Pink or Lavender		
Campanula (Bell Flower)	Kent Belle	Mid, Late	Tall (18-28)	Blue or Purple		
Campanula (Bell Flower)	Superba	Mid, Late	Tall (24-30)	Blue or Purple		
Centaurea (Bachelor's Button)	Mountain Bluet	Early, Mid, Late	Tall (24-30)	Blue or Purple		
Chelone (Turtlehead)	Rosea	Late	Tall (24-36)	Pink or Lavender		
Chelone (Turtlehead)	Alba	Late	Tall (36)	White		
Clematis (Clematis)	Blue Bird	Early, Mid	Tall (10 feet)	Blue or Purple		
Clematis (Clematis)	Radar Love	Early, Mid	Tall (12-15 feet)	Yellow		x
Clematis (Clematis)	*integrifolia*	Early, Mid, Late	Tall (18-36)	Blue or Purple		
Clematis (Clematis)	Alba	Early, Mid, Late	Tall (18-36)	White		
Clematis (Clematis)	Rosea	Early, Mid, Late	Tall (18-36)	Pink or Lavender		
Clematis (Clematis)	Purpurea	Early, Mid	Tall (30)	White	x	
Delphinium (Delphinium)	Magic Fountains Dark Blue-Dark Bee	Mid	Tall (24-40)	Blue or Purple		

Genus	Species or Cultivar	Bloom Time	Height (inches)	Color	Foliage	Fragrance
Delphinium (Delphinium)	Magic Fountains Lilac Pink-White Bee	Mid	Tall (24-40)	Pink or Lavender		
Delphinium (Delphinium)	Magic Fountains Pure White	Mid	Tall (24-40)	White		
Delphinium (Delphinium)	Magic Fountains Sky Blue-White Bee	Mid	Tall (24-40)	Blue or Purple		
Dicentra (Bleeding Heart)	Gold Heart	Mid	Tall (24-30)	Pink or Lavender	x	
Dicentra (Bleeding Heart)	*spectabilis*	Mid	Tall (30)	Pink or Lavender		
Dicentra (Bleeding Heart)	Alba	Mid	Tall (30)	White		
Dicentra (Bleeding Heart)	Valentine	Mid	Tall (30)	Red		
Filipendula (Meadowsweet)	Elegans	Early	Tall (28)	Pink or Lavender	x	
Filipendula (Meadowsweet)	Variegata	Early	Tall (36-48)	White	x	
Filipendula (Meadowsweet)	Venusta	Early	Tall (60)	Pink or Lavender	x	
Gentiana (Gentian)	True Blue	Late	Tall (30)	Blue or Purple		
Hemerocallis (Day Lily)	Flava	Early, Mid	Tall (30)	Yellow	x	x
Hemerocallis (Day Lily)	Hyperion	Late	Tall (36-42)	Yellow	x	x
Hesperis (Sweet Rocket)	*matronalis*	Early	Tall (36)	Pink or Lavender		x
Hosta (Plantain Lily)	True Blue	Mid	Tall (24-30)	White	x	
Iris (Iris)	Snow Queen	Mid	Tall (24-30)	White	x	
Iris (Iris)	Butter and Sugar	Mid	Tall (24-30)	Yellow	x	
Iris (Iris)	Caesar's Brother	Mid	Tall (24-39)	Blue or Purple	x	

Genus	Species or Cultivar	Bloom Time	Height (inches)	Color	Foliage	Fragrance
Iris (Iris)	Ruffled Velvet	Mid	Tall (30)	Blue or Purple	x	
Leymus (Wild Rye)	*arenarius*	Mid	Tall (24-36)	Yellow	x	
Ligularia (Ligularia)	Desdemona	Mid, Late	Tall (30-36)	Yellow		
Ligularia (Ligularia)	Little Rocket	Mid	Tall (30)	Yellow		
Ligularia (Ligularia)	Britt-Marie Crawford	Late	Tall (36-40)	Yellow	x	
Ligularia (Ligularia)	Othello	Late	Tall (36)	Yellow	x	
Ligularia (Ligularia)	The Rocket	Mid	Tall (72)	Yellow		
Lilium (Lily)	Apricot Fudge	Mid, late	Tall (24-36)	Orange or Peach		
Lilium (Lily)	Fata Morgana	Mid, Late	Tall (36-48)	Yellow		
Lilium (Lily)	Conca d'Or	Mid, late	Tall (36-60)	Yellow		
Lilium (Lily)	Landini	Mid, Late	Tall (42)	Red		
Lilium (Lily)	Blackout	Mid, Late	Tall (48)	Red		
Lilium (Lily)	Citronelle	Late	Tall (48)	Yellow		
Lilium (Lily)	Elodie	Mid, Late	Tall (48)	Pink or Lavender		
Lilium (Lily)	Pink Tiger	Late	Tall (48)	Pink or Lavender		
Lilium (Lily)	Splendens	Late	Tall (48)	Orange or Peach		
Lychnis (Campion)	Dusky Salmon	Mid, Late	Tall (48)	Orange or Peach		
Lychnis (Campion)	Maltese Cross	Mid	Tall (48)	Red		
Lythrum (Purple Loosestrife)	Rosy Gem	Late	Tall (48-60)	Pink or Lavender		
Meconopsis (Himalayan Blue Poppy)	*betonicifolia*	Mid, Late	Tall (30-48)	Blue or Purple		
Meconopsis (Himalayan Blue Poppy)	Lingholm	Mid, Late	Tall (36-48)	Blue or Purple		
Nepeta (Nepeta)	Blue Dreams	Mid, Late	Tall (24-36)	Blue or Purple		x
Nepeta (Nepeta)	Pink Dreams	Mid, Late	Tall (24-36)	Pink or Lavender		x

Genus	Species or Cultivar	Bloom Time	Height (inches)	Color	Foliage	Fragrance
Nepeta (Nepeta)	*siberica*	Mid, Late	Tall (36)	Blue or Purple		x
Nepeta (Nepeta)	Souvenir D' Andre Chaudrón	Mid, Late	Tall (36)	Blue or Purple		x
Paeonia (Peony)	Sorbet	Mid	Tall (28)	Pink or Lavender		x
Paeonia (Peony)	Kopper Kettle	Mid	Tall (32)	Orange or Peach		x
Paeonia (Peony)	Bartzella	Mid	Tall (34)	Yellow		x
Paeonia (Peony)	Buckeye Belle	Mid	Tall (34)	Red		x
Paeonia (Peony)	Coral Charm	Mid	Tall (36)	Orange or Peach		x
Paeonia (Peony)	Jana	Early	Tall (36)	Pink or Lavender		
Paeonia (Peony)	Karl Rosenfeld	Mid	Tall (38)	Red		x
Paeonia (Peony)	Festiva Maxima	Mid	Tall (40)	White		x
Papaver (Poppy)	Brilliant	Mid	Tall (32-36)	Orange or Peach		
Papaver (Poppy)	Patty's Plum	Mid	Tall (28-32)	Pink or Lavender		
Papaver (Poppy)	Princess Louise	Mid	Tall (24)	Orange or Peach		
Phlomis (Phlomis)	*tuberosa*	Mid	Tall (36-48)	Pink or Lavender		
Physostegia (Obedient Plant)	Variegata	Late	Tall (24-36)	Pink or Lavender	x	
Tanacetum (Tansy)	Crispum	Mid, Late	Tall (24-36)	Yellow	x	
Tanacetum (Tansy)	Isla Gold	Mid, Late	Tall (36-48)	Yellow	x	
Tanacetum (Tansy)	*vulgare*	Mid, Late	Tall (36-48)	Yellow		
Thalictrum (Meadow Rue)	Anne	Mid	Tall (84)	Pink or Lavender	x	
Thalictrum (Meadow Rue)	*aquilegifolium*	Mid	Tall (48)	Pink or Lavender	x	

Genus	Species or Cultivar	Bloom Time	Height (inches)	Color	Foliage	Fragrance
Thalictrum (Meadow Rue)	Black Stockings	Mid	Tall (48)	Pink or Lavender	x	
Thalictrum (Meadow Rue)	Flavum	Mid, Late	Tall (48)	Yellow	x	
Thalictrum (Meadow Rue)	Hewitt's Double	Mid, Late	Tall (48)	Blue or Purple	x	
Thalictrum (Meadow Rue)	Splendide	Mid, Late	Tall (48-72)	Pink or Lavender	x	
Trollius (Globeflower)	Lemon Queen	Mid	Tall (18-36)	Yellow		
Trollius (Globeflower)	Golden Queen	Late	Tall (36)	Orange or Peach		
Veronica (Speedwell)	Pink Damask	Mid, Late	Tall (24-36)	Pink or Lavender		
Veronica (Speedwell)	Charlotte	Mid, Late	Tall (30)	White		
Veronicastrum (Culver Root)	Apollo	Late	Tall (59)	Blue or Purple		
Veronicastrum (Culver Root)	Red Arrow	Late	Tall (49)	Pink or Lavender		
Veronicastrum (Culver Root)	Erica	Late	Tall (59)	Pink or Lavender		
Veronicastrum (Culver Root)	Fascination	Late	Tall (59)	Blue or Purple		

List your own species and cultivars here:

Genus	Species or Cultivar	Bloom Time	Height (inches)	Color	Foliage	Fragrance

List your own species and cultivars here:

Genus	Species or Cultivar	Bloom Time	Height (inches)	Color	Foliage	Fragrance

CHAPTER 14

Color Charts

Blue or Purple

Genus	Species or Cultivar	Bloom Time	Height (inches)	Color	Foliage	Fragrance
Aconitum (Monkshood)	Arendsii	Late	Tall (40)	Blue or Purple		
Aconitum (Monkshood)	Blue and White Bicolor	Late	Tall (48)	Blue or Purple		
Aconitum (Monkshood)	Blue Lagoon	Late	Short (10-12)	Blue or Purple		
Aconitum (Monkshood)	Bressingham Spire	Late	Tall (30-36)	Blue or Purple		
Aconitum (Monkshood)	Stainless Steel	Late	Tall (40)	Blue or Purple		
Allium (Ornamental Onion)	Purple Sensation	Early	Tall (24-36)	Blue or Purple		x
Aquilegia (Columbine)	Cameo Blue-White	Early	Short (6-8)	Blue or Purple		
Aquilegia (Columbine)	Colorado Violet and White	Early, Mid	Tall (24-28)	Blue or Purple		
Aquilegia (Columbine)	Rocky Mountain Blue	Early, Mid	Medium (24)	Blue or Purple		

Genus	Species or Cultivar	Bloom Time	Height (inches)	Color	Foliage	Fragrance
Aquilegia (Columbine)	Winky Double Dark Blue-White	Early, Mid	Short (12)	Blue or Purple		
Aquilegia (Columbine)	Woodside Gold	Early, Mid	Medium (18-24)	Blue or Purple	x	
Brunnera (Siberian Bugloss)	Alexander's Great	Early	Medium (16)	Blue or Purple	x	
Brunnera (Siberian Bugloss)	Jack Frost	Early	Medium (16)	Blue or Purple	x	
Campanula (Bell Flower)	Campbell	Mid, Late	Medium (16-18)	Blue or Purple		
Campanula (Bell Flower)	Genti Twisterbell	Mid, Late	Medium (16-18)	Blue or Purple		
Campanula (Bell Flower)	Kent Belle	Mid, Late	Tall (18-28)	Blue or Purple		
Campanula (Bell Flower)	Olympia	Mid, Late	Short (6-12)	Blue or Purple		
Campanula (Bell Flower)	Superba	Mid, Late	Tall (24-30)	Blue or Purple		
Centaurea (Bachelor's Button)	Black Sprite	Early, Mid, Late	Medium (16)	Blue or Purple		
Centaurea (Bachelor's Button)	Mountain Bluet	Early, Mid, Late	Tall (24-30)	Blue or Purple		
Clematis (Clematis)	Blue Bird	Early, Mid	Tall (10 feet)	Blue or Purple		
Clematis (Clematis)	*integrifolia*	Early, Mid, Late	Tall (18-36)	Blue or Purple		
Delphinium (Delphinium)	Blue Butterfly	Mid	Medium (16)	Blue or Purple		
Delphinium (Delphinium)	Magic Fountains Dark Blue-Dark Bee	Mid	Tall (24-40)	Blue or Purple		

Genus	Species or Cultivar	Bloom Time	Height (inches)	Color	Foliage	Fragrance
Delphinium (Delphinium)	Magic Fountains Sky Blue-White Bee	Mid	Tall (24-40)	Blue or Purple		
Delphinium (Delphinium)	Summer Blues	Mid	Short (12)	Blue or Purple		
Delphinium (Delphinium)	Summer Nights	Mid	Short (12)	Blue or Purple		
Gentiana (Gentian)	*septemfida*	Late	Short (8-12)	Blue or Purple		
Gentiana (Gentian)	True Blue	Late	Tall (30)	Blue or Purple		
Geranium (Cranesbill)	Nimbus	Mid, Late	Medium (16-24)	Blue or Purple		
Hemerocallis (Day Lily)	Little Grapette	Mid	Short (12)	Blue or Purple	x	
Hosta (Plantain Lily)	Guacamole	Mid	Medium (12-24)	Blue or Purple	x	
Iris (Iris)	Caesar's Brother	Mid	Tall (24-39)	Blue or Purple	x	
Iris (Iris)	Ruffled Velvet	Mid	Tall (30)	Blue or Purple	x	
Iris (Iris)	*setosa*	Early	Medium (12-24)	Blue or Purple		
Meconopsis (Himalayan Blue Poppy)	*betonicifolia*	Mid, Late	Tall (30-48)	Blue or Purple		
Meconopsis (Himalayan Blue Poppy)	Lingholm	Mid, Late	Tall (36-48)	Blue or Purple		
Myosotis (Forget-Me-Not)	*alpestris*	Mid	Short (6-10)	Blue or Purple		
Nepeta (Nepeta)	Blue Dreams	Mid, Late	Tall (24-36)	Blue or Purple		x
Nepeta (Nepeta)	Dropmore Blue	Mid, Late	Medium (24)	Blue or Purple		x
Nepeta (Nepeta)	*siberica*	Mid, Late	Tall (36)	Blue or Purple		x

Genus	Species or Cultivar	Bloom Time	Height (inches)	Color	Foliage	Fragrance
Nepeta (Nepeta)	Souvenir D' Andre Chaudrón	Mid, Late	Tall (36)	Blue or Purple		x
Nepeta (Nepeta)	Walker's Low	Mid, Late	Medium (24)	Blue or Purple		x
Phlox (Phlox)	Blue Emerald	Early, Mid	Short (6)	Blue or Purple		
Phlox (Phlox)	North Hills	Early, Mid	Short (4-8)	Blue or Purple, White		
Phlox (Phlox)	Sherwood Purple	Mid, late	Short (6-10)	Blue or Purple		x
Polemonium (Jacob's Ladder)	Bressingham Purple	Early, Mid	Medium (15)	Blue or Purple		x
Polemonium (Jacob's Ladder)	Touch of Class	Early, Mid	Medium (15-18)	Blue or Purple	x	x
Pulsatilla (Pasque Flower)	*vulgaris*	Early	Short (10)	Blue or Purple		
Thalictrum (Meadow Rue)	Hewitt's Double	Mid, Late	Tall (48)	Blue or Purple	x	
Veronica (Speedwell)	Bicolor Explosion	Mid, Late	Medium (15-18)	Blue or Purple		
Veronica (Speedwell)	Blue Bomb	Mid, late	Medium (15-18)	Blue or Purple		
Veronica (Speedwell)	*gentianoides*	Early	Medium (18-20)	Blue or Purple		
Veronica (Speedwell)	Purpleicious	Mid, Late	Medium (20)	Blue or Purple		
Veronica (Speedwell)	Royal Candles	Mid, Late	Medium (16-18)	Blue or Purple		
Veronica (Speedwell)	Spicata Blue	Mid	Medium (18-24)	Blue or Purple		
Veronica (Speedwell)	Ulster Blue	Mid	Short (6-8)	Blue or Purple		
Veronica (Speedwell)	Waterperry Blue	Early	Short (6-8)	Blue or Purple		

Genus	Species or Cultivar	Bloom Time	Height (inches)	Color	Foliage	Fragrance
Veronicastrum (Culver Root)	Apollo	Late	Tall (59)	Blue or Purple		
Veronicastrum (Culver Root)	Fascination	Late	Tall (59)	Blue or Purple		

List your own species and cultivars here:

Genus	Species or Cultivar	Bloom Time	Height (inches)	Color	Foliage	Fragrance

Pink or Lavender

Genus	Species or Cultivar	Bloom Time	Height	Color	Foliage	Fragrance
Achillea (Yarrow)	Appleblossom	Early, Mid, Late	Tall (18-30)	Pink or Lavender		x
Achillea (Yarrow)	Love Parade	Early, Mid, Late	Tall (18-30)	Pink or Lavender		x
Achillea (Yarrow)	Saucy Seduction	Early, Mid, Late	Tall (27)	Pink or Lavender		x
Aconitum (Monkshood)	Pink Sensation	Late	Tall (40-48)	Pink or Lavender		
Actaea (Bugbane)	Pink Spike	Late	Tall (42-60)	Pink or Lavender	x	
Allium (Ornamental Onion)	Millenium	Late	Medium (12-18)	Pink or Lavender		x
Allium (Ornamental Onion)	*senescens*	Mid	Short (6-12)	Pink or Lavender		x
Anemone (Windflower)	Robustissima	Late	Tall (32)	Pink or Lavender		
Aquilegia (Columbine)	Cameo Pink-White	Early	Short (6-8)	Pink or Lavender		
Aquilegia (Columbine)	Nora Barlow	Early, Mid	Tall (30)	Pink or Lavender		
Aquilegia (Columbine)	Songbird Robin	Early, Mid	Medium (16-24)	Pink or Lavender		
Aquilegia (Columbine)	Swan Pink and Yellow	Early, Mid	Medium (20-24)	Pink or Lavender, Yellow		
Aquilegia (Columbine)	Winky Double Rose-White	Early, Mid	Short (12)	Pink or Lavender		
Astilbe (False Spirea)	Chocolate Shogun	Mid, Late	Medium (18-24)	Pink or Lavender	x	
Astilbe (False Spirea)	Colorflash	Late	Medium (20)	Pink or Lavender	x	
Astilbe (False Spirea)	Maggie Daley	Late	Tall (28)	Pink or Lavender		
Astilbe (False Spirea)	Peach Blossom	Mid, late	Medium (24)	Pink or Lavender		

Genus	Species or Cultivar	Bloom Time	Height	Color	Foliage	Fragrance
Astilbe (False Spirea)	Rhythm and Blues	Late	Tall (26)	Pink or Lavender		
Bergenia (Pigsqueak)	Winterglow	Early	Medium (12-15)	Pink or Lavender	x	
Campanula (Bell Flower)	Pink Octopus	Mid, Late	Short (12)	Pink or Lavender		
Campanula (Bell Flower)	Silver Bells	Mid, Late	Medium (15)	Pink or Lavender	x	x
Campanula (Bell Flower)	*takesimana*	Mid, Late	Medium (24)	Pink or Lavender		
Centaurea (Bachelor's Button)	John Coutts	Early, Mid, Late	Medium (20)	Pink or Lavender		
Chelone (Turtlehead)	Rosea	Late	Tall (24-36)	Pink or Lavender		
Chelone (Turtlehead)	Tiny Tortuga	Late	Medium (14-16)	Pink or Lavender		
Clematis (Clematis)	Rosea	Early, Mid, Late	Tall (18-36)	Pink or Lavender		
Delphinium (Delphinium)	Magic Fountains Lilac Pink-White Bee	Mid	Tall (24-40)	Pink or Lavender		
Delphinium (Delphinium)	Summer Morning	Mid	Short (12)	Pink or Lavender		
Dianthus (Pinks)	Pink Maiden	Mid, Late	Short (6-8)	Pink or Lavender		
Dianthus (Pinks)	Red Maiden	Mid, Late	Short (6-8)	Pink or Lavender		
Dicentra (Bleeding Heart)	Candy Hearts	Mid	Short (10-12)	Pink or Lavender	x	
Dicentra (Bleeding Heart)	Gold Heart	Mid	Tall (24-30)	Pink or Lavender	x	
Dicentra (Bleeding Heart)	*spectabilis*	Mid	Tall (30)	Pink or Lavender		

Genus	Species or Cultivar	Bloom Time	Height	Color	Foliage	Fragrance
Dodecatheon (Shooting Star)	*meadia*	Early	Short (6-12)	Pink or Lavender		
Dodecatheon (Shooting Star)	Aphrodite	Early	Medium (18)	Pink or Lavender		
Filipendula (Meadowsweet)	Kahome	Early	Short (12)	Pink or Lavender	x	
Filipendula (Meadowsweet)	Elegans	Early	Tall (28)	Pink or Lavender	x	
Filipendula (Meadowsweet)	Venusta	Early	Tall (60)	Pink or Lavender	x	
Geranium (Cranesbill)	Birch Double	Mid	Short (10-12)	Pink or Lavender		
Geranium (Cranesbill)	Lakwijk Star	Mid, Late	Medium (12-18)	Pink or Lavender	x	
Hesperis (Rocket)	*matronalis*	Early	Tall (36)	Pink or Lavender		x
Lamium (Dead Nettle)	Beacon Silver	Early, Mid, Late	Short (6-8)	Pink or Lavender	x	
Lamium (Dead Nettle)	Pink Pewter	Early, Mid, Late	Short (6-8)	Pink or Lavender	x	
Lewisia (Bitterroot)	Little Plum	Mid-Late	Short (6)	Pink or Lavender		
Lilium (Lily)	Elodie	Mid, Late	Tall (48)	Pink or Lavender		
Lilium (Lily)	Pink Tiger	Late	Tall (48)	Pink or Lavender		
Lilium (Lily)	Tango Passions	Mid, Late	Medium (14-16)	Pink or Lavender		
Lythrum (Purple Loosestrife)	Rosy Gem	Late	Tall (48-60)	Pink or Lavender		
Nepeta (Nepeta)	Pink Dreams	Mid, Late	Tall (24-36)	Pink or Lavender		
Paeonia (Peony)	Jana	Early	Tall (36)	Pink or Lavender		
Paeonia (Peony)	Sorbet	Mid	Tall (28)	Pink or Lavender		x

Genus	Species or Cultivar	Bloom Time	Height	Color	Foliage	Fragrance
Papaver (Poppy)	Little Patty's Plum	Mid	Medium (20)	Pink or Lavender		
Papaver (Poppy)	Patty's Plum	Mid	Tall (32-36)	Pink or Lavender		
Phlomis (Phlomis)	*tuberosa*	Mid	Tall (36-48)	Pink or Lavender		
Physostegia (Obedient Plant)	Bouquet Rose	Late	Medium (24)	Pink or Lavender		
Physostegia (Obedient Plant)	Variegata	Late	Tall (24-36)	Pink or Lavender	x	
Primula (Primrose)	*matthioli*	Early	Short (10)	Pink or Lavender		
Tanacetum (Tansy)	Robinson's Pink	Mid, Late	Medium (18-24)	Pink or Lavender		
Tanacetum (Tansy)	Robinson's Red	Mid, Late	Medium (18-24)	Pink or Lavender		
Thalictrum (Meadow Rue)	Anne	Mid	Tall (84)	Pink or Lavender	x	
Thalictrum (Meadow Rue)	*aquilegifolium*	Mid	Tall (48)	Pink or Lavender	x	
Thalictrum (Meadow Rue)	Black Stockings	Mid	Tall (48)	Pink or Lavender	x	
Thalictrum (Meadow Rue)	Splendide	Mid, Late	Tall (48-72)	Pink or Lavender	x	
Veronica (Speedwell)	Giles van Hees	Mid	Short (6-8)	Pink or Lavender		
Veronica (Speedwell)	Pink Bomb	Mid, Late	Medium (15-18)	Pink or Lavender		
Veronica (Speedwell)	Pink Damask	Mid, Late	Tall (24-36)	Pink or Lavender		
Veronica (Speedwell)	Red Fox	Mid	Medium (18)	Pink or Lavender		
Veronica (Speedwell)	Spicata Rose	Mid	Medium (18-24)	Pink or Lavender		

Genus	Species or Cultivar	Bloom Time	Height	Color	Foliage	Fragrance
Veronicastrum (Culver Root)	Erica	Late	Tall (59)	Pink or Lavender		
Veronicastrum (Culver Root)	Red Arrow	Late	Tall (49)	Pink or Lavender		

List your own species and cultivars here:

Genus	Species or Cultivar	Bloom Time	Height (inches)	Color	Foliage	Fragrance

Orange or Peach

Genus	Species or Cultivar	Bloom Time	Height (inches)	Color	Foliage	Fragrance
Achillea (Yarrow)	Terra Cotta	Early, Mid, Late	Tall (30-36)	Orange or Peach		x
Hemerocallis (Day Lily)	Mauna Loa	Late	Medium (22)	Orange or Peach	x	
Lewisia (Bitterroot)	Little Peach	Mid, Late	Short (6)	Orange or Peach		
Lilium (Lily)	Apricot Fudge	Mid, Late	Tall (24-36)	Orange or Peach		
Lilium (Lily)	Lily Looks™ Tiny Moon	Mid, Late	Medium (12-14)	Orange or Peach		
Lilium (Lily)	Matrix	Mid, Late	Medium (16)	Orange or Peach		
Lilium (Lily)	Splendens	Late	Tall (48)	Orange or Peach		
Lychnis (Campion)	Dusky Salmon	Mid, Late	Tall (48)	Orange or Peach		
Lychnis (Campion)	Lumina Salmon Shades	Mid, late	Medium (12-15)	Orange or Peach		
Lychnis (Campion)	Orange Gnome	Mid, Late	Medium (12-15)	Orange or Peach		
Paeonia (Peony)	Coral Charm	Mid	Tall (36)	Orange or Peach		x
Paeonia (Peony)	Kopper Kettle	Mid	Tall (32)	Orange or Peach		x
Papaver (Poppy)	Brilliant	Mid	Tall (32-36)	Orange or Peach		
Papaver (Poppy)	Princess Louise	Mid	Tall (24)	Orange or Peach		
Potentilla (Cinquefoil)	William Rollinson	Mid, Late	Medium (16)	Orange or Peach		
Sedum (Stonecrop)	Variegatum	Mid, Late	Short (5)	Orange or Peach	x	

Genus	Species or Cultivar	Bloom Time	Height (inches)	Color	Foliage	Fragrance
Trollius (Globeflower)	Golden Queen	Late	Tall (36)	Orange or Peach		
Trollius (Globeflower)	*ledebourii*	Mid, Late	Medium (18-24)	Orange or Peach		

List your own species and cultivars here:

Genus	Species or Cultivar	Bloom Time	Height (inches)	Color	Foliage	Fragrance

Red

Genus	Species or Cultivar	Bloom Time	Height (inches)	Color	Foliage	Fragrance
Achillea (Yarrow)	Laura	Early, Mid, Late	Tall (24)	Red		x
Achillea (Yarrow)	Paprika	Early, Mid, Late	Medium (18-24)	Red		x
Aquilegia (Columbine)	Songbird Cardinal	Early, Mid	Medium (16-24)	Red		
Astilbe (False Spirea)	Fanal	Mid, Late	Medium (24)	Red		
Campanula (Bell Flower)	Cherry Bells	Mid, Late	Medium (16-18)	Red		
Dianthus (Pinks)	Arctic Fire	Mid, Late	Short (6-8)	Red, White		
Dicentra (Bleeding Heart)	Burning Hearts	Mid	Short (10-12)	Red	x	
Dicentra (Bleeding Heart)	Valentine	Mid	Tall (30)	Red		
Lilium (Lily)	Blackout	Mid, Late	Tall (48)	Red		
Lilium (Lily)	Landini	Mid, Late	Tall (42)	Red		
Lychnis (Campion)	Maltese Cross	Mid	Tall (48)	Red		
Lychnis (Campion)	Molten Lava	Mid, Late	Medium (12-15)	Red		
Lychnis (Campion)	Vesuvius	Mid, Late	Medium (12-15)	Red		
Paeonia (Peony)	Buckeye Belle	Mid	Tall (34)	Red		x
Paeonia (Peony)	Karl Rosenfeld	Mid	Tall (38)	Red		x
Papaver (Poppy)	Allegro	Mid	Short (10-12)	Red		
Potentilla (Cinquefoil)	Monarch's Velvet	Mid, Late	Medium (10-15)	Red		
Pulsatilla (Pasque Flower)	Rubra	Mid	Short (10)	Red		
Sedum (Stonecrop)	Tricolor	Mid, Late	Short (4)	Red	x	

List your own species and cultivars here:

Genus	Species or Cultivar	Bloom Time	Height (inches)	Color	Foliage	Fragrance

Yellow

Genus	Species or Cultivar	Bloom Time	Height (inches)	Color	Foliage	Fragrance
Achillea (Yarrow)	Sunny Seduction	Early, Mid, Late	Tall (27)	Yellow		x
Aquilegia (Columbine)	Swan Pink and Yellow	Early, Mid	Medium (20-24)	Pink or Lavender, Yellow		
Aquilegia (Columbine)	Swan Yellow	Early, Mid	Medium (20-24)	Yellow		
Artemesia (Wormwood)	Silver Brocade	Mid	Short (6-12)	Yellow	x	
Artemesia (Wormwood)	Silver Mound	Mid	Short (10)	Yellow	x	
Artemesia (Wormwood)	Valerie Finnis	Mid	Medium (15-18)	Yellow	x	
Clematis (Clematis)	Radar Love	Early, Mid	Tall (12-15 feet)	Yellow		x
Draba (Whitlow-grass)	*siberica*	Early, Late	Short (6)	Yellow		
Galium (Bedstraw)	*verum*	Early, Late	Medium (10-24)	Yellow		
Hemerocallis (Day Lily)	Flava	Early, Mid	Tall (30)	Yellow	x	x
Hemerocallis (Day Lily)	Fragrant Returns	Mid, Late	Medium (18)	Yellow	x	x
Hemerocallis (Day Lily)	Hyperion	Late	Tall (36-42)	Yellow	x	x
Hemerocallis (Day Lily)	Stella de Oro	Early, Mid, Late	Medium (12-18)	Yellow		
Iris (Iris)	Butter and Sugar	Mid	Tall (24-30)	Yellow		x
Leymus (Wild Rye)	*arenarius*	Mid	Tall (24-36)	Yellow		x
Ligularia (Ligularia)	Britt-Marie Crawford	Late	Tall (36-40)	Yellow		x
Ligularia (Ligularia)	Desdemona	Mid, Late	Tall (30-36)	Yellow		
Ligularia (Ligularia)	Little Rocket	Mid	Tall (30)	Yellow		
Ligularia (Ligularia)	Othello	Late	Tall (36)	Yellow		x
Ligularia (Ligularia)	The Rocket	Mid	Tall (72)	Yellow		
Lilium (Lily)	Citronelle	Late	Tall (48)	Yellow		
Lilium (Lily)	Conca d'Or	Mid, late	Tall (36-60)	Yellow		
Lilium (Lily)	Fata Morgana	Mid, Late	Tall (36-48)	Yellow		
Lilium (Lily)	Golden Matrix	Mid, Late	Medium (16)	Yellow		

Genus	Species or Cultivar	Bloom Time	Height (inches)	Color	Foliage	Fragrance
Lysimachia (Loosestrife)	Alexander	Mid, Late	Medium (12-24)	Yellow		
Lysimachia (Loosestrife)	Firecracker	Mid, Late	Medium (12-24)	Yellow		
Paeonia (Peony)	Bartzella	Mid	Tall (34)	Yellow		x
Primula (Primrose)	*florindae*	Early, Mid	Medium (20)	Yellow		x
Primula (Primrose)	*sikkimensis*	Early, Mid	Medium (20)	Yellow		x
Solidago (Goldenrod)	Little Lemon	Late	Short (12)	Yellow		
Tanacetum (Tansy)	Crispum	Mid, Late	Tall (24-36)	Yellow	x	
Tanacetum (Tansy)	Isla Gold	Mid, Late	Tall (36-48)	Yellow	x	
Tanacetum (Tansy)	*vulgare*	Mid, Late	Tall (36-48)	Yellow		
Thalictrum (Meadow Rue)	Flavum	Mid, Late	Tall (48)	Yellow		x
Trollius (Globeflower)	Earliest of All	Early	Medium (24)	Yellow		
Trollius (Globeflower)	*europaeus*	Early	Medium (24)	Yellow		
Trollius (Globeflower)	Lemon Queen	Mid	Tall (18-36)	Yellow		
Trollius (Globeflower)	*pumilus*	Early	Short (6-8)	Yellow		
Trollius (Globeflower)	Superbus	Mid	Medium (24)	Yellow		

List your own species and cultivars here:

Genus	Species or Cultivar	Bloom Time	Height (inches)	Color	Foliage	Fragrance

White

Genus	Species or Cultivar	Bloom Time	Height (inches)	Color	Foliage	Fragrance
Actaea (Bugbane)	Black Negligee	Late	Tall (42-60)	White	x	
Aegopodium (Bishop's Weed)	Variegata	Early, Mid	Medium (16)	White	x	
Allium (Ornamental Onion)	*altaicum*	Mid	Tall (24-36)	White		x
Anemone (Windflower)	Snowdrop	Early	Medium (12-15)	White		
Aruncus (Goat's Beard)	*aethusifolius*	Mid	Short (10)	White	x	
Aruncus (Goat's Beard)	*dioicus*	Mid	Tall (60)	White	x	
Aruncus (Goat's Beard)	Horatio	Mid	Tall (48)	White	x	
Aruncus (Goat's Beard)	Kneiffii	Mid	Tall (24-36)	White	x	
Centaurea (Bachelor's Button)	Amethyst in Snow	Early, Mid, Late	Medium (14-16)	White		
Cerastium (Snow-in-Summer)	*tomentosum*	Early	Short (6)	White	x	
Chelone (Turtlehead)	Alba	Late	Tall (36)	White		
Clematis (Clematis)	Alba	Early, Mid, Late	Tall (18-36)	White		
Clematis (Clematis)	Purpurea	Early, Mid	Tall (30)	White	x	
Delphinium (Delphinium)	Magic Fountains Pure White	Mid	Tall (24-40)	White		
Dianthus (Pinks)	Arctic Fire	Mid, Late	Short (6-8)	Red, White		
Dicentra (Bleeding Heart)	Alba	Mid	Tall (30)	White		
Filipendula (Meadowsweet)	Variegata	Early	Tall (36-48)	White	x	
Geranium (Cranesbill)	Double Jewel	Mid	Short (12)	White		
Hosta (Plantain Lily)	True Blue	Mid	Tall (24-30)	White	x	
Iris (Iris)	Snow Queen	Mid	Tall (24-30)	White	x	
Lamium (Dead Nettle)	White Nancy	Early, Mid, Late	Short (6-8)	White	x	
Paeonia (Peony)	Festiva Maxima	Mid	Tall (40)	White		x
Phalaris (Ribbon Grass)	Dwarf Garters	Late	Short ((10-15)	White	x	
Phalaris (Ribbon Grass)	Picta	Late	Medium (24)	White	x	

Genus	Species or Cultivar	Bloom Time	Height (inches)	Color	Foliage	Fragrance
Phalaris (Ribbon Grass)	Strawberries and Cream	Late	Medium (24)	White	x	
Phlox (Phlox)	North Hills	Early, Mid	Short (4-8)	Blue or Purple, White		
Physostegia (Obedient Plant)	Crystal Peak White	Late	Medium (16)	White		
Polygonatum (Solomon's Seal)	Variegatum	Mid	Medium (18-24)	White	x	
Pulsatilla (Pasque Flower)	Alba	Early	Short (10)	White		
Trollius (Globeflower)	Alabaster	Mid	Medium (24)	White		
Veronica (Speedwell)	Charlotte	Mid, Late	Tall (30)	White		
Veronica (Speedwell)	Icicle White	Mid, Late	Medium (18)	White		

List your own species and cultivars here:

Genus	Species or Cultivar	Bloom Time	Height (inches)	Color	Foliage	Fragrance

List your own species and cultivars here:

Genus	Species or Cultivar	Bloom Time	Height (inches)	Color	Foliage	Fragrance

PART IV

Using the Charts to
Build Five Perennial Gardens

Lilium 'Fata Morgana'
 with a backdrop of
Achillea 'Appleblossom' and the
foliage of *Aegopodium* 'Variegata.'

CHAPTER 15

Gardening with the Charts

It is a general rule for any perennial garden that in terms of bloom time, about one-third of the plants should be Early Season, one-third should be Mid Season, and one-third should be Late Season. This ensures that at least one-third of your garden will always be blooming. If some of the chosen perennials are plants that span more than one bloom time category, an even larger percentage of your garden will be blooming at some points during the season (e.g., yarrow, capable of blooming from June through August).

A corollary of this rule is that these bloom times should be distributed evenly across space in your garden, assuring an equal distribution of color at any one time. One way to achieve this is to divide your garden into equal front, middle, and back sections (or rows), and to be sure that the three bloom times are represented equally in each section.

Further, within each row or section of the garden, plants with the same bloom time should be placed symmetrically or dispersed evenly. This keeps the viewer's eye and interest moving within the garden. For example, do not plant the one-third of your plants that are early bloomers all together at one end of a row, but instead intersperse them evenly with the mid and late season bloomers through the length of the row.

The most effective distribution of heights is dependent somewhat on the viewing point or points for the garden. Most common is a pattern of short in front grading through medium in the middle to tall in the back. However, the arrangement of heights is really governed by the setting and position of the garden. Once the viewpoint has been established, the only crucial rule is that a tall plant should not block the view of one that is shorter.

This future perennial garden is an empty canvas at this point. Hoses have been stretched out to form boundaries of smaller garden beds within this approximately 1,200 square feet of planting area (top left).

The decision was made to lift the geotextile fabric and to scoop out a dry creek bed before installing plants (top right).

Once the position of the first beds had been established, the Charts were used to begin choosing the plants (center left).

Here the pattern formed by the hoses has been chalked on the geotextile fabric so the hoses can be used to lay out other parts of the garden. Some of the plants have been installed and stepping stone steps are being constructed (center right).

The dry stream has been filled with rocks. Bark nuggets have been used to conceal the geotextile fabric in the planted area and fine bark mulch has been placed on the walking path. The next step is defining more of the small garden spaces and filling them with plants whose choice is based on the Charts (bottom).

The color palette is primarily up to the gardener's taste and I firmly believe that there is justification for any palette. However, there are a few guideposts to at least consider. Some of these are addressed in Chapter 9: "Design at the Medium Level." I would add here that in my experience, a color theme is important, although it can be tempting to have a one-of-everything approach. It is especially easy to fall into this if you gather perennials from nurseries and friends before you have a plan. Often, the plants that are in bloom at a given moment are most difficult to avoid randomly acquiring. They may not all work together in your garden symphony once you have a venue ready. Success with color, whatever your choice, really comes from having a plan.

We will now use the charts to choose the plants for five different perennial gardens. Each garden is fourteen feet in length and six feet in width. Each is viewed from one of the long sides and the other long side backs up against a five-foot-high wooden fence.

The exposure is full sun on a south-facing hillside in Fairbanks, Alaska. The garden is divided into three rows that run its length and that are positioned at two-feet intervals from front to back.

I begin my own planning process by sketching out the dimensions of my garden on gridded paper, At this point, the garden image is very diagrammatic. When the garden is actually planted, each plant will be moved slightly to one side or the other of the one behind it so that no plant is exactly in front of or behind another. Part of the decision-making process involved in this tweaking of the final plant spacing will be based on the mature size of each plant. In the completed garden, the plants will not be exactly on two-feet centers as they are in the diagram.

With pencil, ruler, paper, and charts in hand, we are ready to start drawing out gardens.

Evening view of this developing garden. River rock has been used to outline the position of future beds (top left).

Mid September view from the south deck of the greenhouse over the newly planted garden. River rock outlines future beds, paths have been covered with shredded bark mulch, and most herbaceous perennials are cut back and ready for winter (top right).

CHAPTER 16

The Starter Garden

For this first garden, I begin by referring to the Height Charts. In the Starter Garden (see Figure 6) I am not going to spend a lot of time on color choice, though I will aim for a theme that stays constant through the season.

In the back row against the fence I will have seven tall perennials and, of course, about one-third should be early bloomers, one-third mid season bloomers, and one-third late bloomers. Using the Tall Chart, I choose my first plant arbitrarily, the only criterion at this point being that it is tall. I do have my own personal bias, though, and I choose *Achillea* 'Laura,' one of my favorite yarrows. It is an early-mid-late season bloomer with red flowers. I want to make the back row very symmetrical, as a way to anchor the garden, which is not going to be so symmetrical going forward. I place this same yarrow cultivar on either side of the middle spot in the back row. I choose *Hesperis matronalis* for the middle spot in the back row. The lavender-pink blooms will be a nice contrast with the red of the early yarrow flowers for the brief time they may be blooming together. *Hesperis* will bloom profusely and then probably need to be cut back in mid summer once the foliage starts deteriorating. Since the yarrow blooms all season and has a very full, fluffy growth form, it will do a great job of filling the void left by the *Hesperis* after it blooms. I choose *Aconitum* 'Blue and White Bicolor' for either side of the yarrow. This is a late bloomer with a linear growth form, which will contrast nicely with the thick, bushy yarrow. On each end of the back row, I choose *Ligularia* 'The Rocket' from the Tall Chart. Its growth form is less linear than the monkshood but more contained and vertical than the yarrow. With yellow spikes mid season, it completes our back row. If we count our varieties by bloom times, we have three early, four mid, and four late. You can confirm these bloom times by looking at the Bloom Time column on the Tall Chart. Since some of our plants (like yarrow) span more than one

FIGURE 6

Starter Garden

Consistent Colors Through the Season: Blue – Pink –Red – Yellow – White

N

BACK

MID *Ligularia* 'The Rocket'	LATE *Aconitum* 'Blue and White Bicolor'	EARLY-LATE *Achillera* 'Laura'	EARLY *Hesperis matronalis* (Lavender)	EARLY-LATE *Achillera* 'Laura'	LATE *Aconitum* 'Blue and White Bicolor'	MID *Ligularia* 'The Rocket'
EARLY *Anemone* Snowdrop	EARLY-LATE *Hemerocallis* 'Stella de Oro'	MID-LATE *Lilium* 'Tango Passions'	EARLY-LATE *Achillea* 'The Pearl'	EARLY-MID *Aquilegia* 'Songbird Robin'	MID-LATE *Hemerocallis* 'Fragrant Returns'	EARLY-MID *Aquilegia* 'Swan Pink and Yellow'
MID *Veronica* 'Ulster Blue'	MID-LATE *Campanula* 'Pink Octopus'	EARLY-LATE *Draba siberica* (Yellow)	EARLY-MID *Aquilegia* 'Winky Double Dark Blue-White'	EARLY-LATE *Draba siberica* (Yellow)	LATE *Solidago* 'Little Lemon'	MID *Veronica* 'Ulster Blue'

(Bloom times: Early=11, Mid=14, Late=12)   FRONT

bloom time, they get counted in more than one bloom category. It is a nice benefit to have bloom times that overlap like this, but the most important criterion that has been met is that at least one-third of the plants in the row are blooming at any given time.

In the middle row, I will use the Medium Height Chart. Because the *Hesperis* will be missing for part of the season, I select a long-blooming fluffy plant, *Achillea* 'The Pearl,' for the center spot in this row right in front of it. This also repeats one of the back row colors, the white in the 'Blue and White Bicolor' monkshood. On one side of 'The Pearl' I place *Lilium* 'Tango Passions,' which the Medium Height Chart shows is a mid-late season bloomer in shades of pink and lavender. To echo these colors and to give a feeling of repetition but with a different plant, I chose *Aquilegia* 'Songbird Robin' to plant on the other side of 'The Pearl'. This plant has pink flowers and an early-mid bloom time. On each side of the lily and the columbine I achieve repetition with *Hemerocallis* 'Stella de Oro' and *Hemerocallis* 'Fragrant Returns'. These have similar growth forms, a subtle difference in the shade of yellow color in the blooms, and a slightly different bloom time. On the left end of this middle row I add *Anemone*

Some of the players in the Starter Garden. From left to right: *Achillea* 'The Pearl,' *Draba siberica*, *Solidago* 'Little Lemon,' *Hemerocallis* sp., and *Achillea* 'Laura.'

Snowdrop to give early blooms, to pick up the white in 'The Pearl' and to give a growth form that contrasts with the daylily. On the opposite end I place *Aquilegia* 'Swan Pink and Yellow,' which also contrasts in growth form with its daylily neighbor and picks up both the yellow of the daylilies and the pink on either side of 'The Pearl'. We have a fairly balanced bloom time arrangement now in the middle row, with five early, six mid, and four late bloomers. This array of bloom times is provided by seven plants, most of which bloom during more than one of the three bloom time categories.

I use the Short Chart as my guide for the front row. In the middle of this row I place *Aquilegia* 'Winky Double Dark Blue-White,' which provides a blue flower in early-mid season. On each side of this I add *Draba siberica*, adhering more tightly to symmetry again and giving us a very early yellow. Now I move away from complete symmetry by placing *Campanula* 'Pink Octopus' to the left of the left side *Draba* and *Solidago* 'Little Lemon,' a very late yellow bloomer, to the right of the right side *Draba*. To return again to total symmetry, I add *Veronica* 'Ulster Blue' to each end of the front row. This will provide both mid and late season spikes of blue. The front row has three early, four mid, and four late season bloomers.

In all three rows the predominant colors are blue, pink, red, yellow, and white. These are distributed fairly evenly through the garden both spatially and temporally.

CHAPTER 17
The Chamomile Tea Garden

This garden (see Figure 7) will feature pastel colors and fewer strong linear forms than were in the Starter Garden. The Chamomile Tea Garden, as its name suggests, will be one in which we create a calm, restful mood by the choice of plant color and form. In choosing the perennials for this garden, I will refer to the Color Charts most frequently as an efficient means of finding the colors I need to create this ambiance. I will start with the plan for the Starter Garden and modify the plant selections where appropriate to morph into the Chamomile Tea Garden.

I start by keeping *Hesperis matronalis,* with its fragrant soft lavender blooms, in the center of the back row. I swap out the red yarrow for the soft peach pink of *Achillea* 'Appleblossom.' For an elegant late blooming addition I put *Chelone* 'Rosea' on the left and *Chelone* 'Alba' on the right. Placing the soft yellow of *Lilium* 'Fata Morgana' on the far left and the bright pink of *Lilium* 'Elodie' on the right (both have double flowers) finishes the back row. Its bloom time distribution is three early, four mid, and six late bloomers; not totally balanced, but each bloom time is represented by at least one-third of the plants.

In the middle row I leave the airy growth form and tiny white flowers of 'The Pearl.' On the left side of this I add the lavender and white clusters of *Campanula* 'Genti Twisterbell' and on the right side I put *Astilbe* 'Peach Blossom,' with its plumes of peach-pink. Both of these are mid-late season bloomers. Next, on the right I position *Aquilegia* 'Swan Yellow' and I balance that with 'Swan Pink and Yellow' on the left side of the row. These columbines give continuity and balance just by being the same series in the genus, even though the colors are slightly different. The end spots in the middle row are filled by *Polemonium* 'Touch of Class' on the right and *Nepeta* 'Dropmore Blue' on the left. The mid season lavender-blue blooms of the *Polemonium* will blend softly with the

FIGURE 7
Chamomile Tea Garden
Consistent Colors Through the Season: Blue – Lavender –Pink – White – Yellow

N
↑
BACK

MID-LATE *Lilium* 'Fata Morgana'	LATE *Chelone* 'Rosea'	EARLY-LATE *Achillea* 'Appleblosson'	EARLY *Hesperis matronalis* (Lavender)	EARLY-LATE *Achillera* 'Appleblossom'	LATE *Chelone* 'Alba'	MID-LATE *Lilium* 'Elodie'
MID-LATE *Nepeta* 'Dropmore Blue'	EARLY-MID *Aquilegia* 'Swan Pink and Yellow'	MID-LATE *Campanula* 'Genti Twisterbell'	EARLY-LATE *Achillea* 'The Pearl'	MID-LATE *Astilbe* 'Peach Blossom'	EARLY-MID *Aquilegia* 'Swan Yellow'	EARLY-MID *Polemonium* 'Touch of Class'
MID *Delphinium* 'Summer Morning'	EARLY *Aquilegia* 'Cameo Blue-White'	EARLY-LATE *Draba siberica* (Yellow)	EARLY *Trollius pumilus* (Yellow)	MID-LATE *Phlox* 'Sherwood Purple'	EARLY *Pulsatilla* 'Alba'	MID-LATE *Campanula* 'Pink Octopus'

(Bloom times: Early=11, Mid=14, Late=13)   FRONT

Clematis integrifolia seed pods, the purples and lavenders of *Campanula* and *Veronica*, and the chartreuse foliage of the *Hosta* blend to create a peaceful perennial garden.

The seedpods of woody shrubs and the lavender blue blossoms of *Nepeta siberica* create a quiet, restful garden (top left).

Blooms in pastel shades, foliage in greens and whites, and an inviting bench create a relaxed come-rest-for-a-moment atmosphere in this garden (top right).

The grays and lavenders of the hardscape provide a backdrop for the pastel shades of the *Veronica*, the *Aegopodium*, the *Achillea*, and a few *Hemerocallis* (bottom left).

In mid season this collection of plants is making a soft but colorful statement. The white of the *Achillea* 'The Pearl' and the variegated leaves of the 'Ivory Halo' dogwood as well as the pale pink of the dwarf delphinium keep it all on the quiet side and are a calming contrast to the brighter colors. Later in the season this garden will show off *Hermerocallis* (bottom right).

pink blooms of 'Elodie,' and the blue of the *Nepeta* will contrast gently with the yellow behind it. The bloom time balance of this row is four early, seven mid, and four late.

In the front row the color balance of the soft pink of *Delphinium* 'Summer Morning' and the pink shades of *Campanula* 'Pink Octopus' will add symmetry. The similar growth forms of *Aquilegia* 'Cameo Blue-White,' *Pulsatilla* 'Alba,' and *Trollius pumilus* add balance to a row in which no plant cultivars repeat. The low-growing habit of *Draba siberica* and *Phlox* 'Sherwood Purple' will, by virtue of growth forms, add unity to the row, and will both share bloom time and echo colors of plants behind and to the sides of them. The bloom time balance here is four early, three mid, and three late.

The Chamomile Tea Garden will show consistent colors throughout the season of blue, lavender, pink, white, and yellow, the color palette being provided by different plants at different points in the season.

CHAPTER 18

The Espresso Garden

Our third garden (see Figure 8) created from this book's charts is the Espresso Garden, a perennial garden whose intense colors will create a visual thrill, as they play off each other in the garden symphony. Our goal is to choose players so that the plants blooming at any given time feature flower colors opposite one another on the color wheel. Of course we'll also need correct heights and a plant palette assuring at least one-third of the plants are blooming at all times.

To create a garden so color dependent, I will first look at our color charts to select the most intense oranges, reds, purples, and yellows. I will place these on my three-row, twenty-one space grid. My initial plant choices are listed below. Remember, this is just my first round of selections, and I will definitely be adding, and probably subtracting, some plants as I continue my consideration of the Espresso Garden.

From the Orange or Peach Chart:

> *Lilium* 'Matrix'
> *Hemerocallis* 'Mauna Loa'
> *Achillea* 'Terra Cotta'
> *Trollius* 'Golden Queen'
> *Sedum* 'Variegatum'

From the Red Chart:

> *Lychnis* 'Vesuvius'
> *Potentilla* 'Monarch's Velvet'

FIGURE 8

Espresso Garden

Consistent Colors Through the Season: Blue – Orange –Red – Violet-Purple – Yellow

N
↑
BACK

MID *Ligularia* 'Little Rocket'	EARLY-LATE *Achillea* 'Terra Cotta'	EARLY-MID *Aquilegia* 'Colorado Violet and White'	EARLY-LATE *Achillea* 'Laura'	LATE *Gentiana* 'True Blue'	LATE *Trollius* 'Golden Queen'	MID *Lychnis* Maltese Cross
EARLY *Trollius* 'Earliest of All'	MID *Delphinium* 'Blue Butterfly'	LATE *Hemerocallis* 'Mauna Loa'	EARLY-LATE *Galium verum* (Yellow)	MID-LATE *Lilium* 'Matrix'	MID-LATE *Veronica* 'Purpleicious'	EARLY-LATE *Hemerocallis* 'Stella de Oro'
LATE *Gentiana septemfida* (Blue)	EARLY *Trollius pumilus* (Yellow)	MID-LATE *Sedum* 'Variegatum'	EARLY-LATE *Draba siberica* (Yellow)	MID-LATE *Sedum* 'Variegatum'	MID *Papaver* 'Allegro'	LATE *Gentiana septemfida* (Blue)

(Bloom times: Early=8, Mid=12, Late=14)   FRONT

From the Yellow Chart:
> *Galium verum*
> *Hemerocallis* 'Flava'

From the Blue or Purple Chart:
> *Aquilegia* 'Colorado Violet and White'
> *Delphinium* 'Blue Butterfly'
> *Gentiana* 'True Blue'
> *Gentiana septemfida*
> *Pulsatilla vulgaris*

I first fill in the back row with tall plants from my initial list, adding *Achillea* 'Laura' to anchor the center spot. On the left I'm placing *Aquilegia* "Colorado Violet and White," and on the right I'm adding *Gentiana* 'True Blue.' To the left of the *Aquilegia* goes *Achillea* 'Terra Cotta,' and to the right of the gentian is *Trollius* 'Golden Queen.' All these plants are different genera or cultivars at this point, and I'm achieving symmetry

with color and growth form. The two end spots remain empty, but this row is fairly balanced with respect to bloom time. I will leave this row unfinished for now and move on to medium-height plants in the middle row. In the center of the middle row and in front of the all-season bright red of 'Laura,' I'm placing *Galium verum*, with its bright yellow middle and late-season blooms. To the right I am adding *Lilium* 'Matrix,' whose mid-late season fiery orange blooms will contrast with the late blue of *Gentiana* 'True Blue' and the late yellow of the *Galium*. To its left I will place *Hemerocallis* 'Mauna Loa,' a late-blooming source of orange to stand out against the red behind it and the yellow to its right. To the right of 'Matrix,' I am planting *Veronica* 'Purpleicious,' with a similar bloom time and a definite contrast in color. To the left of 'Mauna Loa' I'm

For stunning color in a perennial garden, Asiatic lilies come to mind immediately (top).

The "espresso" feel in a garden is created with vibrant colors like these provided here by *Verbascum* 'Southern Charm,' *Galium verum* yellow bedstraw, two varieties of *Achillea* including 'Terracotta,' and the dark foliage of 'Diabolo' ninebark (bottom).

adding the cobalt blue of *Delphinium* 'Blue Butterfly,' to contrast with the orange and yellow behind it. This middle row needs some early bloomers and a bit more yellow or red, and to accomplish this I will add *Trollius* 'Earliest of All' on the left. I would also like to fit in *Lychnis* 'Vesuvius' on the right for a touch of scarlet, but this will leave the garden low on early bloomers in the middle row. I search through the Medium Height Chart for early bloomers in my colors and settle on another yellow—*Hemerocallis* 'Stella de Oro.'

In the front row of this garden, I will adhere to stricter symmetry in order to bring together the incomplete cultivar symmetry in the two rows behind it. From my list of first-choice plants, I'm choosing *Pulsatilla vulgaris*, with early purple-blue blooms. This will go in the center, with *Sedum* 'Variegatum' on either side, giving the front row yellow flowers and orange-red seedpods from mid to late season. I'm also adding *Gentiana septemfida* to the two end spaces, and filling the two empty spaces with *Trollius pumilus* on the left and *Draba siberica* on the right. I realize, however, that now the front row has only two mid season bloomers, and so I consult the Short Chart, hoping for a mid season bloomer in orange or red. I am choosing *Papaver* 'Allegro,' a mid-season red. Since the *Sedum* and the *Draba* are prostrate plants, I am rearranging the front row once more. I am removing the *Pulsatilla*, placing the *Draba* in the middle, the *Sedum* on either side of it, the *Trollius* on the left, and the *Papaver* on the right, in front of the *Veronica*. The *Gentiana septemfida* remains at the two end spots. This new and final arrangement also gives a nice undulating flow of heights across the front row.

Returning to the two empty spaces in the back row, I will check the Tall Chart and choose *Lychnis* Maltese Cross for the right end. On the left I am placing *Ligularia* 'Little Rocket,' a midseason blooming plant with spikes of yellow.

Note that a few of the plants that I chose originally were not used, and a few of the plants that I originally placed in the garden were exchanged for others. These decisions were based on some of the original plants' inability to provide correct height, color, or bloom time to complete my composition of this Espresso Garden symphony.

CHAPTER 19

The Chameleon Garden

In our fourth garden design (see Figure 9) the predominant colors of the garden will change through the season, and so I call it the Chameleon Garden. This garden demonstrates clearly that managing bloom time for specific color expression is a powerful and crucial tool in perennial design. My Chameleon Garden example is a small garden, but the concept can be employed even more effectively in larger gardens and in long border beds. In the latter situation, bloom time choice can change the colors of different parts of the border during the season. For example, one color palette might start at one end of the border and move through it, reaching the opposite end in late summer or early fall. Consider also an extreme example such as playing host to two weddings in your perennial garden, one early in the summer and one late, with entirely different color themes. It would indeed be possible to micromanage your garden bloom times to accommodate these two color palettes. Understanding and managing bloom time is the key to success when composing your perennial garden symphony.

When choosing players for the Chameleon Garden, I rely heavily on bloom time and color charts. I begin by choosing specific color palettes for each of three bloom times. My initial choices are:

> Early season: pink, yellow, and white
> Mid: blue, orange, red, and a touch of yellow
> Late: orange, blue, pink, and a touch of red

First I choose plants whose blooms provide the early season colors. In the front row of short plants, I group early bloomers in the middle, with all three of my early season colors represented. In the second row of medium-height plants, I have white at one end,

FIGURE 9

Chameleon Garden

Colors Change Through the Season: Early: Pink – Yellow –White

Mid: Blue –Orange – Red with a touch of yellow

Late: Orange – Blue – Pink with a touch of red

N

↑

BACK

LATE *Trollius* 'Golden Queen'	EARLY-MID *Hemerocallis* 'Flava'	MID-LATE *Lilium* 'Blackout'	EARLY *Hesperis matronalis* (Lavender)	MID-LATE *Nepeta siberica* (Blue)	MID *Lychnis* Maltese Cross	LATE *Aconitum* 'Pink Sensation'
EARLY *Anemone* Snowdrop	MID-LATE *Lychnis* 'Molten Lava'	MID *Veronica* 'Spicata Blue'	LATE *Hemerocallis* 'Mauna Loa'	LATE *Chelone* 'Tiny Tortuga'	MID-LATE *Lilium* 'Matrix'	EARLY *Trollius europaeus* (Yellow)
LATE *Gentiana septemfida* (Blue)	MID *Delphinium* 'Summer Nights'	EARLY *Aquilegia* 'Cameo Pink- White'	EARLY *Cerastium tomentosum* (White)	EARLY *Trollius pumilus* (Yellow)	MID-LATE *Lychnis* 'Orange Gnome'	LATE *Aconitum* 'Blue Lagoon'

(Bloom times: Early=7, Mid=9, Late=11)

FRONT

provided by *Anemone* Snowdrop, and yellow at the other end, from *Trollius europaeus*. Early colors in the back row are the yellow of *Hemerocallis* 'Flava' and the lavender-pink of *Hesperis matronalis*.

For midseason colors, I am adding blues and oranges in the front row, with a cobalt blue delphinium and *Lychnis* 'Orange Gnome." To the middle row I add red, blue, and orange with mid-season blooming *Lychnis* 'Molten Lava,' a blue *Veronica*, and the color saturated *Lilium* 'Matrix.' To provide a source of mid-season red, blue, and orange-red in the back row, I pop in the deep red lily 'Blackout,' the tall blue of *Nepeta siberica*, and the scarlet red of *Lychnis* Maltese Cross. A touch of yellow continues with *Hemerocallis* 'Flava.'

For the late season color show, I add more blue in the front row with a gentian and with *Aconitum*, 'Blue Lagoon.' Across the garden, several of the orange bloom-ing perennials continue into late summer, but I add *Hemerocallis* 'Mauna Loa' to the middle row and Trollius 'Golden Queen' to the back row, to freshen up the orange. I also add *Chelone* 'Tiny Tortuga' and *Aconitum* 'Pink Sensation' to the middle and back

Some of the players in the Chameleon Garden. *Lychnis* 'Molten Lava' (top), *Aquilegia* 'Cameo Pink-White' (bottom left), and *Nepeta siberica* (bottom right).

rows, respectively, and *Aquilegia* 'Cameo Pink-White' to the front for the pink part of the palette. This late stage of the garden will also still have a touch of red, provided by 'Molten Lava' and 'Blackout.'

The distribution of bloom times in each row is fairly balanced:
Front row: three early, two mid, and three late
Middle row: two early, three mid, and four late
Back row: two early, four mid, and four late

The colors in this garden change throughout the season, from pink-yellow-white, to blue-orange-red and a bit of yellow, to orange-blue-pink and a touch of red—just as planned.

CHAPTER 20

The Foliage Dominant Garden

Now we will try our hand at using the Garden Symphony Charts to put together a garden (see Figure 10) that is very *foliage* based. I will use the Master Chart, pulling from it some of my favorite predominantly foliage perennials. I will put less emphasis on bloom time, because foliage color will be the dominant feature in the garden. I will also not adhere so strictly to the height charts. My plan is to use tall plants in the back row, the tallest of some of the medium height plants in the middle row, and some shorter medium-height plants in the front row.

When choosing foliage plants, I place dark foliage next to chartreuse. I am intentionally creating a triangle of yellow-green in the center of the garden with *Tanacetum* 'Isla Gold', *Dicentra* 'Gold Heart', and *Hosta* 'Guacamole.' These contrast with the dark-leafed *Actaea* and the rose-pink flowers of *Achillea* 'Saucy Seduction.' In the middle row, the variegated *Phalaris* is balanced by the variegated *Polygonatum*. Both have a very spiky, linear growth form, which is softened by the geraniums I place at each of the end spaces in this row. The front row is balanced by orange or peach blooms on either end;

What catches the eye in this landscape is the texture and foliage provided by Canada Red chokecherry on the right, False Spirea in the center, and Silverberry on the left (bottom left).

The backdrop interest in this garden is provided totally by woody foliage and texture (bottom right).

FIGURE 10

Foliage Garden

N
↑
BACK

EARLY	MID-LATE	LATE	MID-LATE	LATE	MID	MID
Paeonia 'Jana'	*Thalictrum* 'Hewitt's Double'	*Actaea* 'Pink Spike'	*Tanacetum* 'Isla Gold'	*Actaea* 'Black Negligee'	*Thalictrum* 'Black Stockings'	*Dicentra spectabilis*
MID-LATE	LATE	MID	EARLY-LATE	MID	MID	MID-LATE
Geranium 'Nimbus'	*Phalaris* 'Strawberries and Cream'	*Dicentra* 'Gold Heart'	*Achillea* 'Saucy Seduction'	*Hosta* 'Guacamole'	*Polygonatom* 'Variegatum'	*Geranium* 'Lakwijk Star'
MID-LATE	EARLY-LATE	MID-LATE	EARLY-MID	EARLY-MID	EARLY-LATE	MID-LATE
Lily Looks™ 'Tiny Moon'	*Lamium* 'Pink Pewter'	*Campanula* 'Silver Bells'	*Aegopodium* 'Variegata'	*Aquilegia* 'Winky Double Rose-White'	*Lamium* 'Silver Beacon'	*Lychnis* 'Lumina Salmon Shades'

(Bloom times: Early=6, Mid=17, Late=15)

FRONT

Textures and foliage working together in this mixed perennial bed with *Actaea*, *Solidago*, and *Lamium*. Annual scarlet runner beans on the trellis in the background (opposite, top left).

A foliage dominant landscape at Glacier Gardens in Juneau, Alaska (opposite, top right).

'Amber Jubilee' ninebark and a variety of junipers and Russian Cypress frame this annual garden of phlox. The foliage frame is what "pops out" the pastel phlox (opposite, middle right).

The alpine landscape in fall (Tangle Lakes area along the Denali Highway, Alaska) is one of the best reminders of the power of foliage in a perennial landscape (bottom).

the gray foliage of the *Lamium*, which picks up the silver in the foliage of *Campanula* 'Silver Bells;' and the clear celery-green and white foliage of the *Aegopodium* in the middle.

I finish the back row on one end with the *Paeonia* 'Jana,' whose foliage and seedpods add as much interest as do the pink flowers, and with *Dicentra spectabilis* on the opposite end for midseason pink and summer-long lush foliage. Just in from the end spots, I am placing *Thalictrum* 'Hewitt's Double' to give mid and late season blooms and interesting seedpods and foliage. Predominant colors through the season will be blues, pinks, purples, white, and yellows, with foliage providing a great show of variegated green-white, chartreuse, dark chocolate, and silvery gray.

When putting this garden together, I have used the Master Chart to identify foliage plants, but my second main reference is the height charts. I have also considered the color charts, for choosing colors that will contribute balance. For example, many of the foliage plants I have chosen produce flowers that are pink or lavender. For this reason, I have chosen *Achillea* 'Saucy Seduction' rather than one of my favorites, 'Terra Cotta.' I refer to the bloom time charts the least, with bloom times mostly mid season to late season. This works because a foliage-based garden symphony always has plants playing their part. Their foliage carries the music, even without blooms.

PART V

Supporting the Performance

An annual bed of *Phlox* 'Coral
Reef Mix,' *Digitalis* 'Illumination
Flame,' and *Lupinus* 'Gallery Pink'
in a perennial garden setting.

CHAPTER 21

The Symphony Players: The Plants Themselves

What follows is an alphabetical listing, including brief descriptions, of Fairbanks-hardy perennials that I have grown and have come to love. This is by no means an exhaustive list of all hardy perennials in Interior Alaska. For every species I mention, there will be many others that are also hardy and with which you, the reader, may have already had success. There also exist many cultivars and varieties no one has yet tried to grow in our northern climate but which probably would survive, if not thrive, in the north. So there you have another challenge and potential option for venturing into uncharted gardening territory.

As you plan your perennial garden, you will be drawn to certain varieties on these plant lists, varieties you feel you absolutely must have. Your next endeavor is to search out and procure these specific plants. Some will be readily available commercially, as mature plants from local nurseries, as bare-root plants from online sources, and even as seeds. In the commercial market, however, plant varieties come and go, so there will indeed be plants on this list that are not easily found. This is the time to strike up conversations with local nurseries and botanical gardens. These places periodically divide mature plants in their display gardens and make the divisions available for purchase. These plants that need dividing are most likely older ones, and may no longer be propagated commercially. Watch for plant swaps also. Trade perennials with friends, even if you don't always know the exact name of what you are trading. As long as it's a Fairbanks- hardy plant and you know its color, height, and bloom time, you will have what you need. Lastly, I encourage you to always try new varieties that aren't on my or other northern gardeners' plant lists.

Another consideration during the acquisition of your perennials is initial cost. There is, of course, no gratification more instant than purchasing a mature herbaceous perennial from a local nursery. These plants have the greatest up-front cost, but they will be the quickest for producing a full and finished perennial garden. Bare root plants, sometimes available at local nurseries and box stores as well as online, may take a season or two longer to establish, and their quality may be problematic if they have not been stored correctly—such as hanging on a display rack for an extended period of time. However, they will initially be less expensive than mature plants.

A third option is growing from seed. This has the lowest start-up cost, but many of the newer patented cultivars are unavailable as seed. However, many older varieties are indeed available and can be easily grown from seed. Two such examples are *Myosotis palustris* and *Achillea* 'The Pearl.' Growing perennials from seed requires close attention to specific germination requirements (for example, some may need pre-chilling), and works best if seedlings are first grown in containers and then transplanted as young plants into your garden. A perennial garden planted from seed may take several seasons to achieve the visual effect of a mature garden.

Throughout this book I have used both scientific names and common names for the plants discussed. I will continue this practice with descriptions of individual plants in this section. Each plant description is headed with the scientific name followed by the common name. The advantage of the scientific name is that it applies to just one very specific plant. For example, *Myosotis palustris* designates a forget-me-not species with very defined characteristics, one of which is that it is hardy in Interior Alaska. The common name forget-me-not refers to any number of species, hybrids, and cultivars, most of which are not hardy this far north.

The logic behind my list is not simply that these are familiar favorites of mine. This list is broad enough to illustrate how to design a perennial garden given a palette of plants, but also limited enough that you will not get so lost in plant choices that you never get to the point of putting plants in the ground. Once you master designing and planting with a manageable palette, you can add your own favorites.

As I have explained, most perennials will do well in either sun or shade in northern latitudes, and so I have chosen not to bias and therefore limit your selection of plants based on shade-loving or sun-loving. That being said, there are a few plants that, even in our northern light conditions, require either sunny exposure or shade. In the plant descriptions that follow, I am designating these with the words "sun" or "shade" following the common name. Remember, however, that the need for shade can be met by positioning the plant so there are taller plants between it and incoming sunlight.

Yarrow (Sun)

Yarrows are generally tall, sun-loving plants with long bloom times. One of their tricks is that faded yarrow blooms remain attractive for at least a while, giving the cluster of blooms at any one time a multi-hued look. Periodic deadheading does improve the appearance of the plant and may even extend bloom time.

Achillea 'Laura'

There are numerous species and cultivars of yarrow. Most of my favorites are in the *millefolium* species, with flower colors ranging from yellow, peach, and orange to lavender, pink, and red. Popular cultivars, to name just a few of the many available, include 'Appleblossom,' 'Laura,' Paprika, 'Saucy Seduction,' 'Sunny Seduction,' and 'Terra Cotta.' The fern-like foliage on these varieties has a distinct fragrance. The tall, sometimes rangy growth habit adds a free, wind-blown blast of color to any perennial garden. The *ptarmica* species includes 'The Pearl' and 'Noblessa.' Both of these form clumps or mounds up to twenty-four inches in height, covered with tiny single and double white flowers. 'Noblessa' is definitely the more compact and contained of these two cultivars. These are a good visual substitute for baby's breath in a northern perennial garden. When the white flowers start to fade and turn brown, the whole plant can be sheared to a few inches, and it will grow back and re-bloom.

Achillea 'Terra Cotta'

A third species, *siberica*, includes 'Love Parade.' This is a hardy, lavender-pink flowered yarrow, with shiny green leathery leaves. It is a beautiful filler plant that can be counted on to both stand tall and knit in among its neighbors.

Achillea 'The Pearl'

Monkshood

These are strong, upright plants that produce tall stalks of helmet or monkshood-shaped flowers, primarily in intense blue-purple colors, although 'Pink Sensation' and 'Stainless Steel' are exceptions. All parts of this plant are poisonous, but this does not detract from its beauty as a perennial garden plant.

Monkshood is especially important in the garden symphony because it blooms late in the summer, when the earlier bloomers are no longer contributing color apart from their foliage.

Aconitum 'Blue & White Bicolor'

My favorites in this group include (the first four are cultivars of *A. cammarum,* the fifth is a cultivar of *A. carmichaelii*):

- 'Blue and White Bicolor' is up to forty-eight inches tall, with distinct blue-white bicolor flowers.
- 'Blue Lagoon' grows only ten to twelve inches in height and has deep purple-blue blooms.

Aconitum 'Stainless Steel' upper left of photo with yellow Asiatic lily in foreground

Actaea 'Black Negligee' photographed in late September before a killing frost, but after all the other perennials in the garden have been cut back for fall.

Actaea 'Black Negligee,' mid summer

Actaea ''Black Negligee' contrasted with the yellow foliage of *Dicentra* 'Gold Heart' and the lavender flowers of *Campanula rapunculoides*.

Actaea "Black Negligee' in late August after many earlier blooming perennials have been cut back. Notice the pink-lavender blooms as well as the newly placed layer of grass mulch (right).

- 'Bressingham Spire' is potentially thirty to thirty-six inches in height and produces violet-blue flowers.
- 'Stainless Steel' is forty inches tall and has unusual metallic blue-gray colored blooms.
- 'Arendsii' is forty inches in height, with intense dark blue blooms.
- Sometimes difficult to find for purchase, but a beautiful plant, is a cultivar resulting from a cross of *A. cammarum* and *A. carmichaelii*—'Pink Sensation,' reaching forty to forty-eight inches in height and having pale rose pink blooms.

ACTAEA

Bugbane (this includes the once separate genus *Cimicifuga*)

The *Actaea* we grow this far north are varieties known for their foliage more than their flowers. My two favorites, both cultivars of *A. simplex,* are 'Black Negligee' and 'Pink Spike.' Both have deeply cut foliage, which is a stunning purple-black all season long. The blooms, pale pink to white, and bottlebrush in shape, occur so late in the season that fall frosts often arrive before they do. Both of these cultivars reach a height of forty-two to sixty inches, stand straight and tall without support (even in strong wind and rain) and are stunning contrasts in the perennial garden, especially when paired with lime-green foliage plants and those with bright pastel blooms. More than one visitor to the display gardens at The Plant Kingdom has mistaken these sturdy, noticeable plants for a woody shrub.

AEGOPODIUM

Snow on the Mountain, or Bishop's Weed

The cultivar 'Variegata' in the species *podagraria* is a plant grown primarily for its bright clean foliage. The gray green leaves have clear white margins, and the plant bears white flowers in early spring. Snow on the Mountain is quite adept at spreading by means of rhizomes, and so periodically it must by roped in by the gardener, usually by simply pulling out the advancing margins of its clump. 'Variegata' is a wonderful ground cover, border plant, and backdrop for the bright colored blooms of its neighbors.

Aegopodium 'Variegata'

ALLIUM

Ornamental Onion

Alliums do not always have showy blooms, but their real value lies in the strong linear form and contrast in structure they add to a perennial garden.

Allium altaicum (commonly called Altai onion) is large enough at twenty-four to thirty-six inches to be a focal point in a perennial garden designed to show off specimen plantings. The globe-shaped flower heads full of black seeds (which shed prolifically) add interest all season. The tubular blades of foliage are edible, and they can take the place of green onions or chives for culinary purposes.

Cultivars of *Allium senescens* are only six to twelve inches in height, produce lilac-pink flowers, and have flattened blades that are also edible. 'Millennium' is a named cultivar in this group with rose-purple flower heads, blooming late in the summer. It was named 2018 Perennial Plant of the Year by the Perennial Plant Association.

Allium altaicum

Allium altaicum

ANEMONE

Windflower

Anemone sylvestris, or Snowdrop Anemone, is one of the first perennials to bloom in the spring in a northern perennial garden. Nodding, slightly fragrant white flowers on ten to twelve-inch plants kick off the season. This is followed by white wooly seedpods and a late summer re-bloom, as well as shiny green foliage that remains lush and unblemished all summer. Snowdrop Anemone spreads through rhizomatous roots. The plant is easily propagated by splitting these roots, and it may be necessary to keep these plants in check in the garden by periodically pulling out plantlets spreading beyond their designated space. Every northern perennial garden should have at least one Snowdrop Anemone, not only for its ability to so elegantly usher in the bloom season, but also for its quiet, stately presence in the garden symphony all season long, with a few more surprise blooms in the fall.

Anemone Snowdrop, in May

Anemone Snowdrop, in June

A fall-blooming *Anemone* is 'Robustissima,' a cultivar within the *tomentosa* species. The blooms are mauve pink, and they are held above the dark green shiny foliage. Its potential height is thirty-two inches. The late bloom time for 'Robustissima' is quite the opposite of the early season flowers of Snowdrop Anemone, but both have special value in the perennial garden, because of their ability to extend the bloom season either early or late.

AQUILEGIA
Columbine

Columbine are northern-hardy, very early season bloomers that may be described as woodland plants preferring shade. In Interior Alaska light conditions, columbine are equally successful in sun or shade. There are many species, and many cultivars within them. Most if not all are worth trying to grow in our northern climate. Some of them re-seed freely, although hybrids will not be true from seed. There is also constant hybridization between species, and so columbine quantity and quality in a perennial garden is always evolving

Because of the large variety of bloom colors and plant heights, columbine are the backbone of any perennial garden. These good-natured plants kick off the bloom season with much fanfare and noise, but they continue to add at least a few flowery notes to the tune all season. If they should happen to show signs of powdery mildew after the main bloom, I find it easiest to cut them back to winter level, bag up the diseased foliage, and wait for the emergence of fresh, beautiful, new growth that lasts the rest of the season.

Some of my own favorite columbine for the front of the garden are the 'Cameos,' a cultivar within the *A. flabellata* species. My very favorite is 'Cameo Blue-White,' with its powder blue and white flowers and thick green foliage all on luscious, wide plants growing only about six to eight inches tall. 'Cameo Pink-White' is also a beautiful color and an early blooming front-of-the- garden plant. The 'Winky' series of columbine are double-flowered members of the *A. vulgaris* species, and are only twelve inches tall. 'Winky Double Dark Blue-White' and 'Winky Double Rose-White' are two of my first choices within this cultivar. 'Nora Barlow' is also in this species, but is thirty inches tall with reddish pink, fully double flowers. 'Woodside Gold' is a quite noticeable yellow-leafed *A. vulgaris* cultivar with lavender-blue flowers. This is an unforgettable columbine because of its must-have foliage, adding light to any garden.

In the species *A. caerulea,* there are many beautiful hybrid cultivars available in a variety of colors, whether they are 'Origamis' at fourteen to sixteen inches, 'Swans' at

Aquilegia x hybrida
'Swan Pink and Yellow'

Aquilegia flabellata
'Cameo Blue-White'

Aquilegia caerulea
'Origami Red and White'

Aquilegia hybrid with
Dicentra 'Gold Heart' (left).

Aquilegia vulgaris
'Winkly Double Rose and White'

Aquilegia sp.
late May

Artemesia 'Silver Mound' with
Aquilegia 'Songbird Robin'

twenty to twenty-four inches, or 'Songbirds' at sixteen to twenty-four inches. I find it difficult to design a perennial garden without 'Songbird Robin' (pink and white), or the violet of 'Colorado Violet and White,' or the sky blue of 'Rocky Mountain Blue.' And I also cannot leave out 'Swan Yellow' and the unique 'Swan Pink and Yellow.' The list of columbine is endless and inspiring, and you will inadvertently create a few additional attractive crosses of your own in each garden where you include members of this genus.

Artemesia 'Silver Mound' in mid-July

Artemesia 'Silver Mound' in late fall

Artemesia 'Valerie Finnis'
(right back) with *Nepeta*, *Achillea*, and
Lychnis in background

Aruncus 'Kneiffii' in early May

Aruncus sp. in early September

ARTEMESIA

Wormwood

Artemesia is included in a perennial garden primarily for its foliage. The flowers are insignificant in size and in their gray to yellow color. The foliage of many within the genus is distinctly aromatic, especially when crushed. All of the hybrids and cultivars prefer well-drained soil.

'Silver Mound' (*A. schmidtiana*) has soft silver gray, very tactile foliage that forms a rounded mound about ten inches in height. This is an excellent border plant and a wonderful source of contrasting foliage. The silvery foliage accents any colorful blooms in its presence. 'Silver Brocade' (*A. stelleriana*) is a prostrate, spreading *Artemesia* with silvery white serrated foliage. It ranges from six to twelve inches in height and may spread as much as twenty-four to thirty inches. To maintain its mat-like growth habit, you may trim it back later in the summer, when the plant begins to grow more upright. 'Valerie Finnis' (*A. ludoviciana*) is an upright *Artemesia*, fifteen to eighteen inches tall. It has silver gray leaves that are not serrated, but are a beautiful contrast with the more flowery members of the garden symphony.

ARUNCUS

Goat's Beard

Goat's beard is definitely a multipurpose plant in a perennial garden, even though its blooms do not add vibrant color. Instead, its early summer flowers are creamy plumes, and are followed by cascades of seedpods that lend texture and interest for the rest of the season. Add to this the fall foliage, which can vary from rusty tones to orange and peach.

Goat's beard has still another use to the northern gardener. If your perennial garden is situated in a microclimate not suitable for *Astilbe*, goat's beard can be substituted to successfully accomplish the visual task of *Astilbe* in your garden design.

A. aethusifolius is a goat's beard that works well in a garden border. It is only about ten inches tall, has reddish stems, and produces white flowers. *A. dioicus* is a species that may reach sixty inches in height and produces yellowish-white flower plumes. 'Horatio' is a cultivar of *A. dioicus* that sports golden-green foliage, dark bronze stems, and creamy white flowers, with a potential height of forty-eight inches. This species and its cultivars add impressive stature and structure to the garden, and may be mistaken at first glance as woody shrubs. 'Kneiffii' is a twenty-four to thirty-six-inch tall cultivar of *A. dioicus*. It has unusual finely cut leaves with almost thread-like segments.

ASTILBE

False Spirea

The genus *Astilbe* is an extensive group of plants, with numerous species, hybrids, and cultivars. The flowers are plumes ranging in color from white, pink, and peach to lavender, purple, and burgundy. Heights range from twelve to forty-eight inches. *Astilbe* is not tolerant of excessively dry soil, especially when in containers waiting to be planted. The plants in this genus do not recover well (or at all) from their soil drying out, even if only once.

Many *Astilbe* cultivars I have grown in Fairbanks are in the *A. arendsii* species, but some are cultivars of *A. chinensis* or of *A. japonica*. There are many possibilities in the *Astilbe* genus for an adventurous northern gardener, especially if the microclimate offers close to zone 4 conditions.

Some of my favorites are 'Fanal' (*A. arendsii*), with its red flowers and its potential height of twenty-four inches; 'Maggie Daley' (*A. chinensis*), with bright lavender-purple flowers and a height of twenty-eight inches; 'Rhythm and Blues' (*A. arendsii*), which reaches up to twenty-six inches in height and produces bright pink flowers; and 'Peach Blossom' (*A. japonica*), with salmon-pink flowers and a height of twenty-four inches. Two others that I grow especially for their foliage are 'Chocolate Shogun' (*A. arendsii*), which has chocolate brown leaves, bright pink flowers, and a possible height of eighteen to twenty-four inches, and 'Colorflash' (*A. arendsii*), which has foliage that changes from light green to burgundy-purple-green, and then to gold-orange-russet. Along with this colorful foliage drama, 'Colorflash' produces light pink flower plumes.

The *Astilbe* genus offers varying bloom times, usually designated in perennial catalogs as early, mid, or late. My experience is that only the early and some of the mid season varieties will bloom before the end of the growing season in Interior Alaska, where we consider August late in the season.

BERGENIA

Pigsqueak

Bergenia is a genus considered to be shade-loving elsewhere, but here in our northern climate, it is happy in the sun as well. Its foliage is evergreen, and so it comes out of the snow in the spring shiny and dark green, ready to send up stocks of rose-pink flowers. The growth form is reminiscent of cabbage. Most varieties are in the range of twelve to eighteen inches in height.

There are many pigsqueak species and cultivars that can be grown successfully in the north. This is one of those unique perennials that is useful in a mixed planting, but

Astilbe sp. in early August

Astilbe sp.

Bergenia sp. in early June

Bergenia sp. with *Eschscholzia californica*

which also may be successfully planted as a group or linear planting of just *Bergenia*. This stand-alone ability is because of the foliage that makes its own strong summer-long statement, even after the early summer blooms are gone. Then in the fall, this foliage turns iridescent shades of intense purple and burgundy.

I have grown several varieties of *Bergenia* that differ only slightly, primarily in height and shades of flower color. A common and favorite one of mine is 'Winterglow' (*B. cordifolia*) with its thick, shiny green leaves, a height of twelve to fifteen inches, clusters of lavender-pink flowers, and bronze red fall foliage. This is typical of so many *Bergenia* that will thrive in Interior Alaska and that will play some part in the garden symphony during the entire production.

BRUNNERA

Siberian Bugloss

Brunnera 'Aexander's Great' in late May

Brunnera are most successful as hardy perennials in gardens that have close to a zone 4 microclimate. 'Alexander's Great' is a cultivar of *B. macrophylla* that has been hardy for me in a south exposure garden. This plant is known primarily for its foliage—large (even up to twelve inches across) heart-shaped, silvery leaves with gray veins. Dainty forget-me-not like flowers that appear in early summer or even late spring are typical of this cultivar and of 'Jack Frost,' another *B. macrophylla* I have grown. Both of these cultivars can reach up to sixteen inches in height. Their part in a perennial garden is to provide contrast for the brightly colored blooms and dark foliage of their neighbors. Their foliage definitely adds light, and it draws the visitor's eye in any garden.

CAMPANULA

Bell Flower

Campanula glomerata

There are a huge number of *Campanula* species and hybrids, many of which are not hardy in Interior Alaska. However, there are some that do survive the test of winter, and there are probably numerous more worth trying at least once, especially if your garden is situated in one of the warmer microclimates.

The ones I like most are cultivars of the *C. glomerata* species. These bear clusters of flowers at the top of the flowering stem. 'Superba' has violet-blue flowers and may reach twenty-four to thirty inches in height. 'Genti Twisterbell' is a unique purple-white bicolor that is more compact, at a height of sixteen to eighteen inches. *C. takesimana* is a species with tubular light pink flowers whose interior is decorated with dark spots. Usually not more that twenty-four inches tall, this plant re-seeds and spreads. *C. punctata* cultivars include 'Cherry Bells,' with burgundy-red flowers,

Campanula glomerata
in early August (left).

and 'Kent Belle,' with dark blue flowers. 'Silver Bells' also survives well in the display gardens at The Plant Kingdom, where it draws attention for its fragrant lavender-pink flowers and silvery gray foliage, all presented on a compact fifteen-inch plant. Another *C. punctate* cultivar is 'Pink Octopus,' with bright pink octopus-shaped flowers, shiny green foliage, and a height of about twelve inches. It flowers prolifically and for quite a long time in late summer in Interior Alaska.

'Campbell' is a cultivar of *C. rapunculoides*, featuring violet bell-shaped blooms on spikes that branch low on the stalk, giving a characteristic, almost candelabra effect. This plant can reach sixteen to eighteen inches in height, and has quite a long bloom time in mid season. This is one that may benefit from an early cutback as the foliage degenerates a bit after the blooms are spent. A full re-bloom sometimes follows. Members of this species are considered invasive by some, but the cultivars are somewhat more well-mannered, and of course the gardener must always be ready to corral garden bullies.

Campanula punctata
with *Veronica sp.*

Completely different in appearance is the six to twelve-inch-tall, blue-flowered 'Olympia,' a very cold-hardy cultivar of *C. rotundifolia*, a species also known as the Bluebells of Scotland. This is a front-of-the-border or rock garden plant.

Other species with cultivars definitely worth trialing in the north are *C. persicifolia* and *C. poscharskyana.*

Campanula rapunculoides

Centaurea montana

Centaurea montana in mid June

Cerastium tomentosum

Cerastium tomentosum in late August

Chelone obliqua in late August

CENTAUREA

Bachelor's Button

One of the hardiest and best-known members of the *Centaurea* genus is Mountain Bluet or *C. montana*. This plant produces its intense cornflower–blue flowers nearly all season. Early in the summer, it grows to form an attractive mound up to twenty-four inches tall, but as summer progresses it is prone to erring on the rangy side with some browning on the edges of the leaves. This is the time that the gardener must step in for maintenance in the form of fairly severe cutback. Mountain Bluet will bounce back and continue through the season with a fresh look and new flowers. This plant self-seeds prolifically, a constant reminder to the diligent gardener that a weed is simply a plant in the wrong place. You do not want Mountain Bluet popping up everywhere in your garden. Seedling removal is essential.

There are other cultivars of *C. montana* that have similar forms and growth habit, and that are equally hardy, although they are maybe not quite as aggressive as the blue-flowered species. 'Amethyst in Snow' has pure white flowers with dark purple centers, and is fourteen to sixteen inches in height. 'Black Sprite' sports purple-black flowers on a relatively short sixteen-inch plant. 'John Coutts' is a cultivar of the *C. hypoleuca* species, which reaches twenty inches in height and has fragrant pink flowers.

CERASTIUM

Snow-in-Summer

C. tomentosum is the species of *Cerastium* most commonly grown in northern gardens. Cultivars such as 'Silver Carpet' and 'Yo-Yo' also perform well. *C. tomentosum* is about six inches tall, and it forms a mat of silvery gray foliage that can spread to eighteen inches. Early in summer, small white flowers appear, but once they have bloomed, it is the soft, velvety foliage that marks the plant's place in the garden. As a border plant, the silver foliage serves as contrast for both pastel and jewel-tone blooms, the first combination providing calm and the second acting as a visual wake-up.

CHELONE

Turtlehead

Turtlehead is a plant we all should have in our perennial gardens. Its first attraction is the white or pink flowers that truly are shaped like turtle heads, complete with scales. Secondly, turtlehead is a very late blooming perennial, displaying its blooms at a time when the garden symphony needs strong players with new energy.

'Tiny Tortuga,' a cultivar of *C. obliqua*, is only fourteen to sixteen inches tall, but its reddish stems and fluorescent pink flowers give it a strong presence in the fall perennial garden.

C. obliqua includes two other very hardy cultivars that I have grown. 'Rosea' is twenty-four to thirty-six inches tall with bright pink blooms, and 'Alba' is a stately thirty-six inches with pure white blooms.

Chelone obliqua blossoms

CLEMATIS
Clematis

This is a plant genus much better known in warmer climates, where it offers more choices, including the spectacular large-flowered vining varieties. However, there are unique and beautiful clematis that do grow in the north.

C. integrifolia and its cultivars are upright plants, ranging from eighteen to thirty-six inches in height. The nodding flowers are most commonly blue, but there are cultivars that produce white, pink, or rose blooms. Most *C. integrifolia* begin blooming in early summer, and continue on through fall. The seedpods are very ornamental. This means that as the season advances and there are more seedpods than blooms, this species and its relatives are still playing a part in the symphony. In the shade and nestled in among other plants, *C. integrifolia* may sprawl more than stand upright. The members of this species are herbaceous, and should be cut back to within a few inches of ground level each fall.

Clematis integrifolia

C. recta is another herbaceous clematis species, and the cultivar that I have grown is 'Purpurea.' This elegant plant has burgundy leaves contrasted with clusters of delicate white flowers that are lightly fragrant. 'Purpurea' stretches to thirty inches, and it loves to knit in among its neighbors, using them as support and an opportunity to show off its blooms.

Clematis macropetala
'Bluebird' in early June

'Blue Bird,' a cultivar of *macropetala*, is a climbing clematis that needs the support of a trellis to accommodate its possible ten feet of growth. The lavender-blue flowers have yellow centers and are followed by bad-hair-day seedpods. Often there is a second lesser bloom in late summer. It may be helpful to prune young 'Blue Bird' plants back to a few feet, leaving two or three buds on each stem in an effort to promote root growth the first season. Moose accomplished this for us at The Plant Kingdom for the first few winters of our 'Blue Bird's' life. Then we wised up, and now we wrap this clematis and its trellis with row crop fabric each fall.

Tangutica is a woody yellow-flowered clematis that climbs to as much as twelve or fifteen feet. There are several cultivars, one being 'Radar Love.' These flowers are slightly fragrant and the seedpods are feathery and interesting. Mature 'Blue Bird' and 'Radar Love' should NOT be cut back to ground level in the fall. Selective pruning can be used to remove deadwood and thereby force new growth, which will bloom the following season.

DELPHINIUM

Delphinium

Delphinium
Magic Fountains series, mid July with *Thalictrum*, Asiatic lily, and *Lychnis*

Delphinium Pacific Giants

Delphiniums are very hardy, and they perform at their best in northern latitudes. The Pacific Giant Hybrids (*D. elatum*) are capable of mature heights of up to six feet or more, which means they are also unstable in wind and heavy rain. My thoughts are that plants of this size do not combine well with other perennials. Instead, they belong by themselves along a tall building or along a fence, or possibly with tall shrubs as a backdrop. When they finish blooming in mid to late summer, I suggest cutting them back to fall level and letting their fresh new foliage be their swan song.

The Magic Fountains series (*D. elatum*) has a color range similar to that of the Pacific Giants, including whites, pinks, lavenders, and shades of blue, some with white bees and some with dark bees. The Magic Fountains are only twenty-four to forty inches at maturity. This height is more manageable when combined with other tall perennials, or when used as a specimen plant (but probably with the assistance of some staking for stability). They also benefit from cutting back, at least to some degree, after the blooms are spent. This may encourage a second minor bloom later in the summer, and at the very least it adds feathery, fresh new foliage as a contribution to the garden symphony.

Delphinium
Pacific Giants
(photo courtesy
Stephanie Bluekens, right).

My favorite delphiniums for combination with other perennials are the dwarf cultivars in the *D. grandiflorum* species. 'Blue Butterfly' has deep cobalt blue flowers, and is about sixteen inches tall. The 'Summer' series is twelve inches in height and includes 'Summer Blues,' with sky blue flowers; 'Summer Nights,' with intense blue flowers; and 'Summer Morning,' with soft pink flowers.

Delphiniums are susceptible to aphids and also to powdery mildew. A foliage cutback after blooming can reduce both these problems. Delphiniums may also suffer from the effects of the larval stage of a moth in the genus *Polychrysa*. The larvae feed on the leaves, and then wrap up in the leaves to pupate. These delphinium defoliators are easily controlled with an application of a commercially available Bt-based formulation, administered as a spray or by a hose-end applicator. There are various strains of Bt (*Bacillus thuringiensis*), effective against delphinium defoliators. The success of all of them involves a bacterium, which causes digestive system damage by means of a crystal protein. The Bt must be applied to the leaves while the defoliators are actively feeding on them. At first sign of defoliator activity, treat your delphiniums with Bt, and this typically eliminates the problem.

DIANTHUS

Pinks

My favorites in this group are cultivars of the *D. deltoides* species. These are low-growing ground covers that form mats of stems and flowers, often not more than six or eight inches in height. 'Pink Maiden' and 'Red Maiden' are cultivars that work well for borders in mixed perennial beds, and also in rock gardens. In bloom they are literally covered with small flowers, sometimes for as much as six or eight weeks. When blooms fade, shear the plant for new growth and more blooms. 'Arctic Fire' is another cultivar, and this one has unique white flowers with red centers.

Dianthus
mixed 'Maiden' varieties

DICENTRA

Bleeding Heart (Shade)

Bleeding hearts are shade-loving plants, ranging in size from the ten to twelve inches of some of the *D. formosa* cultivars (such as 'Burning Hearts' and 'Candy Hearts'), up to the thirty-six to forty-eight inches of the *D. spectabilis* species or common bleeding hearts.

Dangling heart-shaped blooms are produced in early to mid summer, and the fern-like foliage persists and sings all summer long, provided the garden setting is shady or cool. This foliage is usually bright green, but in many of the *D. formosa* types it

Dicentra 'Gold Heart'
mixed garden in early August

Dicentra spectabilis

Dicentra 'Gold Heart'

is a blue-green, which of course is accentuated when paired with other bluish foliaged plants.

The species *D. spectabilis,* commonly referred to as Old Fashioned Pink, and its cultivars offer many Interior Alaska-hardy choices. *Spectabilis,* with its pink and white blooms can spread to forty-eight inches. 'Alba' or Old Fashioned White has pure white blooms. 'Valentine,' with a mature height of thirty inches, produces red and white blossoms on red-stemmed branches. The foliage shows burgundy-plum overtones. One of my favorites in the bleeding heart group is 'Gold Heart,' a plant that reaches twenty-four to thirty inches in height, with pink flowers and brilliant gold foliage. It is a spot of sunshine in a shade garden and is particularly stunning when positioned next to dark-foliaged plants like *Ligularia* 'Othello' or *Actaea* 'Black Negligee.'

DODECATHEON
Shooting Star

Dodecatheon meadia with *Bergenia sp.* in background

Dodecatheorn meadia

Shooting stars are some of the first plants to bloom in the late spring or early summer in a northern perennial garden. After a dramatic display of lilac-pink or purple-pink flowers that totally cover the plant, shooting stars melt down gradually, and the plant goes into summer dormancy. For this reason, it is important that shooting stars in a perennial garden be planted in close proximity to perennials that can cover the empty spot for the rest of the summer. This is a member of the garden that plays with all its energy for a few weeks, and then exits the symphony. There are several species of *Dodecatheon* that are potentially hardy in Interior Alaska. The one I have grown most successfully is *D. meadia,* with a height of six to twelve inches and lilac-pink flowers. 'Aphrodite' is one of its cultivars. This plant grows to eighteen inches in height and displays magenta flowers with yellow centers.

Draba siberica on May 14

Close up of *Draba siberica* early spring blooms

DRABA

Whitlow-grass (Sun)

This alpine plant is not well known, but it has great value in a northern perennial garden border or as a rock garden plant. My favorite is *D. sibirica*, which grows low, only a few inches tall, and spreads in a circular mat twelve inches or more in diameter. This plant has tiny, bright yellow flowers produced prolifically and early in the spring. This will likely be the first color of the season in your perennial garden, and it is dramatic. Shear *D. sibirica* after the blooms are spent, and it will re-bloom in the fall. This is definitely a sun-loving plant.

FILIPENDULA

Meadowsweet

There are several species and various cultivars of *Filipendula* that are hardy in Interior Alaska gardens. Their flowers are clusters of tiny pink or white blooms produced in early summer. This is a plant whose main contribution to the garden symphony is the structure and very textured foliage that it adds all season. Although meadowsweets like sun, they do not like drought, and will respond to dry soil with browning on the edge of the leaves, very much like the *Astilbe* genus does.

Filipendula 'Variegata'

'Kahome' (*F. vulgaris*), a dwarf cultivar, is only twelve inches tall, with pink flowers produced early, and foliage that hums softly in the background all summer long. My personal experience has been that, at least in a mixed garden situation, 'Kahome' blooms later than the other members of the genus. Most *Filipendula* are much taller, with the cultivar 'Elegans' (*F. palmata*) producing pink flowers on twenty-eight-inch plants, and 'Venusta' (*F. rubra*) growing to as much as sixty inches, with dark reddish-pink blooms. 'Variegata' (*F. ulmaria*) has deep green leaves with gold centers. This cultivar reaches a height of thirty-six to forty-eight inches with white flower plumes.

Filipendula sp. (center) with *Lychnis* 'Dusky Salmon-Pink'

Galium Yellow Bedstraw on left

Galium Yellow Bedstraw

Gentiana septemfida 'True Blue'

Geranium 'Lakwijk Star'

Geranium 'Lakwijk Star' blossom

GALIUM

Bedstraw (Sun)

Galium verum, commonly called yellow bedstraw, is a plant that may sprawl and ramble in the garden, or that may grow upright in a vase shape. Its ultimate height ranges from ten to twenty-four inches. I like it best when planted among other perennials toward the front of the garden, so that others can support it while it alternates between rambling and knitting among its neighbors or instead pursuing a vertical lifestyle.

Yellow bedstraw produces a mass of bright yellow blooms very early, but oftentimes continues blooming late into the season. Whenever it slows at flowering, it usually benefits from a complete cutback to freshen up the foliage and to encourage re-blooming.

GENTIANA

Gentian

There are several hardy gentians in our northern gardens, but my favorite is the species *G. septemfida* and some of its cultivars. It can be prostrate or upright in growth form, with a total height or length between eight and twelve inches. 'True Blue' is a cultivar that may grow to thirty inches in height. Gentian flowers are bell-shaped, intense blue, and produced in late summer. When gentians are blooming in Interior Alaska, fall is just around the corner. I have grown both *G. dahurica* and *G. cruciata* as well, and they are hardy, but I think *G. septemfida* is the showiest of the lot.

GERANIUM

Cranesbill (or Hardy Geranium)

These are often called hardy geraniums, to distinguish from the popular annual geraniums, which are actually members of the genus *Pelargonium*. There are many species, varieties, and cultivars in the genus *Geranium*, many of which are hardy this far north and many of which are not. I have my favorites, but do not restrict yourself to my list if you enjoy pushing the limits of geranium species that survive in a northern garden. There are many possibilities worth trialing. When you are reading plant tags or catalogs to make your choices, do not base your decision solely on the zone listing. These are not always correct, and they are not the only consideration as to whether a plant is hardy in our climate.

Most hardy geraniums bloom in colors ranging from white to pink, lavender, burgundy, blue, and purple. Some produce single flowers, and some have double flowers.

'Birch Double' (*G. himalayense*) has double pink blooms that appear mid-season, and it contributes to the fall garden symphony with red-orange foliage. 'Nimbus' (a hybrid of *G. collinum* and *G. clarkei* 'Kashmir Purple') is a violet-flowered cultivar that stands quite upright at sixteen to twenty-four inches. 'Double Jewel' (*G. pratense*) is only twelve inches tall and very hardy, and it produces double white flowers. My favorite is 'Lakwijk Star' (*G. wlassovianum*), with large magenta blooms, dark, zoned leaves, and a rounded, mounding growth habit reaching up to eighteen inches in height.

HEMEROCALLIS
Daylily

There are literally thousands of cultivars of daylilies. Across the many different colors and heights, there are also different bloom times. It has been my experience that early blooming daylilies will bloom mid to late summer in Interior Alaska, and mid season bloomers will be blooming only slightly before the fall frost. Therefore, when choosing daylily varieties, avoid those classified as late. They will add vertical structure to the garden but no blooms. The strong, grass-like structure of all daylilies adds nice contrast when mixed with puffier, fluffier plants.

Some daylilies, like 'Stella de Oro,' bloom continuously once they begin, whereas others, like 'Fragrant Returns,' bloom for a few weeks, take a break, and then re-bloom. The re-bloom may not be as spectacular as the first, and it may occur so late that frost is nipping at its heels, if not stopping it in its tracks.

How can I have favorites among daylilies, when there are so many choices—and so many choices that I have not even tried yet? Here are just a few that I have grown and loved. At this time, I am expanding the boundaries of my own perennial garden area, and I plan on adding daylilies, both favorites and new cultivars.

'Stella de Oro' is found in many Interior Alaska perennial gardens. It is very hardy and dependable, and the growth form is compact but substantial, at a height of twelve to eighteen inches. Its blooms are bright yellow and produced all summer long. 'Fragrant Returns' is one I have grown in more than one garden. Its name says everything. Fragrance and re-blooming are reason enough to grow it, but add to that a nice height of eighteen inches, bright lemon-yellow flowers, and a bloom season that starts here in the Interior in July. 'Mauna Loa' is a late July bloomer, with fiery orange blooms and a height of twenty-two inches. 'Little Grapette' is a compact cultivar at only twelve inches, so it may function as a border plant. Its blooms are hot pink to purple, with yellow-orange throats. This is a June to July bloomer in Interior Alaska. 'Hyperion' is a tall daylily, with a potential height of thirty-six to forty-two inches. It is definitely fragrant,

Hemerocallis sp. late August

Hemerocallis 'Stella de Oro'

Hemerocallis flava July

with lemon yellow blooms and narrow grassy foliage. This is an August bloomer in the north.

If I were to choose a favorite among the daylilies in my garden, it would be *H. flava*, sometimes called lemon daylily. The leaves are narrow and strap-like. The mature plant height is thirty inches. The four-inch-wide trumpet-shaped flowers are bright yellow and fragrant. *H. flava* is not only the earliest blooming daylily in most northern gardens, but it also re-blooms. This is a plant that readily naturalizes, and may need to be split every few seasons.

HESPERIS

Sweet Rocket

Hesperis matronalis is a species of *Hesperis* used as an ornamental in perennial gardens. It is not a true perennial, but instead a biennial that also re-seeds. Its value in a perennial garden lies in its very early bloom time, its gorgeous fragrant, lavender flowers, and its height of up to thirty-six inches. Add to this list of attributes the fact that it is very easy to grow. The summer foliage is far from stunning, and this is when other players in the garden symphony must expand their personal space and cover for their fading neighbor. Do not hesitate to cut back the foliage of sweet rocket after it blooms.

Hesperis matronalis with
Trollius europeus

HOSTA

Plantain Lily (Shade)

Hosta is a genus of plants grown primarily for the beauty of its foliage and its stems of lavender, white, or pink flowers, some of which are fragrant. This is a genus with many species, hybrids, and cultivars, and many of these are no doubt hardy in Interior Alaska. Many have never been trialed here.

Hosta 'Guacamole'
in late August after cutback of many
other perennials in the garden

Hostas are considered shade plants in warmer climates, but in the Interior, they do not seem to thrive or even survive in true shade. I have had the best success growing them in a south exposure, but in among taller perennials. In this situation, they enjoy some shade but also warm soil, which in fact they seem to need.

With the *Hosta* group, there is considerable variation in size, leaf structure, growth form, and even leaf color. Some have foliage that is green, others have bluish foliage, and there are others with variegated green-white or green-gold foliage.

'Guacamole' is one that has grown well in the display gardens at The Plant Kingdom, even in fairly sun-exposed situations. It is twenty to twenty-four inches tall, and produces fragrant lavender-purple flowers in mid to late summer. The foliage is a beautiful lime yellow, contrasting well with dark-foliaged plants

Hosta 'Guacamole'

'True Blue' is similar in size, reaching twenty-four to thirty inches, with flowers that are white with a pink stripe, and foliage that is somewhat puckered with a blue-green cast. This bluish color echoes nicely with Blue Globe Spruce, 'Wichita Blue' Juniper, and the Redleaf Rose.

IRIS

Iris

For me, the main beauty of an iris in a perennial garden is its imposing vertical structure. In the display gardens at The Plant Kingdom, we have one Alaska wild iris (*Iris setosa*) and several Siberian cultivars. The native iris has broader leaves, is shorter (twelve to twenty-four inches), and produces its purple-blue flowers earlier than the Siberian. I also think that the foliage of the native *Iris setosa* is more likely to flop and drop out of the symphony after it has bloomed, sometimes requiring a fall cut-back in July. The Siberian iris plants have narrower leaves, grow taller (twenty-four to thirty-six inches), and flower in early summer. They also tend to remain quite neat, tidy, and vertical through the season, unless they are hit with excessive wind and rain, or if they are crowded and in need of splitting. Both native and Siberian iris also have flowers in shades of pink and white, and the Siberians add yellow tones and two-tones to their bloom repertoire.

Native iris in front
Siberian iris in back

Siberian iris late June

There are probably microclimates in Interior Alaska where bearded iris may grow. However, I have had the most experience and success with cultivars of *Iris siberica*, so my favorites come from that species. 'Butter and Sugar' is a cultivar with white and yellow flowers, and is about twenty-four inches at maturity. 'Caesar's Brother' produces violet-blue flowers and is about thirty inches tall. 'Ruffled Velvet' is a tall plant, with a potential of thirty inches, and its blooms are rich violet-blue with gold and white highlights. The flowers are quite large. 'Snow Queen' has pure white flowers with bright yellow centers, and also matures at thirty inches. The iris world is open for trialing by the adventurous perennial gardener whose garden has space for plants on this scale.

Siberian iris in back
Polygonatum variegatum front

LAMIUM

Dead Nettle (Shade)

Lamium is a low growing plant, only six to eight inches in height, but each plant may have a spread of up to thirty-six inches. It is best planted along the front border of a perennial garden, or even as a ground cover separating gardens. Since it spreads by underground stolons, the gardener is in charge of controlling its movement in the garden. Although a shade plant by nature, *Lamium* tolerates sunny locations if it is

Lamium 'Silver Beacon'
Solidago 'Little Lemon'

Lamium 'Silver Beacon'

Lewisia cotyledon' Elise Ruby Red'
(photo courtessy Jennifer Jolis)

Lewisiia longipetala 'Little Plum'

Leymus arenarius
(photo coutesy Susie Zimmerman)

Leymus arenarius
(photo coutesy Susie Zimmerman)

among taller plants.. All the varieties I have grown are cultivars of *L. maculatum*. The yellow-leafed cultivar 'Aureum' is not hardy, but all of the silver-leafed ones seem to winter successfully. My three favorites are 'Beacon Silver,' with lavender flowers; 'Pink Pewter,' which has pink flowers; and 'White Nancy,' with white flowers.

Lamium starts blooming in June and continues into August in the perennial gardens at The Plant Kingdom.

LEWISIA

Bitterroot (Sun)

This genus is a group of succulent plants, including roughly twenty species, as well as many hybrids and cultivars. I was first introduced to *Lewisia* by Walt Mayr. He and his wife, Elsie, operated a greenhouse-nursery in Sutton, Alaska, until they were in their nineties. They grew and experimented with many interesting perennials, but two of their specialties were *Lewisia* and *Trollius*. Numerous times I have made the seven-hundred-mile round trip to Sutton to bring back a van loaded with their unique perennials.

In the commercial market, many *Lewisia* are sold in mixes such as 'Elise Mix,' and so the bloom color of each plant is not known until the first time the plant blooms.

Here I will introduce you to two cultivars that are available as specific colors. Both are cultivars of the species *longipetala*. 'Little Plum' grows only six inches tall, and has pink-purple flowers that are tinted with orange when they first open. 'Little Peach' is the same height, but has peach-pink star-shaped flowers. These are both mounding evergreen plants with strappy leaves. Both bloom in June and then again in late summer. *Lewisia* are sun-lovers, and they must have well-drained soil.

These two characteristics frequently land *Lewisia* in rock gardens. However, we have found that both these cultivars grow quite happily as border plants in south sun in the river loess that is the garden soil at The Plant Kingdom.

LEYMUS

Lyme Grass

L. arenarius, whose common name is blue dune lyme grass, is one of two genera of ornamental grasses I have found to be reliably hardy in Interior Alaska perennial gardens.

The steel blue foliage of this grass can reach twenty-four to thirty-six inches in height. This is a running grass that spreads by rhizomes, and I feel it works best along the edge of a path, a fence, or an entrance drive, rather than being incorporated in a mixed perennial garden. This strength as a visual guide into a garden is enhanced by the blue foliage, which resonates beautifully with other blue-foliaged plants like Dwarf Blue Spruce and Redleaf Rose.

Ligularia 'Othello' in a mixed garden in September (left).

LIGULARIA

Ligularia (Shade)

These are plants that prefer some protection from hot south sun, and from the sun and heat reflected off the side of a building. There are both green-leafed and dark burgundy-leafed cultivars. It has been my experience that the green-leafed ones are more sun tolerant. Moist soil is important to all *Ligularia* in northern gardens.

'Little Rocket,' at thirty inches in height, and 'The Rocket,' at a potential of seventy-two inches, both produce spikes of yellow blooms on dark purple stems. Both are cultivars of *Ligularia stenocephala*. These are the earliest *Ligularia* to bloom in Interior Alaska gardens, and the color show often starts in late June. Removing spent flower spikes keeps the plant looking attractive even after flowering is finished. 'Desdemona' (*L. dentata*) has green leaves with purple undersides, and has golden yellow, daisy-shaped flowers. Its height is about thirty to thirty-six inches. 'Othello' (*L. dentata*) has somewhat darker foliage and is slightly taller, reaching thirty-six inches. The flowers are orange-yellow and also daisy-shaped. 'Desdemona' is more heat tolerant than 'Othello,' a plant that does not hesitate at all to take a wilting posture in hot afternoon sun. 'Britt-Marie Crawford' (*L. dentata*) has dark chocolate-maroon leaves and orange-yellow late summer blooms. This is a tall (thirty-six to forty inches) plant, and presents wonderful contrast in the garden, with its large, round-leafed, and very dark foliage.

Ligularia 'Othello'

Ligularia 'Britt-Marie Crawford'

Ligularia 'The Rocket'

The author with Jim and Marcia Holm and their Conca d'Or' lily (right).

Lilium 'Matrix'

Lilium 'America' and 'Peach Pixie'

Lily Bed at The Plant Kingdom

Lilium 'Elodie'

LILIUM

Lily

The extensive hybridization in this genus has the downside of confusing genetics, as well as inconsistent terminology and classification among the various sources for lily information. The upside is that there are countless colorful and spectacular lilies, most of which are worth trying at least once, even in a northern perennial garden. I will not attempt here to sort out the lily species, hybrids, and cultivars. That is an area open to ongoing exploration as you add to your garden and create new ones. I do want to touch, however, on some of the major classifications to help you negotiate the lily world and incorporate it in your perennial garden.

All the varieties I mention are quite forgiving regarding sun requirements in Interior Alaska, thriving both in south sun and in north exposure light. The blooms last longer, and bloom time is delayed a week or two later, in north versus south exposure habitats.

Asiatic hybrids are extremely hardy and offer a wide assortment of colors, with heights ranging from twelve to forty-eight inches. They are usually mid season bloomers in Interior Alaska. The Lily Looks™ and the Pixie lilies are dwarf members of the Asiatic group, but the other end of the spectrum includes varieties that reach a height of four feet. Like the rest of the lilies we grow here in the north, the flowers are large, colorful, and obvious.

Species lilies typically have downward-facing flowers with re-curved petals, pulled back from the stamens. Tiger lilies, with their heavily spotted petals are in this group, as are the Martagon or Turk's Cap lilies. Tiger lilies are late summer bloomers, and the last of the lily genus to bloom each season. Martagons are early to mid-summer bloomers, and are known for their ability to tolerate shade.

LA hybrids are crosses between Asiatic lilies and longiflorum lilies, and they are considered hardy to at least zone 4, and probably lower. These hybrids boast larger and longer-lasting flowers than the Asiatics, and they often have a light fragrance. OT hybrids are similarly hardy and are sometimes called Orienpets, referencing their mixed parentage of oriental and trumpet lilies. Even though trumpet lilies and oriental lilies are not dependably hardy in northern climates, at least some of the OT hybrids, with their potential of four to six-feet heights and large, fragrant, trumpet-shaped flowers, are hardy even in zone 3 microclimates.

There are so many lilies in so many colors, and with slight differences in bloom times, that I cannot imagine a perennial garden without some of them. Their foliage is a striking upright and very linear addition to the garden. Then their big, showy blooms appear. Once blooms are finished, the foliage often deteriorates, and may even show signs of bacterial or fungal disease. This means it is cutback time.

Lilium 'Fata Morgana'

I love lilies, any and all, and here are some of my favorites. Shades of salmon and peach are some of the most wonderful colors in the garden. For lilies in these shades, consider Lily Looks™ 'Tiny Moon,' in salmon-peach at twelve to fourteen inches; 'Tango Passions,' with peachy-pink flowers that have yellow centers; and 'Apricot Fudge,' with its very unusual double peach-yellow flowers and a noticeable height of twenty-four to thirty-six inches.

Lilium 'Apricot Fudge'

Yellow is a color that grabs your eye, and two lilies that will do that are 'Golden Matrix,' at a compact size of sixteen inches, and the long-blooming 'Fata Morgana,' with double yellow blooms and a height of thirty-six to forty-eight inches.

Intense red lilies are another strong player in the garden. I go to 'Blackout,' with its dark red flowers and spotted centers, or 'Landini,' with flowers so dark purple-red that they are almost black.

Lilium Turk's Cap

'Elodie' is a gorgeous double pink that stands tall at forty-eight inches, and has an amazingly long bloom time.

Another lily I cannot leave out of a garden is 'Matrix,' a sixteen-inch plant whose flowers are intense dark orange with red overtones at the center.

My first choices in Tiger Lilies are 'Pink,' 'Citronelle' (yellow), and 'Splendens' (orange). These classics are later blooming and bold-colored, and stand tall in the symphony.

And if you are thinking tall, experiment with an Orienpet like 'Conca d' Or,' with huge lemon-yellow blossoms that are wonderfully fragrant. This lily easily reaches forty-eight to sixty inches, and blooms prolifically in late summer. If this one is hardy in your garden, you will want to consider adding some of the other amazing colors in this group.

Lilium 'Conca d'Or''

Lychnis Maltese Cross

Lychnis 'Molten Lava'

Lychnis 'Vesuvius'

LYCHNIS

Campion

This is a plant that offers short varieties, which work well at the front of a garden or border and also taller varieties for areas of the garden that need height. My two favorite cultivars in the *L. arkwrightii* species both have dark burgundy ornamental foliage and are twelve to fifteen inches tall. 'Vesuvius' has orange-scarlet flowers, and the blooms of 'Molten Lava' are more cherry red. Both bloom in July and frequently re-bloom later in the summer if they are cut back or at least deadheaded after the first bloom. Other series in this same species are the 'Luminas' and 'Orange Gnome,' both of which are in the twelve to fifteen-inch height range and offer dark and green-leaved varieties in shades of salmon, orange, and red.

The tall *Lychnis* often used in northern perennial gardens include *L. chalcedonica* or Maltese Cross, with scarlet-orange flowers and a mature height of forty-eight inches, and the 'Dusky Salmon' and 'Dusky Pink' series, with salmon or pink flowers and forty-eight inches of height.

Most *Lychnis*, especially the *L. chalcedonica* types, do best if they are cut back to ground level after blooming, because their foliage deteriorates and becomes a liability to the garden.

Lychnis 'Dusky Salmon' (right).

Lysimachia 'Alexander'

LYSIMACHIA

Loosestrife

There are two species of *Lysimachia* I have enjoyed in my own perennial garden.

One is 'Alexander,' a cultivar of *L. punctata*. This is an upright plant, twelve to twenty-four inches tall, with attractive light green leaves edged with creamy white margins that may be tinged with pink in early summer. Many yellow flowers are produced on top of the plants, and here in Interior Alaska, that bloom is in July.

'Firecracker,' a cultivar of *L. ciliata*, has equally interesting foliage that is brown-purple and contrasts stunningly with its lemon yellow flowers. This is a plant that at times is upright (twelve to twenty-four inches) and in other situations is more prostrate. 'Firecracker' is my favorite hardy *Lysimachia*, not only because of the colors, but also because it continues to bloom profusely through the summer, once it begins in late June or early July.

Lysimachia 'Alexander' with *Nepeta subsessilis*

LYTHRUM

Purple Loosestrife

This is a plant with a reputation for being invasive, especially in waterways and in warmer climates. Unfortunately, it has been given the invasive designation in Alaska. However, it has been my experience and that of other gardeners in the Interior (even as far south as Willow) that the named cultivars of *Lythrum* are not invasive in Interior Alaska. I have a beautiful *Lythrum salicaria* 'Rosy Gem' minding its own business and staying in its designated spot in one of my own perennial gardens. I am the envy of some of my gardening friends, who meanwhile struggle to get this supposedly invasive plant to survive in their gardens.

Lysimachia 'Firecracker,' mixed garden

I do not take lightly the concept of invasive plants, but I also feel strongly that just like the word "hardy," the word "invasive" must always refer to a specific set of growing conditions. Alaska encompasses 665,000 square miles, spans twenty degrees of latitude, and qualifies for classification as USDA climate zones 1A through 8A. Add to that a multitude of microclimates. This means that a plant that thrives in one part of the state may not have a hope of surviving in another part. To say a plant is invasive from Sitka to Prudhoe Bay is absurd. To be meaningful and taken seriously, designations of invasive must be based on habitat and microclimates, not on political boundaries.

Lysimachia 'Firecracker'

Do not pass up the opportunity to grow a hybrid like 'Rosy Gem' in your garden. It is a tall (thirty-six-forty-eight inches), late season, long-blooming perennial with multiple spires of rose pink.

Lythrum 'Rosy Gem'

Meconopsis 'Lingholm'
(photo courtesy Kay Sawyer)

Meconopsis sp. in late September

Meconopsis sp.

Myosotis palustris in summer

Myosotis palustris in September

MECONOPSIS

Himalayan Blue Poppy

A native to the alpine regions of the Himalayas, the Himalayan blue poppy is known for its intense sky-blue flowers, a shade of blue like no other flower. There are not many places in the world that provide the growing conditions needed by the Himalayan blue poppies or blue poppies, as they are commonly called. This is a plant that prefers or even demands cool, moist summers, and relatively mild winters. In Alaska, these conditions are better provided south of the Interior, and especially in the Southcentral part of the state. One of the pioneer breeders and growers of this plant in Alaska was Stan Ashmore. His gardens and growing area in the Palmer area have since been handed to fellow grower Kay Sawyer. She is now one of the primary producers and wholesalers of the Himalayan blue poppies grown in Alaska.

On paper, Interior Alaska is not the ideal climate for this plant, but the magic and the beauty of blue poppies appeals to even the most skeptical gardener. Also, from a blue poppy perspective, the effects of climate change in Interior Alaska have been positive, allowing them to spread their range northward, as winters become milder and summers become cooler.

This is a plant you must try—and keep trying, until you figure out how to grow it in your microclimate. Himalayan blue poppies prefer very organic soil that is kept quite damp. They are grown under a shady forest canopy on Kay's farm, but here in Fairbanks we are fairly successfully growing them in mixed perennial gardens in south exposures. The species most commonly grown is *betonicifolia* and its hybrid 'Lingholm.' During the summer of 2018 (a cool, rainy one), I had a 'Lingholm' blooming in one of my north exposure gardens from July 10 to September 24.

MYOSOTIS

Forget-Me-Not

This is a special plant because the native species, *M alpestris*, is Alaska's state flower. The species *M. palustris* is the one I have grown in my perennial gardens. It has the characteristic bright blue flowers that we associate with forget-me-nots. It blooms from early summer, and continues with at least a few flowers well after the main bloom. If it is shorn (but not to full fall cut-back) after the main bloom, it will completely re-bloom later in the summer. *M. palustris* spreads by underground stolons and has a somewhat trailing habit that gives it a six to ten-inch height, with some stems reaching eighteen inches in length. This species also re-seeds prolifically. This is a plant that prefers damp conditions, its natural habitat being in or close to water.

NEPETA

Nepeta (Sun)

The nepetas that I have grown in my Fairbanks perennial garden are a group within the genus that go by the common name of catmints.

My favorite cultivars of the species *N. faassenii* are 'Dropmore Blue' and 'Walker's Low.' These both grow in a rather sprawling vase shape. Blue flowers are produced fairly continuously all season long and even later in the season if the plant is shorn as the initial blooming slows. Both of these cultivars are about twenty-four inches tall.

Cultivars of *N. subsessilis* are bushy and more upright than 'Dropmore Blue' and 'Walker's Low,' and they may grow twenty-four to twenty-six inches tall. This group may also be pruned back after the main bloom, and the reward will be repeat flowering in late summer. Two favorites in this species are 'Blue Dreams,' with tubular blue flowers, and 'Pink Dreams,' with the same flower form in pink.

The *N. siberica* species is very hardy in northern gardens. It commonly reaches a height of thirty-six inches. This species readily spreads from seed. My experience has been that *N. siberica* blooms constantly all summer long, possibly starting a little later than other hardy catmints, but not needing to be shorn mid season to continue blooming. My first experience with *N. siberica* was with its cultivar 'Souvenir d' Andre Chaudrón,' and that is still my favorite catmint, although I have also grown the species from seed.

The leaves of all of these catmints have a distinct fragrance that is attractive to many cats. This is one way to keep your vole patrol close by and engaged.

Nepeta subsessilis

Nepeta 'Souvenir d'Andre Chaudrón'

Nepeta siberica in mixed garden

Nepeta sibirica in August

Nepeta 'Dropmore Blue' with *Lychnis* 'Vesuvius' (left).

Paeonia 'Eden's Perfume'

Paeonia 'Buckeye Belle'

Paeonia in a mixed garden

Paeonia 'Kopper Kettle'

Paeonia anomala 'Jana'

PAEONIA

Peony

The herbaceous peonies most commonly grown in northern climates are the *lactiflora* hybrids, but also hardy are some of the Itoh peonies that represent a cross between herbaceous garden peonies and tree peonies. The Itohs have intense, unique colors not found in the herbaceous types. There are many herbaceous peony varieties that are hardy in Interior Alaska. The Itoh varieties add yellows and spectacular two-tones.

There is some variation in bloom time between varieties, either inherent in the variety or in response to the microclimate. Most years the majority of herbaceous peonies will bloom sometime in midseason (June-July) in Fairbanks. This bloom time is later than in other areas in the northern hemisphere, and it is the key to the developing peony cut flower industry in Alaska. Fresh-cut peony blooms are available in our northern climate during the shoulder season of world peony production in the northern and southern hemispheres.

Peonies may prefer sun, but I grow them quite successfully in a northern exposure garden as well, the main difference in response being bloom time. My north exposure plants bloom as much as two weeks later than those in my south exposure garden. The blooms tend to hold longer on the plants grown in the shade locations. Peony foliage is shiny and dark green all season, and this, coupled with the plant's height and sturdy form, is the reason it contributes structure to a perennial garden long after the spectacular bloom season is past.

My favorite *lactiflora* varieties are 'Buckeye Belle,' with intense dark red, semi-double blooms and a height of thirty-four inches; 'Coral Charm,' which is also semi-double, has peach blooms, and is thirty-six inches tall; 'Karl Rosenfeld,' with double crimson-burgundy blooms, which are very fragrant and produced on a plant that may be up to thirty-eight inches tall; 'Sorbet,' which has double pink blooms tinged with light yellow on twenty-eight inch plants; and 'Festiva Maxima,' with white blooms decorated with a few crimson spots and growing to forty inches in height. Among the Itoh peonies, two of my favorites are 'Bartzella' at thirty-four inches, with intense yellow blooms, and 'Kopper Kettle,' growing to thirty-two inches and displaying unique apricot-orange blooms.

The earliest blooming peony in the Fairbanks area is *Paeonia anomala* 'Jana.' This species has been grown in Fairbanks for more than seventy-five years. It was given its name because it was first grown at the Georgeson Botanical Garden from seeds provided by Jana Gordon. She had grown it herself for nearly sixty years. In early June, this plant produces a mass of single rose-pink flowers, followed by large seedpods that split open later in the season to display shiny black seeds. 'Jana' may be thirty-six inches or more in height, and can fill a width in the garden equal to its height. The foliage color adds burgundy and rust to the garden in the fall. The seeds fall to the ground and provide a plentiful supply of plantlets to share with gardening friends each spring.

There are many, many more varieties of herbaceous and Itoh peonies that thrive in Interior Alaska. If you become, or already are, a peony aficionado, you can fine-tune your collection based on differences in color tones, height, bloom size and form, and subtle bloom time differences. For our purposes, we will focus on the varieties I have mentioned and how we can fit them into a multi species symphony in a perennial garden.

PAPAVER

Poppy (Sun)

Papaver orientale, known by the common name oriental poppy, is the poppy species I have grown in the perennial gardens at The Plant Kingdom and in my own gardens. One characteristic of oriental poppies is that after they have finished their stunning floral display, their foliage deteriorates, and the plants close shop for the rest of the season. In planning a garden, you must prepare for this by making sure that the neighboring plants are large enough to conceal this late season void in the garden. A player so flamboyant early in the performance requires a lot of others to cover for it when it goes missing.

There are many hybrids and cultivars of oriental poppies that thrive in the north. 'Brilliant' has scarlet-orange flowers whose centers are black and cone-like. This is a thirty-two to thirty-six-inch addition to the garden, and it adds color in midsummer. 'Allegro' has scarlet-red blooms that also have mid season timing, but the plant is only ten to twelve inches tall. 'Princess Louise' produces unique salmon-pink blooms mid season, and is about twenty-four inches tall. Two more favorites are 'Patty's Plum' and 'Little Patty's Plum.' Both bloom mid season, and the flowers are a distinct plum color with dark centers. 'Patty's Plum' is twenty-eight to thirty-two inches tall, while 'Little Patty's Plum ' is about twenty inches in height.

Because of the size and intense colors of the flowers of oriental poppies, they fill the same design niche as do the Asiatic lilies. Unlike the lilies, poppies also have large seedpods that add texture and interest to the garden, until the whole plant melts away into late summer dormancy.

Papaver sp. and *Achillea millefolium*

Papaver sp.

Papaver 'Patty's Plum' and *Meconopsis sp.*

Papaver 'Patty's Plum'

Phalaris picta with *Nepeta* 'Dropmore Blue'

Phalaris 'Picta' in mixed garden

Phlomis tuberosa, flower stalks removed

Phlomis tuberosa in bloom

Phlox subulata 'North Hills'

PHALARIS

Ribbon Grass

Phalaris arundinacea 'Picta' is a variegated green and white grass that grows to twenty-four inches tall. It thrives in boggy areas, but it also manages in dry south exposure habitats. This is a plant that spreads by underground stolons, and so it must be kept in check in the garden if it starts to spread beyond the boundaries desired by the gardener in charge.

'Dwarf Garters' is a cultivar that is more compact at ten to fifteen inches, and it spreads more slowly than 'Picta.' 'Feesey' or 'Strawberries and Cream' ribbon grass is the same height as 'Picta' but its white and green foliage has a distinct pink blush, and it does not spread as aggressively as 'Picta.'

Phalaris is used in a perennial garden for both its structure and its foliage. An added contribution is the late summer pink-white inflorescences that appear.

PHLOMIS

Phlomis

Phlomis tuberosa is a plant locally known by the common name Russian salvia, but probably more widely known as Jerusalem sage. The species name comes from the numerous small tubers that grow from its roots. This is a plant noticeable in a perennial garden because of its height of four feet and its nearly equal spread. The whorls of pink flowers borne on tall stalks are very popular with bees and other pollinators.

My favorite Russian salvia plant is one that I grow in a north exposure garden somewhat shaded by buildings and other plants. I diligently remove all the flower stalks as soon as they poke above the giant leaves. The result is an immense, rounded foliage plant with arrowhead-shaped dark green leaves. This plant of mine has no blossoms but it has a commanding voice in my shade garden symphony.

PHLOX

Phlox

This is a genus especially popular in warmer climates because of the species *P. paniculata* or garden phlox. Unfortunately, I have not found the many beautiful cultivars of this species to be dependably hardy in Fairbanks. However, I continue to trial various garden phlox cultivars.

My best success has been with some of the low-growing phlox. 'Sherwood Purple' is a cultivar of *P. stolonifera* with a height of six to ten inches, and is a must-have because of its very fragrant lavender-blue flowers that pop out in midsummer. This is a plant that can be shorn after the initial bloom as a way of encouraging a re-bloom. 'Blue Emerald' is a *stolonifera* cultivar about six inches in height and up to eighteen inches in diameter. Both cultivars are stoloniferous or mat-forming plants derived from a woodland heritage, so they tolerate shade. In the *P. subulata* species is 'North Hills,' a four to eight-inch tall plant that produces unique white flowers with violet-purple eyes. It is an early bloomer that loves sun and that will consider re-blooming if shorn after the primary bloom.

Phlox stolonifera 'Blue Emerald'

PHYSOSTEGIA

Obedient Plant

This is a plant that should be included in your perennial garden if for no other reason than it is an end-of-the-season bloomer, coming in loud and clear when the other players in the garden are beginning to tire. The tubular flowers are produced on elegant spikes, and the entire plant stands sturdy and upright through the season.

'Crystal Peak White' (*P. virginiana*) is a compact variety, only about sixteen inches tall. It is an earlier bloomer than some of the pink-flowered varieties like 'Bouquet Rose,' which is also taller at twenty-four inches. A third cultivar of *P. virginiana* that we grow in our display gardens at The Plant Kingdom is 'Variegata,' which displays creamy white stripes on gray foliage, has rose-pink flowers and achieves an impressive height of twenty-four to thirty-six inches.

Physostegia 'Bouquet Rose'

Polemonium 'Touch of Class'

POLEMONIUM

Jacob's Ladder

The common name of this genus comes from the pattern of alternating leaflets arranged like a ladder along the elongated leaves.

Add to this the sage green leaves with white edges that come with the cultivar 'Touch of Class' (*Polemonium reptans*), and you have a solid player in your symphony. Pink buds open into soft blue flowers that are produced for a large part of the early and mid summer season. 'Touch of Class' is one of several popular variegated *Polemonium* cultivars, and for me it has been more powdery mildew-free and more dependably hardy than the rest. 'Bressingham Purple' (*Polemonium caeruleum*) has dark purple-green spring foliage, which turns green later in the season. Both these cultivars are about fifteen inches tall and thrive in cool climates, and even in full shade. The blooms have a light fragrance.

Polemonium' Touch of Class'

Polemoniun caeruleum

Polygonatum 'Variegatum'

Potentilla 'Monarch's Velvet'

Potentilla megalantha 'Nana'

Primula sikkimensis

Primula matthioli

POLYGONATUM

Solomon's Seal

'Variegatum' is a cultivar of the species *Polygonatum odoratum*, which is quite hardy in Interior Alaska. Even though it may be a sleeper for more than one season, it eventually establishes and spreads out from the center in a circular pattern. It has arching stems with white-edged, green leaves. Pendulous, small, white, slightly fragrant flowers dangle from the stems in early summer. The contribution from Solomon's seal continues all season because of the linear, upright structure and the bright foliage. A miniature relative is the species *P. humile*, which is also extremely hardy in the north. The leaves of this dwarf are green, flowers are white, and the whole plant is at the most eight to ten inches tall.

POTENTILLA

Cinquefoil

Here we are considering the herbaceous cinquefoils as opposed to the woody species. There are many species of cinquefoil and probably quite a number of these and their cultivars are worth trialing in northern gardens. The herbaceous cinquefoils have strawberry-like foliage, and they tend to grow in clumps with trailing stems.

'Monarch's Velvet' (*Potentilla thurberi*) is a cultivar that has two-tone flowers saturated with burgundy-maroon pigment. This plant is in the range of ten to fifteen inches tall. Another cultivar is 'William Rollinson' (*Potentilla atrosanguinea*), which has double, deep orange blooms with contrasting yellow centers. It grows and sprawls to about sixteen inches, 'Nana' is a compact yellow-flowered cultivar. Cinquefoils are quite at home in a cool, northern climate. Even though they are never covered with blooms, the ones they do produce have an unforgettable intensity of color.

PRIMULA

Primrose (Shade)

I have experimented with *P. sikkimensis* and *P. florindae*. Both are about twenty inches tall and have fragrant bright yellow flowers. My success has been marginal, but I still believe these and other hybrids and cultivars are worth trialing in northern gardens, especially in those with microclimates close to zone 4.

Primula matthioli (alpine bells) is a plant in the family Primulaceae, that has more recently been included in the genus *Primula* rather than *Cortusa*. It has light green leaves that are rounded but with scalloping. This plant has a very primrose-like presence, and it grows to about ten inches, with flowers on long stems clustered at the top, and usually hanging from one side of that stem. These pendulous flowers are purple-pink and bell-shaped. Blooms are produced in early spring, If you have a shady perennial garden and are struggling with other *Primula*, you might want to try alpine bells, especially if you have a microclimates close to zone 4.

PULSATILLA

Pasque Flower

Pulsatilla vulgaris, (also listed as *Anemone pulsatilla* by some sources), at ten inches tall, produces some of the first flowers of spring, and thereby earns its place in the front border of any northern perennial garden. The fuzzy stems, finely cut lacy foliage, and velvet purple flowers are even more reasons to grow this plant. There are two cultivars of *P. vulgaris*, 'Alba' with white flowers and 'Rubra' with wine red flowers. 'Rubra' may bloom slightly later than the others. Pasque flower seedpods, silky and feathery, are spectacular and odd by themselves, and play a part all on their own in the garden symphony.

SEDUM

Stonecrop (Sun)

Although some of the more upright *Sedum* cultivars are popular in temperate climate gardens, it is the low-growing spreading species of *Sedum* that I have found most hardy in this northern habitat.

My favorite is *S. kamtschaticum* 'Variegatum.' The small, fleshy leaves are green and edged with white, so they are themselves ornamental. The orange-yellow flowers in early summer are followed by red-orange seedpods so colorful at first glance they may be mistaken for blooms, so this cultivar is listed on the Orange or Peach Color Charts. Short (five inches) and wide (twelve to twenty-four inches), this little plant plays its part all season long. *S. spurium* 'Tricolor' has green foliage that is noticeably white and pink edged. Its flowers are pink, and the total plant size is about four inches tall and twelve inches in spread. There are undoubtedly other cultivars of both these species, and others that will perform in the north, offering huge opportunity to gambling gardeners.

Sedum kamtschaticum (non-variegated).

Pulsatilla vulgaris opening

Pulsatilla vulgaris open in May

Sedum mixed prostrate

Sedum kamtschaticum 'Variegatum'

Sedum kamtschaticum 'Variegatum'

Solidago 'Litttle Lemon'

Solidago 'Little Lemon'

Solidago 'Little Lemon' from top

Tanacetum vulgare Common Tansy

Tanacetum 'Crispum'

Goldenrod (Sun)

This perennial is a late bloomer and a spectacular one, with spikes of bright yellow flowers. I have had the most success with 'Little Lemon' (*Solidago* x 'Dansolitlem'), a twelve-inch-tall cultivar, which produces a mass of bright yellow blooms as the growing season winds down. I have also grown 'Laurin' (*Solidago* hyb.), which winters reliably but whose blooms open so late that the plant freezes to death before showing any color.

TANACETUM

Tansy (Sun)

This is a genus of plants whose numbers expanded with the addition of plants that were once considered part of the genus *Chrysanthemum*.

T. coccineum, commonly called the painted daisies, includes several cultivars that thrive in the sun in Fairbanks and the rest of the Interior. 'Robinson's Red' and 'Robinson's Pink' have blooms that are daisy-shaped and deep rose or light pink, respectively. The flowers of both have yellow centers. These plants reach eighteen to twenty-four inches in height and bloom in mid season. Once they have bloomed, much as in the case of *Delphinium* and *Lychnis*, the plant should be trimmed to fall cutback height. Fresh, feathery foliage will spring back and maybe even a few more blooms will appear as well.

Tanacetum 'Robinson's Pink' (photo courtesy Brenda Adams).

T. vulgare is a species that looks very different from *T. coccineum*, though both have foliage that is fragrant and feathery. These are the plants most often associated with the common name tansy. The species has button type flowers, is three to four feet tall, and spreads quickly by rhizomes. It is a back-of-the-garden plant that may need physical support once it reaches full height. *T. vulgare* is also one that may benefit from a full cut-back once it has bloomed. My favorite tansy is 'Isla Gold,' a cultivar of *T. vulgare,* which has yellow foliage, especially bright early in the spring. It is quite noticeable when planted next to the very contrasting dark foliage of 'Diabolo' ninebark or of *Actaea* 'Black Negligee.' 'Isla Gold' is a similar height to the species, but does not spread as easily. Of the three members of the *vulgare* species grown in Interior Alaska, the cultivar 'Crispum' is the most compact. Its name describes it well because it stands straight and tall, with curled leaf margins that give the light green foliage a neat, crisp appearance. The button-shaped yellow flowers are often a little later in the season than those of the species or of 'Isla Gold,' and the bloom period is relatively long.

Tanacetum 'Robinsons Red'

Tanacetum 'Isla Gold'

Tanacetum 'Isla Gold' (lower left corner of photo) and 'Crispum' (upper left back of garden).

Thalictrum aguilegifolium
blossoms (right).

Thalictrum 'Splendide'

Thalictrum 'Flavum'

Thalictrum 'Black Stockings'

THALICTRUM

Meadow Rue

Meadow rue thrives in Interior Alaska and is probably a zone 3 or possibly a zone 2 plant, even though various authors, plant catalogs, and plant tags describe it as zone 5. Zone designations are only as reliable as the information on which they are based. When I trial a new perennial in my garden, the reported zone is only one of its characteristics that I consider in making my choice. If the plant has a hardy sounding resume, and has close relatives that are hardy, I figure it's worth the gamble, especially considering the multitude of microclimates and the wild card of climate change.

Most meadow rues are tall plants, with attractive foliage that is reminiscent of columbine, and produce plumes of lavender-pink flowers, followed by decorative pendulous seedpods.

The species *T. aquilegifolium* has lilac-pink flowers and can grow to forty-eight inches in height. 'Hewitt's Double,' a *T. delavayi* cultivar is equally tall but with violet double flowers. Also in the species *T. delavayi* is 'Splendide.' This cultivar is capable of heights of four to six feet, and may need support. It produces clouds of showy lavender purple flowers from mid summer into September. 'Anne' (*Thalictrum hyb.*) and 'Black Stockings' (*T. aquilegifolium*) both have dark stems, though 'Anne' has an amazing potential height of seven feet and has pink flowers. 'Black Stockings' only grows to four feet and has lavender blooms. *T. flavum* is four feet tall with bluish gray foliage. It is unusual among the meadow rue in that it has yellow flowers and they are fragrant.

Meadow rues are mid season bloomers, but foliage and seedpods and their sturdy, tall growth habit all contribute to the garden before and after their bloom season.

TROLLIUS

Globeflower

The plants in this genus grow well in sun or shade. *Trollius* was a common plant in many of the early perennial gardens planted in Interior Alaska. Most have globe-shaped, orange or yellow flowers. The species *T. pumilus* has more flattened, five-petaled flowers that are bright golden yellow. *T. pumilus* is only about six to eight inches tall. I have found it to be a little less hardy than many of the other *Trollius* species. It is a perfect plant to play the part of the early bloomer in the front row of a perennial garden, so if you can grow it successfully, by all means include it in your garden.

I have found *Trollius* to be stubborn about germinating in a greenhouse, but left on its own, the species spreads readily through the garden by seed. Here again is a situation in which the gardener must remember the working definition of "weed."

Trollius is one of those members of the garden symphony whose foliage may become a bit shabby once the main bloom season is complete. The solution to this is a partial or full cutback of the bloomed-out plant.

The yellow-flowered species and cultivars seem to bloom earlier than the orange ones in many cases. 'Earliest of All' is an early season bloomer with orange-yellow flowers and a height of about twenty-four inches. *T. europaeus* is another early season bloomer, with yellow blooms and a height of twenty-four inches. 'Superbus' is a cultivar of this species with similar color and height, but it is more floriferous than the species. 'Alabaster' (*Trollius* x *cultorum*) is a white-flowered early summer bloomer that reaches about twenty-four inches in height. 'Lemon Queen' (*Trollius* x *cultorum*)

Trollius europaeus

Trollius chinensis 'Golden Queen'

Trollius chinensis and
Achillea 'Terra Cotta'

Trollius europaeus

Trollius chinensis (left).

Veronica 'Giles van Hees' on the left, *Lysimachia* 'Vesuvius' center, and *Veronica* 'Ulster Blue' on the right.

has very double lemon yellow flowers, may reach eighteen to thirty inches in height, and with deadheading may participate in the symphony again late in the season. *T. ledebourii* produces orange flowers that are at their peak a week or two later than the varieties I have mentioned so far. It grows eighteen to twenty-four inches tall. The latest blooming *Trollius* in many Interior gardens is 'Golden Queen,' a cultivar of the *T. chinensis* species. Rich orange flowers on tall thirty-six-inch plants make a showy July display.

VERONICA

Speedwell

There are numerous species and cultivars in the speedwells. Most are happiest in sunny locations, produce spikes of flowers that are popular with bees, and will re-bloom to some extent if deadheaded. Some are susceptible to powdery mildew as the season wears on, and may benefit from early cutback.

The following seven cultivars are all in the species *Veronica spicata*. 'Ulster Blue' and 'Giles van Hees' produce spikes of cobalt blue and rose pink, respectively, and the entire plant is only about six inches tall. 'Royal Candles' has vibrant blue flower spikes and belongs in the sixteen to eighteen-inch tall row of the garden. 'Purpleicious' has saturated purple flower spikes, and may reach up to twenty inches in height. 'Red Fox' has rose-red spikes and is about eighteen inches tall. Both 'Spicata Rose' and 'Spicata Blue' have a potential height of twenty to twenty-four inches and bloom midseason. 'Charlotte' (*V. longifolia*) has white and green variegated leaves with spikes of clear white flowers. This plant may reach thirty inches in height. 'Icicle White' also has pure white flowers but lacks the variegated foliage, is in the *V. spicata* species, and grows only to eighteen inches in height. This is a reliable re-bloomer if cut back after the first bloom has finished. 'Pink Damask' is another *V. spicata* cultivar. It is a late bloomer with clear shell-pink spikes of flowers and a height of twenty-four to thirty-six inches. It is one of my favorites and is not always readily available for sale, so grab one if you have the chance.

Veronica spicata
with *Clematis integrifolia*

New in the last few years are *V. spicata* hybrids with multi-branched plumes of flowers. This flower form tends to lengthen the bloom season, especially if the individual spikes are deadheaded as they fade. 'Blue Bomb,' 'Pink Bomb,' and 'Bicolor Explosion' all have this type of flower and range in height from fifteen to eighteen inches.

Veronica spicata mixed

V. gentianoides is the earliest speedwell to bloom. This plant shows masses of pale blue flowers on a plant eighteen to twenty inches tall. The foliage is not a noticeable contribution to the garden music once the blooms have faded. At that point the flower stocks and possibly the whole plant should be cut back.

'Waterperry Blue' (*V. surculosa*) is an early summer bloomer that is low growing with dark green foliage and white-eyed, intense blue flowers (not produced in spikes).

Veronica 'Pink Damask'

VERONICASTRUM

Culver Root

This is a tall, sturdy plant that may reach five feet in height but that does not need support, even in wind and rain. It produces many spikes of lavender, lilac, rose, purple, or white in mid to late season. The central flower spike on each flower stalk is surrounded by a whorl of side spikes that bloom after the central one is fading.

Veronicastrum sp.

Bees love this plant. It is a strong part of the symphony when planted at the back of the garden or as a focal point. With its stature and form, *Veronicastrum* carries its weight even before and after the blooms are showing off.

CHAPTER 22

Planting

Timing the Planting

One of the great advantages of perennials is that they can be planted much earlier and later in the season than annuals. This is assuming that they have been hardened off. If you are planting a perennial garden while there is still danger of frost and the plant in your hands has never lived anywhere but in the controlled environment of a greenhouse, you must harden it off before planting. Hardening off involves gradually exposing the plant to more and more time outdoors in ambient temperatures for a period of a week or so. A hardened-off perennial can be planted outdoors successfully, as long as the soil is thawed enough to pack it in tightly around the roots once the plant is in the ground. In Interior Alaska these days, the perennial planting season can extend from as early as mid to late April into late September or early October, depending on the year.

Some gardeners are hesitant to plant so late in the fall because they fear that the perennial cannot establish. However, at this late point in the season, the perennial is well into its winter dormancy. Actively growing and establishing is not something it will be or should be doing whether newly planted or not. You may wonder, "So why plant in the fall if the plant is not going to be growing at that time of year?" If you put a perennial in the ground in the fall, it will most likely be coming out of dormancy and starting to grow in the spring long before you, the gardener, would be working in your garden.

Both the cooler temperatures and minimal hot sun exposure typical of fall help a plant transition into new surroundings much more easily. Combine this with their state of dormancy, and fall-planted perennials just go through a lot less transplant shock.

And finally, in northern climates, fall is busy, but spring may be even crazier as we sprint from the starting line to get all of our summer projects accomplished in the few

This mixture of herbaceous and woody perennials was planted in early September from containerized plants. This photo was taken a year later (top right)

One of the paths in the garden one year after installation (center left).

A view of the path shown from the opposite end. This photo was taken during the summer five years later (center right).

A view from inside the garden one year after planting (bottom left).

The same view four years later than the previous photo (five years after installation, bottom right).

months ahead. Imagine having a perennial garden pop to life without your help first thing in the spring. Planting in the fall essentially gains you a season quite painlessly.

I want to clarify that properly hardened containerized perennials make the transition to a new garden setting with less transplant shock during the spring and fall, but they also are very successful during the summer. On the other hand, if you are digging established perennials out of a garden and moving them, you will have the greatest success and be kindest to the plants if you do it in the spring or fall.

The Weed Question

So we know now that any time we can work the soil, we can plant (hardened off) perennials. The next decision is weed control. You will not be tilling a perennial garden each season, as you would be an annual garden, where every spring you can, at least visually, free your garden of weeds with a spade or a rototiller. Whether you are planting your perennial garden in freshly purchased topsoil or in an area that has been tilled and that was previously covered with vegetation, uninvited opportunistic plants will be a force that you cannot ignore even within the first season. Planning for weed control before you plant is part of your garden design. There are various ways to accomplish this. Let me describe two methods I have used in our display gardens at The Plant Kingdom and in my personal gardens. For me it is a choice of planting directly in the soil and adding an organic mulch, or laying down a woven geotextile fabric and planting through it. Both methods have their selling points.

When I plant a garden of any type directly in the soil, I automatically assume I am going to be using an organic mulch. My favorite type is grass clippings, bagged as I mow my lawn. Of course these grass clippings must not come from a lawn that is kept dandelion-free with herbicides. Herbicides that kill dandelions will also have a negative effect on the seedlings in your garden. Yes, I use mulch that contains dandelion and other weed seeds, but they will only be in the mulch, so with regular scouting I keep them from rooting down into the soil.

Grass clippings are an amazing and often wasted resource. Used as a mulch in any garden, they help retain moisture, block out weeds, and add nutrients as they compost. They are best used fresh off the lawn because even after sitting in a pile for just a few hours, they will start composting, heating up, and getting quite slimy. When planting a new garden, annual or perennial, I layer four to six inches of clippings over the entire garden surface and then push them aside at any spot that I am putting a plant. After packing the soil in around the plant's roots, I push the clippings back into place and up around the plant's stem. One of the main advantages of this method of preparing the planting area is that it makes adding and modifying plant placement very easy. Maybe it is also best used in a perennial garden that will represent a collection of plants growing and tangling into each other rather than one with large empty spaces where plants are displayed more as individual specimens. Some of the perennials in your garden will drop viable seed each season. Depending on your vision for the garden, the grass mulch method may require diligent removal of these volunteer seedlings to prevent their rooting through the mulch.

A second way to prepare your garden stage before putting plants in the soil is to lay a woven geotextile fabric on the planting surface. Here I want to caution you that, if you use a geotextile fabric, be sure it is of a quality that will truly prevent weeds coming through it and that does not break down over time. My favorite is commercial grade woven geotextile fabric used to stabilize road beds. As time passes, plant debris and dust will collect on top of the fabric, and weed seeds can take root in this new micro-environment. However, they are easily dislodged with the sweep of a hand or a broom, because their roots can go no further than the surface of the fabric.

When planting through a geotextile fabric, simply cut an X shape in the fabric and fold back the points to make an opening large enough for the size of your plant's root ball and with some extra space for getting a trowel in to dig out the soil. Once

An established perennial garden to which grass clippings are added once or twice per season to replace the layer underneath that has composted in place (bottom left).

A layer of about four to six inches of fresh grass clippings has been spread on this area of garden prior to planting. I have found it is more efficient to plant through the mulch layer rather than packing the grass clippings around the plants after they are installed (bottom right).

the soil is excavated, insert the plant, pack the soil in tightly around its roots, and then fold the tabs or corners of the fabric triangle back out so they contact the stem of the plant. Then sweep away any excess soil on top of the fabric. The final touch is to add a decorative mulch. This decorative mulch should be added after planting so as to reduce the mixing of excavated soil with the mulch. My favorite is cedar bark nuggets in the medium or large-size grade. They add an organic feel, are tidy and attractive, are easily moved around for picking out any weeds that establish from seeds falling onto the garden, and are quickly freshened up with the addition of a few new bags of nuggets each spring. Decorative gravel or rock may be used as the top mulch on geotextile fabric, but the problem with each of these occurs when debris and seeds settle in among them. It is much easier to swish bark nuggets around to dislodge weeds than it is to do the same with gravel. Of course weeding around larger rocks is even less fun. I have also been known to avoid any decorative mulch on top of a fabric, and instead to just wait for a couple of seasons for the resident plant foliage to grow and conceal the fabric. This works especially well with low growing, spreading junipers.

There are several other considerations when making the decision on weed control. Woven geotextile fabric prevents re-seeding and spreading of plants. This

In this garden the geotextile fabric was laid first and then the "bones" of the garden were installed. Over the next several seasons, pavers were installed and herbaceous perennials were planted through the fabric (top left).

Here there are varying degrees of maturity among the plantings. Above the retaining wall, the junipers are spreading to cover the fabric mulch but the area where the fabric is exposed is still open, weed-free, waiting for the perennials that will complete the garden (top right).

A new perennial garden whose surface has been covered with geotextile fabric. The area where pavers will be installed has been cut out and removed so that soil could be excavated. The piece of fabric that was cut from this area will be put back in place before sand and pavers are layered on top (bottom left).

The island garden is underlain with geotextile fabric. It was the last part of the entire project that was completed, so in the interim, decorative bark nugget mulch was spread on the geotextile for aesthetic purposes. When it was finally planted, the bark was all swept off and then replaced once the plants were installed. This kept the bark nuggets from getting mixed with soil during the planting process (bottom right).

A one-year old perennial garden planted through geotextile fabric with ornamental bark mulch on the surface. Eventually these plants will be large enough that the bark will not be so visible.

can be an advantage or a disadvantage, depending on your vision for your garden. A fabric-covered garden is slightly more tedious to plant, both originally and when adding plants later. You must cut a hole in the fabric each time you place a plant and brush away the decorative mulch in the case of adding to an already completed garden.

Planting for the Future

The spacing of perennials in a garden is much different than for annuals. Most herbaceous perennials require several seasons to reach their mature size, and of course for woody perennials it takes even longer. One often-quoted adage for perennials is:

> The first year they sleep,
> The second year they creep,
> And the third year they leap.

This is all relative, of course, and depending on the perennials and the growing conditions, plants may "sleep" or "creep" an extra year or two, and so the "leap" to mature size may be several years out. The original spacing must allow for this increasing space requirement as the garden ages.

Another consideration for spacing is whether the ultimate visual goal is a garden made up of specimen plants with lots of negative space or a garden of plants intertwined and knitted together, so that the blossoms of one may be poking above the foliage of another.

Perennial display with disclaimer posted (top left).

A section of my garden several years after the junipers were planted (center left).

The same area of my garden shown four years later (center right).

A view to the east in my garden four years after planting (bottom left).

The same view to the east five years later (bottom right).

A small secluded perennial seating area at one end of a vegetable garden. This photo was taken a few weeks after the perennials were planted in mid summer (top left).

The same perennial garden one year later (top right).

Remember too that you can remove plants, and that you can add plants even in a perennial garden. If you are adding plants, be sure they are large enough to establish in the company of mature neighbors. This may necessitate some temporary trimming back of those neighbors.

As a general guide, I usually allot twelve to twenty-four inches in all directions between herbaceous perennials. Even with this amount of space, there will be a continuum of foliage and color within a few seasons.

Finally: Plants in the Dirt

Once you are ready to put your plants into the soil, dig the hole in the garden an inch or two wider and deeper than either the pot the plant is in or the size of the root ball (if it is a recently dug plant). Slide the plant out of the pot, and use your finger to loosen the root ball, actually pulling it apart so the roots are spread to the sides as you push them firmly down into the hole. I often add a handful of compost at this point, either my own worm castings or a bagged commercial type, and mix it in with the soil that I am packing in around the newly disturbed roots. Position the plant so that the soil line is at the same place relative to the plant stem as it was in the pot, but so that it is below grade, providing a bowl or moat around the plant. This allows water to collect and sink in slowly rather than run off when you water it or rain falls. Water the plant well as soon as it is in place so that water is percolating down and pushing any loose soil up against the roots, filling in remaining air pockets.

Newly planted perennials do not need a large dose of fertilizer. Besides adding compost to the soil as I position the plant in the garden, I sometimes add a mild strength solution of organic fertilizer as part of initial watering. Reducing the stress related to transplanting is what is most important at this time, when roots are

establishing and gaining the ability to take up water and nutrients. There are three ways to reduce this shock:

1) Keep the plant well hydrated for the first few weeks.

2) Consider covering the newly planted area with row crop fabric for a few days, to protect from desiccation, especially if there is excessive sun or wind. There are several manufacturers of this fabric. I am most familiar with DeWitt fabric in the weight of 1.5 ounces per square foot. This white fabric allows water and about fifty percent of natural light to reach the plant, and it protects from wind. It is reuseable season after season, and it is also very useful in hardening off plants and protecting from light frosts.

3) Reduce the foliage burden on the roots by cutting back excess foliage, especially in the case of dug rather than containerized plants. This leaves the roots with less foliage to support while they are getting established. The degree of cutback can be as extreme as fall cutback levels.

The *Campanula* and the *Hosta* have enough space around them that they appear as specimen plantings with the bark mulch showing clearly. Within a few more seasons, they will probably encroach upon each other's spaces, cover the mulch, and visually share blossoms (top left).

The perennials in this garden have knit together so tightly, it appears as if lily and yarrow blossoms are attached to the foliage of the Snow on the Mountain (top center).

The two island beds in the middle of this pathway are ready for plants to go into the soil through the geotextile fabric (top right).

CHAPTER 23

Supplementing Herbaceous Perennial Gardens

Supplementing the Color in Your Perennial Garden

One way to extend the season of bloom in your perennial garden is to plant fall bulbs. These are bulbs that are planted in the fall and that bloom in the spring. They begin their rooting phase in the last weeks before the ground freezes, complete their rooting in early spring as soon as the ground thaws, and bloom when herbaceous perennials are just starting to wake up.

In Interior Alaska, fall bulbs would include various varieties of *Allium, Muscari, Galanthus, Scilla*, daffodils, and tulips. Here in Fairbanks, I personally have had success with a variety of the Trumpet daffodils and the Emperor tulips. *Tulipa tarda* is a

Tulips in mid-May in a first year bulb planting.

A bed of Emperor tulips and *Muscari* situated in the entrance area of a large perennial garden. In early June this bed is planted with annuals to add another area of brilliant color and to cover the fading foliage of the bulbs.

species tulip that grows eight to twelve inches tall, has bright yellow and white flowers, blooms very early in the spring, and naturalizes quite successfully in Interior Alaska. A stunning allium that can be planted as a fall bulb for early spring blooms is 'Purple Sensation' (*Allium aflatunense*). This plant reaches a height of two to three feet, naturalizes in the Fairbanks area, and has iridescent purple flowers that form globes as large as four inches across. The foliage fades away after blooming, but the tall flower stems of this allium, topped by spherical seed pods, remain all summer to contribute their small but unique part to the summer symphony. I have not had much success with *Crocus* in my garden, but they are definitely hardy in more southern regions of the state.

Allium 'Purple Sensation' flower heads (top left).

Allium 'Purple Sensation' spherical heads of seed pods (top right).

Fall bulbs can be planted in among the perennials in your garden (preferably not one covered with geotextile fabric), and they will be the first plants to emerge in the spring. Flower color, form, and size, as well as the height, form, and texture of the plant should be considered in your planting layout for the bulbs. They will be the primary players in your garden for a week or two. As they begin to fade, herbaceous perennials will be pushing out of the soil. Once these bulbs have bloomed, leave the foliage to grow and build up the bulbs for the following season. Emerging perennials will cover this foliage as it slowly withers and becomes unsightly.

Conventional wisdom concerning fall bulb planting should be modified when you are planting in northern climates. In Interior Alaska, fall bulbs should be planted in late August or early September, once the soil temperature is in the mid to low 50-degree Fahrenheit range. This is earlier than is normally recommended, and earlier than the instructions on bulb packaging will advise. This is also early enough that the entire selection of fall bulbs may not yet be harvested and available for sale at garden centers. However, our bulbs must be planted within this time frame in order to accomplish some of their rooting before the ground freezes. Once established and happy in their location, most bulbs will naturalize, so you will not have to re-plant them, although it seems gardeners are always adding new varieties in any empty spot of soil.

Most fall bulb packaging will include information on how deep to plant. This also needs to be modified for northern climates. Rather than several inches deep, fall bulbs must be buried only an inch or two deep, so that they are in the layer of soil that thaws first in the spring. This allows them to warm up and finish their rooting. One

The "Nose Bed" at The Plant Kingdom one early autumn day. The colorful foliage of many of its resident plants provides the color and beauty in a garden that has few blooming flowers at this point in the season.

The dominant contrast and color here are provided almost entirely by foliage (below, top).

The foliage of the *Aegopodium* is a perfect all-season accompaniment for the long blooming yarrow (below, bottom).

way to assure early spring soil warmth for your bulbs is to plant them in an area with high early spring sun exposure. Warm, well-drained soil is crucial to fall bulb success. The area of your garden that is first bare of snow in the spring is the place to plant your bulbs in early fall.

The success of your fall bulb planting can be further enhanced by covering the planted area with row crop fabric. Row crop fabric, or frost protection fabric as it may also be called, in the 1.5 ounce per square foot weight adds frost protection (six to eight degrees above ambient) and transmits about 50% of the light. This will protect young plants in the spring if their warm exposure encourages them to emerge while there is still the possibility of hard frost at night.

Another way to add color to your perennial garden is through foliage with on-going visual contributions. Foliage plants may be what saves your perennial display in a brief (but seemingly endless) stretch of time when, for some reason, no one in your garden symphony is playing.

Incorporating annuals here and there in your perennial garden is still another acceptable way to add color, extend the season, and fill in those moments of unanticipated bloom silence. One way to do this is to plant the annuals right in the perennial bed. Another way is to intersperse perennial and annual beds in a larger landscape. This assures color in the landscape even if the perennial area itself momentarily has a weak symphony. The latter is my preferred method. For me it showcases the beauty of both annuals and perennials in a purer sense. It also avoids the messiness of planting annuals among established perennials, and then pulling them out in the fall with the incumbent hazard of uprooting small perennials as well as any fall bulbs that may be busily rooting out of sight underground.

In this mixed perennial garden, the yellow green of the *Dicentra* and the dark chocolate of the *Actaea* catch the eye almost more quickly than the flowers do (top left).

This garden is a combination of annual beds and perennial beds (top right).

The bed in the lower left of the photo is a combination of annuals and perennials (center left).

A more expansive view of the garden shown center left, but in late fall. At this time, it is the fall foliage of the woody shrubs and the blooms of the annuals that are carrying the symphony (center right).

An annual bed in full glory surrounded by perennial beds in late summer (bottom left).

An annual bed situated among perennial beds (bottom right).

Individual annual and perennial beds supporting each other in the garden symphony.

This photo of shrubs and trees being bedded down for winter storage leaves no doubt that woody plants are capable of adding wonderful color and texture to a garden landscape.

Woody Plants and the Herbaceous Perennial Garden

Woody plants, shrubs and even trees, can also be incorporated into a perennial garden design. Trees can be used to enhance the surrounding setting of the garden, and shrubs may be used as a backdrop or even in close proximity to herbaceous perennials that have a robust growth habit. Trees and shrubs are often considered the "bones" of the garden, because of their strong and obvious year-round presence.

My favorite way to use trees is in a larger setting, so that there is plenty of space for their spreading roots and for the canopy of shade that they will create. The herbaceous garden needs to be far enough from resident trees that it does not suffer in the competition for resources. Like their herbaceous relatives, many trees have a specific bloom time. Here in Interior Alaska, pears, crab apples, apples, chokecherries, and mountain ash bloom profusely, roughly in that chronological order. Some, such as the crab apples and chokecherries, include fragrance as part of their appeal. Most lilacs are actually shrubs, but there are also a few tree forms. Lilac trees and many varieties of the shrub forms reach a size that makes them more useful as focal points and privacy curtains, rather than as close neighbors of perennial gardens. Within the lilac genus, there is quite a range of bloom times. Common Purples (*Syringa vulgaris*) bloom right after the chokecherries, but others such as 'Golden Eclipse' Japanese Tree

Lilac (*S. reticulata*) and three *Syringa x prestoniae* cultivars—'Minuet,' 'Donald Wyman,' and 'James MacFarlane'—reach peak bloom up to several weeks later. A new introduction from a few years ago is 'Bloomerang®' (*Syringa* x 'Penda'), which blooms in early spring and then, with pruning of these blooms, re-blooms in late summer. The leaf color, bark, and berries of some trees may be as important ornamental attributes as the blooms. Examples are the red-purple summer and fall foliage of the Schubert or Canada Red Chokecherry (*Prunus virginiana*), the oranges and reds of Amur Maple (*Acer ginnala*) foliage, the brilliant red seed pods and fall foliage of the Hot Wings Tatarian Maple (*Acer tataricum* 'Gar Ann'), the golden bark of the Amur Chokecherry (*Prunus maackii*), the bright red berries of the Showy Mountain Ash (*Sorbus decora*), and the blue-gray, highly textured foliage of the 'Wichita Blue' Juniper (*Juniperus scopulorum*). Trees are efficient competitors for nutrients, water, and light, so keep this foremost in your thoughts as you choose their location in the landscape. A tree that provides desired shade in its youth may overstep its boundaries, and a few years later it may be creating excessive shade for a sun-loving perennial garden.

There are many woody shrubs that are not candidates for planting in close proximity to an herbaceous perennial garden, simply because of their mature size and the accompanying competition for resources. Their best and very effective use may be

Ornamental trees and shrubs may also provide fruit and berries. These apples are from a 'Norland' apple tree.

In early September, a *Hydrangea* 'Pink Diamond' is in full bloom, the Showy Mountain Ash shows bright red berries, and *Chelone*, a late blooming herbaceous perennial (back center of photo), is adding the final notes to the garden symphony.

An Amur maple in fall foliage brightens a corner of the landscape.

Syringa 'Asessippi' is one of the earliest blooming lilacs.

in the larger garden setting as focal points, as protection from wind and sun, and as a backdrop. Position them strategically so they are a positive visual element in the garden as a whole, but far enough away to avoid scooping up nutrients and water and crowding out their herbaceous neighbors.

It is tempting when planting a new perennial garden to crowd the plants, so that it looks instantly full. In the case of herbaceous plants, there is the chance that hungry voles or a lack of snow cover or some other unfriendly event will take a few of your plants over time. Besides that, herbaceous perennials are relatively easy to remove in the first few years if they are too crowded. Woody shrubs, on the other hand, are more tenacious and a little more difficult to extract from their rooting spot. They also have lots of potential size increase, so space shrubs even to the point of seeming sparse the first few years. You can always add more later.

Some of my favorite shrubs include many spireas; the Ninebarks (*Physocarpus*); Blizzard Mock Orange (*Philadelphus lewisii*); Summer Glow Tamarisk (*Tamarix ramosissima*); prostrate and short upright junipers; hardy roses including the Morden Series, the Pavement series, the Red Leaf Rose (*Rosa glauca*), and the *R. rugosa* hybrids as well as several climbers such as 'William Baffin' (Explorer Series) and 'Ramblin'

Fragrant 'Blizzard' Mock Orange and *Spirea* 'Goldmound' act as a border here but they can also be the backdrop for herbaceous perennials. In the upper left is a Showy Mountain Ash.

In winter it is woody plants that are the musicians—changing with each additional snowfall (top left).

The woody foliage is the texture–rich setting for this lavender *Thalictrum* blossom (top center).

Woody shrubs are providing the structure of "garden rooms." A view here from one room to another (top right).

Physocarpus 'Diabolo' and 'Nugget' have early summer blossoms, but their foliage is why they are the bones of the garden symphony (bottom left).

Purple Leaf Sand Cherry, Red Leaf Rose, and Blue Globe Spruce add to the symphony with foliage color and texture (bottom right).

The crescendo in the symphony as the end approaches (opposite top).

Leaves are what create the ambiance in this garden vignette (opposite bottom).

Red;' and some of the *Hydrangea paniculata* cultivars, including 'Pink Diamond,' 'Limelight,' and 'Peegee.' Honeysuckles as a group add distinctive bark and berries, and this includes the Haskap Berries (*Lonicera caerulea kamtschatica*), prized for their fruit by both birds and humans. Purple Leaf Sand Cherry (*Prunus x cistena*) adds dark burgundy foliage, whereas Nanking Cherry (*Prunus tomentosa*) adds blooms and fruit. All of these favorites of mine have colorful blooms, beautiful foliage, or fragrance, or are edible, or all of the above. They create an ambiance and physical presence that enhances the garden setting. They help set the stage for the garden symphony.

Another great strength of these woody shrubs, which combine well with herbaceous perennials, is their use in creating garden rooms. A large garden may include secluded spaces, garden rooms, connected by paths and natural pass throughs. Woody shrubs function well as the "walls" or visual divisions between these garden rooms.

Berry-producing shrubs and trees bring their own music to the garden because of their great appeal to birds. Robins nest near my Haskap Berry shrub and deftly snag the berries under the watchful eyes of my cats. In the fall, robins, Bohemian waxwings, and even ravens settle into my yard to devour the berries still hanging on the chokecherries, the crab apples, and the Showy Mountain Ash.

CHAPTER 24

Maintenance

Maintenance and Ongoing Care

I have talked with customers at The Plant Kingdom who have decided to switch from annual gardening to perennial gardening. "Because," they explain, "I'm tired of maintenance and I want a garden that is maintenance-free." Of course the plants for a maintenance-free garden would be best purchased at a silk flower shop, although even those will require dusting. I do not say this, however, because this frustrated gardener is now standing in my live-plant filled nursery giving me the opportunity to deliver the news that perennials are not maintenance-free, but that they will more than amply reward any time the gardener devotes to them.

A glass of wine and a garden (bottom left).

The joy of hands in the dirt (bottom right).

In this era of instant gratification, many of us sometimes wish for a beautiful garden to be transported magically into our yard, growing and blooming carefree all summer long. In this garden of our dreams, our only duty would be to stroll through sipping our wine or our tea, enjoying the fragrance, and cutting colorful bouquets. As perfect as this may sound, the satisfaction and joy of gardening comes from the doing—the planting, the weeding, the watering, the hands in the dirt. Don't cheat yourself. Reap the benefits of gardening from the ground up.

Let's look at maintenance in a perennial garden on a seasonal basis.

Perennial Spring Tasks

Springtime in a perennial garden is busy. A lot is happening as the plants come out of dormancy and start to send new growth up out of the soil. Water and nutrients are required to support this high-energy process. For a while, the melting snow will hydrate your perennials, but once the snow has melted, it is time to turn on the outside faucets and hook up hoses so you can keep your busy plants well-watered. If you have already spread an organic slow release fertilizer the previous fall, you should not need to fertilize in the spring. If you did not, you may wish to add a light dose of liquid feed fertilizer as new growth emerges.

In late spring, when all of your woody perennials are leafed out, you can assess what branches or sections were the victims of winter damage and remove them with pruning shears. This is also a good time to do general pruning and shaping on all shrubs and trees because you know what has survived the winter weather and winter grazers like voles and moose. Fall pruning may be more typical in other climates, but here in the north, where winter weather will do some pruning of its own, I prefer to do some pruning and shaping in the spring, when I can base my decisions on the condition of the plant after surviving the winter and as it heads into the growing season.

This is a season when you can also enjoy one of the advantages of your perennial garden—no planting in the spring. The players in your garden symphony take their places and prepare to play their parts with minimal help from the gardener.

Staying on Top of Summer Maintenance

Continue your diligence about watering. This not only keeps the plants hydrated but also washes into the soil the slow release fertilizer that you sprinkled on the garden the preceding fall. On rainy days, check with your finger to see how deep in the soil the rainwater has penetrated. You may be surprised at how dry the soil is, even after what seems like a heavy rain. You may find yourself wearing a raincoat and wielding a hose.

The top three photos of the same garden were taken at two-week intervals.

Here in late April there is no above ground growth visible yet. All of the herbaceous perennials were cut back in the fall and granular fertilizer was applied at that time (top).

Here in mid-May some of the herbaceous perennials are showing foliage growth, most of the woody shrubs are leafed out and the 'Pink Spires' crabapple is in full bloom (center, left).

In late May the Snowdrop Anemone and the yellow *Trollius* are in full bloom while the crabapple is fading. The foliage of the ninebarks and purple leaf sand cherry are giving strong support to this garden symphony (center, right).

Here is the same garden in late June. Peonies, yarrow, and catmint are in full bloom. Notice that the garden is freshly watered, a vital summer task for the gardener (bottom left).

Again, here is the same garden in mid-July, typically the warmest part of the summer. The yarrow and the catmint are still blooming and the symphony is receiving colorful support from the foliage of the woody shrubs. Notice the paver path has been kept free of weeds (bottom right).

In this late spring garden woody plants have leafed out, and it is now easy to determine what parts need pruning because of winter weather damage or vole and moose attacks.

I usually water with liquid fertilizer one or two times during the growing season. If you did spread granular fertilizer the fall before, this added feeding may not be crucial. However, excessive rainfall may wash that fertilizer through the soil more rapidly than normal, and so adding liquid fertilize later in the summer can be a needed boost in a very wet growing season.

Weeding, an essential summer task, is probably the most dreaded word associated with gardening. The two keys to minimizing weeding pain are:

1)   Use a weed barrier mulch (like grass clippings or geotextile fabric), and

2)   Keep current on the weeding that does need to be done. Do not let weeds take over. Weeding is an endeavor for which the phrase "Nip it in the bud" says everything.

My approach to weeding is to devote a little time to it each day. In addition, once a week I dedicate several hours to removing all the dandelions out of my paver and rock paths, or on my hands and knees in the vegetable garden, scouring for embryonic

weeds, or layering on more grass clippings in garden areas where original clippings have composted in place making the weed barrier thin. Weeding should be viewed as an excuse to hang out in your garden, rather than as dreaded maintenance.

Early summer is the time to replace perennials that for some reason did not survive the winter. Occasionally, gardeners will come to The Plant Kingdom in mid May with the sad news that most of their perennials did not survive the winter. The reality is that you cannot know if perennials that are not showing growth in mid May have survived or not. Warm air temperatures do not mean warm soil temperatures, especially if it is a spring where warm air temperatures occurred suddenly. The soil warms much more slowly than the air. The soil temperature below the first few inches of the surface takes even longer, and in fact it may take a drenching spring rain to wash the heat from the top few inches down to the level of plant roots.

The spring of 2013 in Fairbanks might better have been described as late winter 2013. Well below freezing night temperatures persisted into mid May or later. A *Dicentra spectabilis* on the north side of my house had not yet emerged by the time my other perennials showed green growth. This was a plant that had been there many years, that had survived the minimum egress window trauma I described earlier, and that had been the focal point of the garden in which it lived. I was not surprised that it stayed hidden in May, because the north exposure snow pack was still covering the garden late into that month. By the end of June, I was debating what I might plant to replace it. Fortunately, other projects got in the way. On July 11, I spotted the tiny green shoots of my bleeding heart poking through the bark mulch. A few seasons later, that very plant covered an area four feet square and reached a height of four to five feet. This bleeding heart represents the extreme, but I would give any herbaceous perennial until June 15 to emerge. If you choose to replace it at that point, plant the replacement to one side of the original plant, just in case it still emerges, as did my bleeding heart.

This border perennial bed has a thick layer of grass clippings in mid July. It has already had new clippings added to it once this season (top left).

In late August another thick layer of grass mulch is being added to this bed in much the same manner that it was done earlier in the summer (top center).

Summer is the time to freshen up bark mulch as has been done here near the base of the steps (top right).

This is the *Dicentra spectabilis* that did not emerge until July 11 the summer of 2013.

In the perennial bed on the left some of the plants have finished blooming and their foliage was deteriorating so they have been cut back. The result is a neater, tidier look with room for other perennials to use the space as they prepare to play their part in the symphony of blooms.

At The Plant Kingdom, in our display gardens we have several clumps of Asiatic lilies with more than one flower color in the clump. These are lilies that were heavily damaged by hungry voles during the winter and that emerged barely visible in the spring as grassy shoots. We planted a new lily next to them, but by the following season or two, the grassy shoots, propagated from seeds or scales, had matured, and the original lily cultivar was blooming again along with its replacement.

Removing spent blossoms, or deadheading, is not as necessary to keep perennials blooming as it is with annuals. However, deadheading keeps the plant and your garden neat and tidy. It also may encourage longer bloom time in some species. In the case of plants with large, heavy blossoms like peonies and roses, spent flowers left on the plant are a great place for fungal diseases to establish, something the gardener does not want to encourage.

There are situations during the summer when it is advisable to reduce the amount of foliage on a plant or to cut it back even as much as in fall. The foliage of some perennials deteriorates or dies after the plant blooms. Examples are delphiniums, *Lychnis*, shooting star, oriental poppies, and painted daisies. For many of these, the best management technique is to cut them back to within a few inches of the ground once this deterioration is obvious. Often they will send up new attractive foliage that will be a positive contribution to the music in your garden for the rest of the season. Removing old foliage at the base of some of the larger perennials during the growing season encourages air circulation, which in turn discourages fungal diseases. An overgrown garden may also make it easier for non-plant-friendly insects to hide from predators. Removing excess foliage as the summer progresses and as plants pass their prime makes it easier for predatory insects and birds to search among your perennials for plant pests.

Fall Cleanup and Preparing for Winter

Fall is a busy time for both perennial plants and gardeners. Time invested in the fall will set you up for a perennial garden that pops to life on its own in the spring.

The best time to divide perennials is in the fall as they are nearing dormancy. Spring is also a possibility, but disturbing perennials as they are coming out of dormancy may delay their bloom time. Also, spring emergence may happen before conditions are amenable to your spending time in your garden. Our focus here is perennials that are thriving. Each season they are larger, and maybe they are becoming the bullies of the garden, crowding out their neighbors. This calls for some active management on the part of the gardener. These plants must be split, and fall is the best time to do this.

Some plants can be split by literally cutting the root ball into pieces. The Siberian iris in photos on the opposite page was dug up and split into half a dozen chunks. One of the pieces was replanted in the garden, and the others were potted and sold. This iris was about six years old and substantial enough that the tool of choice was a cross cut saw. For plants that have eyes on the woody root, such as herbaceous peonies, the root should be split so that each of the pieces has one or more eyes. In the case of Asiatic lilies and other perennials propagated by bulbs or corms, the plant can be dug up, and the clump of bulbs at its base can be gently pulled apart, with individual bulbs then being replanted separately. Some perennials can grow for years without needing to be split, whereas others must be brought back into check every few seasons.

Here is the same garden shown on page 273 in early August. *Gentiana septemfida* is blooming and the yarrows are starting to fade (top).

The same garden the third week in August. Now *Gentiana* 'True Blue' (lower left of photo) is participating in the symphony. Many of the perennials that have finished blooming have been cut back in preparation for winter (bottom left).

In this photo all the herbaceous perennials have been cut back except for the blooming gentians. The 'Pink Spires' crab apple has been wrapped for moose protection (bottom right).

The tools of choice for splitting a Siberian iris (left).

More tools were brought in to split this five or six year old *Iris* 'Caesar's Brother' (right).

As the growing season closes and winter approaches, all herbaceous perennials (NOT the woody ones) should be cut back to within a few inches of the ground. This is called fall cutback. In my own garden, I begin fall cutback on some plants as early as mid-August, if they have finished blooming and their foliage is degenerating. By early September, I go through my gardens every day and selectively cut back, leaving the plants that are still flowering or showing attractive foliage, or both. Depending on the speed with which winter is approaching, I may leave the latest blooming and still beautiful perennials into late September. The gamble is the weather, and the goal is to maximize the length of the season, but not to be cutting back your garden in freezing rain and snow.

Cutting back foliage in fall has many advantages. Your garden will be neat and tidy in the spring, with no slimy, dead foliage infested with fungal disease or the eggs of insect pests. Cutting all of your herbaceous perennials to the same level makes for even distribution of granular fertilizer when you spread it over your beds. With no foliage in the way, you can sprinkle a granular slow release organic fertilizer evenly throughout the garden at a rate of about 3#/100 square feet. This fertilizer will start washing into the garden soil with the spring snowmelt. This is the only time during the year that you need to add granular fertilizer to your garden, and it is the easiest time. If you choose to add compost instead, fall is also the time, since the soil is hidden by neither snow nor foliage.

Continuing to water your perennial garden in the fall is wise, especially if the weather is warm and dry. Although the above-ground parts of plants are no longer eye-catching with color, there is much going on underground as the plant negotiates winter dormancy. Do not store your hoses away for the winter without assuring that your garden is well-hydrated.

To mulch or not to mulch? This is a question for any fall gardener who is shutting down a garden for winter. One way of adding protection from wind and extreme cold

in the winter is indeed to add mulch. Mulch in this context is some material functioning as an insulation medium. Snow, falling and accumulating naturally, or being tossed (but not compacted) on to the garden surface with a shovel is, in my opinion, the best insulating mulch. Perhaps it was my son's grade school science project that convinced me of the insulating value of a thick blanket of undisturbed snow. This family project involved making a square vertical excavation through four feet of snow, covering the open top with several layers of rigid foam insulation, and then opening it once each day to read the thermometers inserted at intervals from top to ground level in the snow wall. Even in this low-tech investigation, the negative 30 degrees Fahrenheit at the top of the snow pack and the 20 degrees Fahrenheit at ground level were very convincing. Snow equals warm—or at least warmer.

Where there is no snow cover on a perennial garden in the winter, such as up against a house in the snow shadow of the eaves, mulch may need to be added. My preferred method is to use 1.5-ounce row crop fabric to cover the garden. Anchor the fabric along the edges with rocks or bricks, and then toss snow on top when shoveling nearby walkways. The row crop fabric can be lifted off the garden as soon as the snow melts in the spring. However, the porous nature of this fabric also allows you to leave it in place until there are a few inches of green growth on the plants under it. This is particularly helpful in spring weather, which teases with a few warm days and then reverts to one more taste of winter.

Leaves and straw can also be used as insulating mulch. It is wise to put down a layer of row crop fabric first. This separates the organic mulch, with its accompanying weed seeds, from the garden plants, and prevents the seeds from making their way into your garden. One problem with leaves and straw as mulch is that they may insulate against the cold in winter but they also insulate against heat in the spring, and therefore keep the soil underneath them cooler later into the season. Think about brushing a pile of leaves with your foot as you walk through a wooded area in the early spring right after the snow has gone. Often that pile of leaves will be the last holdout of ice and frozen soil. If you do use leaves and straw for mulch, plan to scrape them away in the spring, so that sunlight can warm the soil underneath.

Insects, Disease, and Other Bad Guys in the Garden

And then there is that dark subject of disease and insects in your garden. I do not find disease to be a big problem in the short season of northern gardens, especially with the use of some simple management techniques. Encouraging air circulation is one of the best preventatives for fungal diseases. Removing excess foliage so that sun and

In this late August photo, all of the herbaceous perennials have been cut back for winter but the woody shrubs are left intact (opposite, top left).

A perennial garden in which most of the herbaceous perennials have been cut back for winter. The late-blooming *Solidago* 'Little Lemon' has been spared for a few more days. Annuals have been pulled from the bed on the right and a fresh layer of grass clippings has been added to block weeds that may try to emerge during a warm September (opposite, top right).

These are pots of perennials that have been cut back for the winter, giving the opportunity to see what fall cut back really means (opposite, center left).

Perennial beds covered in late fall with row crop fabric (opposite, center right).

Trees are wrapped with row crop fabric for moose protection through the winter (opposite, bottom left).

The best insulating mulch . . . and it's free (opposite, bottom right)!

Ladybug on patrol in a perennial garden (top left).

Ladybugs inside a greenhouse feeding on a mixture of peanut butter powder and powdered sugar, waiting for some tasty aphids (top right).

wind can penetrate the plant canopy is one tool for doing this. Removing any diseased foliage, bagging it, and putting it in the garbage is another preventative practice. There is an assortment of organic certified fungicides available, but most are not systemic. This means their efficacy is based on contact, and they will knock the fungus back but they will not eradicate it. I have used a mild dilution of horticultural fine oil and I have used baking soda dissolved in water as deterrents to powdery mildew on plants in my garden. Preventative measures, however, are the wisest line of defense.

Insect pests are part of gardening. As you approach this problem, set your goal not for eradication (not even the most lethal pesticides will accomplish this), but for control. The point is that a thousand aphids are a problem, but a plant can nevertheless live just fine with ten aphids.

Your first tool is to practice preventative measures, and this includes being proactive in scouting for insect pests. Keep your garden weed-free and sufficiently watered (so plants are not stressed), trimmed back and deadheaded, and free of decaying plant debris. Don't overfeed with high nitrogen fertilizers. Excessive use of high-analysis fertilizers encourages soft, succulent growth and thin cell walls in new tissue. Aphids and other sucking insects love thin cell walls. Lower analysis, organic fertilizers tend to encourage more controlled growth with thicker cell walls, which are more difficult for sucking insects to penetrate. Keep your eyes open for pests while you are weeding or deadheading or walking through your garden. Pinch off infected leaves and squish aphids on flower buds. These are all part of "bad bug" control.

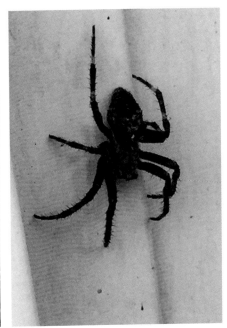

Attracting birds and other natural insect predators and parasites to your garden is a very effective means of keeping plant-damaging insects at bay. There are several ways to encourage these species to police your garden. First, do not use pesticides, which will harm the "good bugs" and birds just as they do the insects feeding on your plants. Even herbicides can be harmful to species you want to attract to your garden. Second, grow a wide variety of flowering annuals, perennials, shrubs, and trees in your yard. They will encourage a diverse insect and bird population.

The most common insect pest we encounter in Interior Alaska gardens is various species of the aforementioned aphids. If you find yourself with an infestation of these on some of your perennials, the first level of action is physically washing them off with a blast from a garden hose. More aggressive action is spraying a solution of liquid dish soap (about one tablespoon of soap per gallon of water) on heavily infected plants, contacting all surfaces. The soap desiccates the aphids but only those it contacts. Wait two hours and then wash the soapy water off with a garden hose. This MUST be done in the evening or in the shade or on a very cloudy day because sunlight will burn plants covered with soap.

Voles are larger pests that can be quite destructive in a perennial garden. They may nibble, or even gobble, foliage and stems in the summer. They may even cause damage in the winter, when they burrow down and chew the roots of perennials or feed on the bark at the base of woody shrubs.

A varied plant palette in your garden will attract a variety of birds, some feeding on seeds (including weed seeds) and some feeding on insects (top left).

Spiders and many insects are the "good bugs" that you want to encourage in your garden (top right).

One of the best deterrents for voles is a resident cat. This is the solution in my own garden. At The Plant Kingdom, when we are experiencing an especially destructive vole population, we sometimes resort to snap traps baited with peanut butter or cheese, depending on the preference of the target voles. We check these traps regularly in case a vole has been caught but not killed or in case a bird has been lured in and caught by a toe. Poisons should never be set out for voles, as they are not species specific, and any scavenger that feeds on a poisoned vole will also be harmed. It probably goes without saying that sticky traps should never be used simply because they are inhumane. For the most part snap traps kill quickly. A garden is a place of peace and happiness, so I think that if killing must occur, it should be quick and cause minimal suffering to the victim.

During the process of splitting this Siberian iris, we found a vole nest lined with remnants of row crop fabric. The iris was thriving. Apparently the benefits of the root aeration with vole tunnels and the addition of vole manure fertilizer outweighed the nibbling on the roots (top left).

The vole patrol, wondering if the voles on the outside of the fence might taste better. (top right)

Voles in my garden usually do not need to worry about winter hunters, but here is an exception (bottom).

This mountain ash was wrapped for moose protection for the first ten years of its life until we could no longer reach the top with our ten feet of step ladder. Because of its size, we used both clothespins and lightweight rope to hold the fabric in place and anchor it against wind. In recent years we have only wrapped the lower trunk to prevent moose gnawing it in winter.

Some gardeners subscribe to the use of cayenne pepper placed in vole burrows and at places in the garden that they are feeding. I have been partially successful using cayenne pepper at the mouth of a vole burrow that was the point of entry into their favorite part of my garden.

Voles also do not like sharp rocks, and so there have been attempts to surround lily bulbs underground and on the planting surface with a barrier of rock shards. Another physical barrier is hardware cloth lining the planting hole with sharp rock placed on the surface around the stem of the plant. These methods can be quite cumbersome and time-consuming to install.

The largest plant pest of all in Interior Alaska gardens is moose. Moose can be especially destructive on shrubs and trees in the winter, late spring, and early fall. In the summer months, their most likely target is vegetable gardens, but plants in hanging baskets and annual and perennial gardens may also be part of the menu.

For fairly effective winter moose protection, I wrap young trees and even some shrubs with the 1.5-ounce row crop fabric described in Chapters 22 and 23. I drive a fence stake into the ground next to the tree. The stake must be as tall as the tree. I then spiral the row crop fabric tightly around the stake and the tree as one unit and hold the fabric in place with clothespins. The stake prevents the tree from bending and breaking under icy snow load. This works amazingly well. I have had trouble with wind snapping off the clothespins but only rarely has a moose removed one.

Before my garden and before my fence, a moose at the front door was not unusual (top left).

These young shrubs had a difficult time gaining any growth before I fenced my yard (top right).

This calf moose's mother parked it for a nap outside my fence one spring afternoon. She went around the corner and fed on my compost pile. I keep this pile outside the fence to decrease the temptation for them to jump my fence and to show my willingness to share at least my compost (opposite).

There are various commercially available liquid sprays that are designed for application on shrubs and trees to deter moose feeding. I have heard of some degree of success with these, but they do need to be re-applied regularly.

The most effective moose protection is a fence. A farm fence that is six feet tall has kept moose out of my very delicious looking yard for twelve years. My compost pile is outside the fence and moose paw through it regularly. They also occasionally browse on the tree branches overhanging the fence. None have attempted to come inside—yet. There is always the option of a taller, stronger fence. We do not have moose-proof fencing at The Plant Kingdom, but we have not had moose destruction in our herbaceous perennial beds. We wrap our young trees each fall until they reach a size that is difficult to wrap. For me, the investment in a fence has been worth the protection from moose that it has provided for the shrubs, trees, vegetables, and perennials growing in my yard. However, you can indeed successfully grow an herbaceous perennial garden in an unfenced yard.

Lilium 'Conca d' Or,' *Astilbe* 'Colorflash,' and *Solidago* 'Little Lemon' in a one-year old perennial garden.

REFERENCES

Much of what I have written here comes from personal experience in my own garden and in the display gardens at The Plant Kingdom greenhouse. My years in the horticulture industry, reading trade magazines, attending symposia, and talking with gardeners of all sorts have further influenced my approach to perennial gardening. In putting together *Northern Garden Symphony*, I have supplemented and corroborated my personal knowledge with a variety of references. What follows is a list of those reference texts that have been most important, and that I have found myself referring to most often.

Armitage, Allan M. *Herbaceous Perennial Plants*. Champaign, IL: Stipes Publishing, 1997.

Bron and Sons Nursery Co. 2018 Catalog. www.bronandsons.com.

Center Greenhouse Young Plant Program 201/-2018. www.CenterGreenhouse.com.

Darwin Plants Bare Root Perennials 2018 Catalogue. www.darwinplants.com.

De Vroomen Grower Catalog 2019. www.devroomen.com.

Growing Colors Spring 2018 Catalog. www.growingcolors.com.

Gulley Greenhouse 2018 Young Plant Catalog.www.gulleygreenhouse.com.

Netherland Bulb Company 2018 Grower Catalog. www.netherlandbulb.com. (http://digitalcommons.unl.edu/natrespapers/563)

Rettig, Molly. "Higher Temperatures are Lengthening Alaska's Growing Season." Fairbanks: *Fairbanks Daily News Miner.* mrettig@newsminer .com, August 1, 2010.

Rijinbeek and Son 2018-2019 Catalog. www.rijinbeek.com.

Swift Greenhouse, Inc. Predictable Perennials 2018-2019 Catalog. www.swiftegreenhouses.com.

Wendler, Gird and Martha Shulski. "A Century of Climate Change for Fairbanks, Alaska." *University of Nebraska–Lincoln Papers in Natural Resources.*563. 2009.

Cyndie Warbelow has lived in Alaska all of her life. She grew up in villages near the Arctic Circle, then later lived along the Alaska Highway where her family operated a roadhouse and bush flying service.

After earning a B.S. in Biology from the University of Alaska and an M.S. in Zoology from the University of Michigan, Warbelow returned to Alaska. She first lived in Fairbanks working for a biological consulting company and teaching at the Tanana Valley Community College. Her venture into horticulture began when she moved east of Fairbanks to Two Rivers, and with her family developed a truck farming operation and helped establish the Tanana Valley Farmers Market. The farming business grew into a general store, a café, and a greenhouse-nursery.

In 1998, after selling the Two Rivers business, Warbelow built The Plant Kingdom Greenhouse and Nursery, now a well-known spot to buy locally grown plants in Fairbanks. She soon started teaching perennial garden design at many locations including The Plant Kingdom, the Cooperative Extension, Master Gardeners, the National Garden Club, and local garden groups. Warbelow now teaches classes and consults in garden design.